T0126153

# Keeping Faith
## with the
# Psalms

# Keeping Faith
## with the
# Psalms

## Deepen Your
## Relationship with
## God Using
## the Book of Psalms

## Daniel F. Polish

*For People of All Faiths, All Backgrounds*

**JEWISH LIGHTS** Publishing

Woodstock, Vermont

*Keeping Faith with the Psalms: Deepen Your Relationship with God Using the Book of Psalms*

2004 First Printing
© 2004 by Daniel F. Polish

**Library of Congress Cataloging-in-Publication Data**
Polish, Daniel F.
Keeping faith with the Psalms : deepen your relationship with God using the Book of Psalms / Daniel F. Polish.
p.    cm.
Includes index.
ISBN 1-58023-179-9
1. Bible. O.T. Psalms—Criticism, interpretation, etc. 2. Spiritual life—Judaism. 3. Judaism—Doctrines. I. Title.
BS1430.52.P65 2003
223'.206—dc22                                              2003015275

Grateful acknowledgment is given to the following sources for permission to use material: "Momento Mori," written by Moishe Leib Halpern and "Text," written by Aaron Zeitlin," from *Voices within the Ark: The Modern Jewish Poets*, edited by Howard Schwartz and Anthony Rudolf, © 1980. Translated by Ruth Whitman. Used by permission of Ruth Whitman. "I Will Go Away," written by Zvi Shargel, from *Voices within the Ark: The Modern Jewish Poets*, edited by Howard Schwartz and Anthony Rudolf, © 1980. Used by permission of Howard Schwartz. "Isaac Leybush Peretz," written by Moyshe-Leyb Halpern, from *Voices within the Ark: The Modern Jewish Poets*, edited by Howard Schwartz and Anthony Rudolf, © 1980. Translated by Kathryn Hellerstein. Used by permission of Kathryn Hellerstein. *Gitanjali*, written by Rabindranath Tagore, and extract by Joshua Loth Liebman, from *Gates of Prayer—Shaarai Tefila: The New Union Prayerbook for Weekdays, Sabbaths and Festivals*, edited by Chaim Stern, © 1975. Used by permission of CCAR Press. *Selected Poems of Yankev Glatshteyn*, © 1987, The Jewish Publication Society. "God Is a Sad Maharal," "Like a Mousetrap," reprinted with the permission of the publisher, The Jewish Publication Society. Every effort has been made to trace and acknowledge copyright holders of all material used in this book. The publisher apologizes for any errors or omissions that may remain, and asks that any omissions be brought to their attention so they may be corrected in future editions.

10  9  8  7  6  5  4  3  2  1

Printed in Canada

*For People of All Faiths, All Backgrounds*
Published by Jewish Lights Publishing
A Division of LongHill Partners, Inc.
Sunset Farm Offices, Route 4, P.O. Box 237
Woodstock, VT 05091
Tel (802) 457-4000        Fax (802) 457-4004
www.jewishlights.com

*For my wife, Gail*
     *my* Peshe Gittel

*My inspiration for writing this book*

*As she is my inspiration for so many things*

*Who has brought so much that is beautiful
     and lovely into my life*

*With gratitude and love.*

# Contents

# Introduction

The Psalms of David
The songs he sang,
So beautifully
Rang and rang
At God's Mercy Seat.
They came to a lowly house
In a humble street,
They came to a workshop,
To the Synagogue at prayer,
To the watchman on the hill,
To the market square.
All sang Psalms,
As King David sang,
To the glory of God
And the glory of man
The Psalms of David,
King David's song,
The song of all Jews,
To all peoples belong.
They belong to the world.
The Psalms—a thought—
Man's cry for help
Has comfort brought.
The Psalms—plea and praise,
Of many and one,
All together and alone.
Through our days,
Our Psalms sing sweet.
King David's song
We repeat.

(A. Almi, "Psalms")

"Of making many books there is no end" (*Koheleth*/Ecclesiastes
12:12). When we read *Koheleth*/Ecclesiastes, we usually assume that
the author of those words was a reader like ourselves, complaining
about the fact that the flow of books seemed endless. Or, as one
current slogan reads, "so many books, so little time" (although at
the time *Koheleth*/Ecclesiastes was written, this was hardly likely).
But for anyone who has ever written a book, the statement takes on
a different meaning. No book is ever actually ended. No work is
really finished or complete—certainly in the author's mind.

As soon as my book *Bringing the Psalms to Life: How to
Understand and Use the Book of Psalms* (Jewish Lights Publishing) was
in proofs, I knew I had more I wanted to say about the psalms—or
rather, more that the psalms wanted to have said about them.
*Bringing the Psalms to Life* was about relating Psalms to the personal
experiences of our lives and the emotions with which we react to
them. This new book tries to relate Psalms in the same way to the
religious questions that all of us ask at some point in our spiritual
journey. In addition to helping us deal with the challenges that
arise in the course of our lives, Psalms can also help us think about
some of the most perplexing questions of religious belief: How do
we know God? How can we think about God? The Book of Psalms
also offers us the opportunity to confront hard and important religious dilemmas: How do we deal with the fact of our mortality?
How do we understand what makes a life righteous? What sense
can we make of the idea of an afterlife? How do we account for the
presence of evil in our world? Looking at these questions helps us
enter further into the Book of Psalms. I am not suggesting that
there is such a thing as a consistent way of answering religious
questions in the Book of Psalms. Clearly, Psalms does not have a
consistent perspective on the most important religious issues—or
one single way of understanding issues. Still, the Book of Psalms
does offer us important resources from which we can draw perspectives and insights to help us refine our own understanding. We

can use Psalms to help us shape our own personal religious world-views.

If you have opened this book with no sense of what the Book of Psalms is about—where it came from, who wrote it, and so on—you will not find those questions answered here. There are many good books that I would send you to for answers, including the first chapter of my own earlier book. If you are looking for a book that explains why generations of people have turned to psalms for comfort and inspiration—again, you will find those issues explored in my earlier book. *Keeping Faith with the Psalms* addresses a more specific question: What beliefs make up our own personal theology? In this book we will explore what the Book of Psalms can contribute to that quest.

Many times the Book of Psalms talks in questioning tones rather than in terms of certainty. For every

Surely goodness and mercy shall follow me all the days of
   my life;
And I shall dwell in the house of the Lord forever.

(Psalm 23:6)

we find verses whose character is one of uncertainty or perplexity—often urgently so.

What is man, that Thou art mindful of him?
And the son of man, that Thou thinkest of him?

(Psalm 8:5)

Lord, who shall sojourn in Thy tabernacle?
Who shall dwell upon Thy holy mountain?

(Psalm 15:1)

> Who shall ascend into the mountain of the Lord?
> And who shall stand in His holy place?

(Psalm 24:3)

These verses of Psalms reflect another facet of our lives—the desire to understand the important issues, to gain clarity about the things that matter most to us. Part of being a person of faith involves not only the desire for intimacy with God but also the desire to understand more about God and the questions that flow from our relationship with God. The Book of Psalms offers us glimpses of ways we can answer these "ultimate questions" and from these glimpses build structures of faith in which we can live our religious lives.

There is one very important way that the Book of Psalms is different from other books of the Bible—especially the books of the Torah (the Five Books of Moses). In those earlier books, God is an active participant in human affairs, and people know God through interacting with God. In Psalms, as in our own experience, God is not the protagonist of the drama; rather, the psalmists talk to God and talk about God. Psalms is more like our own faith experience than other books of the Bible. In Psalms, a number of ways to understand God are presented and elaborated upon. As a result, Psalms can be a very important resource for us as we work at developing our own religious understanding.

In *Bringing the Psalms to Life,* I suggested that the Book of Psalms was beloved by generations of readers because it offered solace in times of trouble and held out hope for rescue and redemption. Perhaps another reason that Psalms was beloved was because it helped believers answer some of the hard questions that faith raises. Belief is not "steady-state": unwavering and unchanging. And faith does not mean that we don't have a desire for clearer understanding of the concepts that make up our religious perspective.

Reading through Psalms does not offer us a presentation of one systematic way of understanding things religiously. But it does offer us facets of truth, aspects of answers, glimmers of deep understanding to questions that arise naturally from living a life of faith.

Psalms offers us the resources with which to shape our own personal theology—our own understanding of God and the way God operates in the world and in our lives. If Psalms can offer us help in that very human—and very authentically religious—quest, how can it not be beloved to us? The psalms are written in the first person singular. As we read the psalms, we read about the understandings and faith affirmations of a figure called "I." If we read these declarations with an open heart, the psalms offer us the opportunity to become that "I" and to try on the various religious ideas put forward by that "I."

Which of these voices is truly our own? In taking the role of the various "I"s of Psalms we discover which faith stances are really appropriate to us: which ones fit us, resonate with us, and express the unstated affirmations that we have been carrying around within us. By reading psalms as if they were our own, we come to learn which understandings belong to us. From the threads of the spoken word, we can weave our own garment of faith. All of us have need of such a garment in the chill of the world in which we live.

## A Word on the Yiddish Poems

You will find a good number of Yiddish poems appearing in this book, which is supposed to be, after all, about a more ancient literature. Each chapter opens with a Yiddish poem that evokes the theme that will be discussed in that chapter, and I have used Yiddish poems or other Yiddish literary creations to illustrate some of the ideas presented here. I have done this for a number of reasons. First, I think of Yiddish literature as a more recent part of the continuum of Jewish expression that has its origins in the Bible. Also, I believe that the way we look at the Book of Psalms can be reframed in an important way by looking at it as a body of poems in the whole universe of specifically Jewish poetry that is so eloquently represented by the creativity of Yiddish poetry in more recent times. Perhaps, in some way, I see myself expanding the canon of psalms to include Jewish poetic creations of a more recent composition.

I also want to take the opportunity to introduce this wonderful resource of the human spirit to readers who might not otherwise meet it. "But why," you might ask, "have you selected Yiddish poetry? If it is Jewish poetry you want people to read, surely there are Jewish poems in other languages." I decided to limit myself specifically to Yiddish because of its tragic history in our age. Here is a language that was virtually exterminated in the fires of the *Shoah*/Holocaust. So many of those who wrote in Yiddish, and most of the audience who conducted their cultural life in Yiddish, were driven from this earth. I was moved by the opportunity to let a small piece of this cultural universe live again.

## A Note on Translation

The translation that I have used in this book is almost entirely from the Jewish Publication Society translation of *The Holy Scriptures* (1917). In a very few instances I have modified the translation for clarity.

The JPS has published a more recent translation (*Tanakh,* 1985); but I prefer the older one for its more poetic quality, the majesty of its language, the graphic quality of its images, and the cadence of its verses. The older translation uses what we today recognize as "masculine language" in speaking about God. This is in marked contrast to the language I have employed throughout the book; I hope you, the reader, will find as I do that the poetic quality of the older JPS translation is worth the price of this dissonance.

# PART I
# THE QUEST FOR GOD: USING THE PSALMS TO KNOW GOD

# SEARCHING FOR THE PRESENCE OF GOD

O God where shall I find you
hid is Your lofty place

These words, filled with yearning, begin a poem by the medieval author Yehuda Halevi. Centuries later, those very words form the beginning of the poem *Gitanjali* by the Indian author Rabindranath Tagore: "Lord where can I find you?" For many of us the question of where we can find God is a real and personal part of our lives. All people have times when the religious certainty they once had eludes them. And many people discover that the challenge of finding God is an ongoing part of their spiritual lives. The search for God and the hunt for doorways into the presence of God is a crucial part of what it is to be a human being. And the Book of Psalms offers some guideposts for us as we pursue that quest.

Some people can be characterized by the story told by the Chasidic Rabbi Baruch of Mezbizh:

Rabbi Baruch, the grandson of the Ba'al Shem Tov, the founder of Chasidism, had a grandson named Yehiel. One day Yehiel was playing hide-and-seek with a friend. Yehiel hid and waited for the other boy to find him. After he had waited for a very long time, he finally came out of his hiding place but could find no trace of his playmate. He quickly understood that the other boy had not been looking for him from the very start. Crying, he ran to his grandfather to tell Rabbi Baruch of the faithlessness of his friend. Rabbi Baruch told him, "It is the same way with God."

There are times when this story captures the relationship between God and human beings. Often we don't look for God in our lives. We don't "see" God or are indifferent to the reality of God and oblivious to God's presence in our world—and in our lives. The Chasidic Rabbi Levi Yitzchak of Berditchev once undertook a bold and dramatic action as a result of his sense that many people did not look for God—and let God "hide" from them:

Rabbi Levi Yitzchak of Berditchev once put out a call that all of the Jews of Berditchev were to gather at noon on the following day in the main square of the town. He had an announcement of the utmost importance to make, and he wanted everyone to be there. Merchants were to close their shops. Artisans were to leave their work. If parents had children too young to be left alone, they should bring them along. People wondered what could be so important that the rabbi would summon them all. Had he learned that, God forbid, a pogrom was being planned? Or was a new tax to be imposed on Jews? Maybe their rabbi was going to leave them. Or maybe he had become gravely ill? Or had he learned somehow of the time of the Messiah's arrival? Whatever it was, it was certainly of great importance. And, as could be expected, at noon the next day all the Jews of Berditchev were gathered in the town square, waiting with bated breath. At exactly noon the rabbi rose and announced, "I, Levi Yitzchak, son of Sarah of Berditchev, have gathered you here today in order to tell you ... that there is a God in the world."

But just as often stories like the one about Rabbi Baruch and his grandson do not seem right at all. God is hidden all right, but we human beings are not indifferent. Instead, we struggle to find God, but don't know where God could be. When we are in quest of God, where can we begin to look? We will look at a number of doorways that the Book of Psalms opens for us as a starting point in our quest. Perhaps one of them—or all of them—may be helpful to you on your own search, as you answer the question, "O God where shall I find You?"

# 1

# MEETING GOD IN NATURE

I look up to the sky and its stars,
And down to the earth and the things that creep there.
And I consider in my heart how their creation
Was planned with wisdom in every detail.
See the heavens above like a tent,
Constructed with loops and with hooks,
And the moon with its stars, like a shepherdess
Driving her sheep to pasture;
The moon itself among the clouds,
Like a ship sailing under its banners;
The clouds like a girl in her garden
Moving, and watering the myrtle-trees;
The dew-mist—a woman shaking
Drops from her hair on the ground....

(Shmuel Hanagid, "I Look Up to the Sky")

This poem by the medieval poet Shmuel Hanagid (993–1036) reflects a sense of wonder at our natural world. The sky speaks to Shmuel Hanagid of creation—and creation becomes a signpost pointing toward the Creator. So, too, can the world around us become a doorway to God's presence. The psalms offer examples of this same way of finding God, and they put it into words for us.

Psalm 98 is devoted to complete and absolute rejoicing. That theme of rejoicing is established from the psalm's opening words, "Sing unto the Lord a new song for He hath done marvelous things" (verse 1). We have specific reasons for exalting God so enthusiastically:

> 3 He hath remembered His mercy
> And His faithfulness toward the house of Israel;
> All the ends of the earth have seen the salvation of our God.
> 4 Shout unto the Lord, all the earth;
> Break forth and sing for joy, yea, sing praises....
> 7 Let the sea roar, and the fulness thereof;
> The world, and they that dwell therein;
> 8 Let the rivers clap their hands;
> Let the mountains sing for joy together.
>
> (Psalm 98:3–4, 7–8)

Psalm 98 is part of a series of psalms—93 and 95–100—that extol God in terms of being a ruler. Many modern biblical scholars characterize Psalms 47, 93, and 96–99 as "royal enthronement psalms," which take the human phenomenon of the coronation of a king and project it onto God. Thus, this group of psalms is sung when we, as it were, enthrone God as our sovereign. Significantly, the sixteenth-century Kabbalists of Safed—early exponents of the Jewish mystical tradition who lived in the upper mountains of the Galilee—introduced the practice of including Psalms 29 and 95–99 in the liturgy that they used to welcome Shabbat, a practice continued in Jewish liturgies to this day.

What is striking about Psalm 98 is how it chooses to talk about God in the context of nature. All the ends of the earth have seen the work of God. The physical world bears witness to God. And it is the earth itself that praises God. In verse 4 the praises are offered by the totality of the earth. In verses 7 and 8, individual elements of the natural world are depicted as singing God's praises. Some of the ways these elements of the natural world are presented are familiar to us. Some of the ways they praise God differ very much from what we experience. We are certainly accustomed to referring to the sea as "roaring." That is often how the ocean sounds to us. But we probably do not experience rivers as clapping their hands or mountains as singing. Perhaps the author of Psalm 98 is taking some poetic license, expanding upon the sounds we do hear in the world of nature, including rivers as they rush along their courses and mountains when the wind blows through them. Or perhaps the author is suggesting that even elements of the natural world are moved to behave in ways outside of their normal patterns when they are roused to exalt God. In either case, these images are part of a pattern we see elsewhere in the Bible, for instance, in Isaiah 55:12, where "the mountains and the hills break forth ... into singing, and all the trees of the field ... clap their hands," and elsewhere in Psalms. In Psalm 98 it is clear that one significant place we can begin to meet God is in the realm of creation—that realm which is, in many senses of the phrase, our natural environment.

This theme of God as encountered in nature explains why Psalm 98 is included in both the "enthronement" cycle and in the Jewish liturgy for Shabbat. For nature, the work of creation, represents God's greatest achievement. When we "enthrone" God as our sovereign, we remind ourselves of the greatest gift our ruler has given us: the natural world and the many elements that comprise it.

As we prepare to welcome the seventh day, it is equally fitting to talk about God as we experience God in the natural world that God created. In Jewish tradition, Shabbat is called *Zecher l'maasei v'resheet,* a reminder of (or tribute to) the works of creation. In the Genesis 1 account of creation, Shabbat is described as the final piece of God's work of creating—the culmination of the six days of labor that preceded it. How appropriate, then, to welcome

Shabbat with a testimonial to that world of nature—even to imagine that those works of creation were giving praise themselves.

## The Heavens Express Themselves

To the literal-minded reader, the first half of Psalm 19 must appear very perplexing. Its message may seem hard for us to grasp. After all, what sense can the literalist expect to make of a text that begins with the sky talking, then later includes the paradoxical statement that "there is no speech, there are no words." The images that are employed in Psalm 19, however, convey a deep and important teaching:

> 2 The heavens declare the glory of God,
> And the firmament showeth His handiwork;
> 3 Day unto day uttereth speech,
> And night unto night revealeth knowledge;
> 4 There is no speech, there are no words,
> Neither is their voice heard.
> 5 Their line is gone out through all the earth,
> And their words to the end of the world.
> In them hath He set a tent for the sun,
> 6 Which is as a bridegroom coming out of his chamber,
> And rejoiceth as a strong man to run his course.
> 7 His going forth is from the end of the heaven,
> And his circuit unto the ends of it;
> And there is nothing hid from the heat thereof.
>
> (Psalm 19:2–7)

The remainder of Psalm 19 is a reflection on an entirely different theme, the subject of finding God through Torah. Here let us focus on the first verses. Verse 4 sets the basic theme: "There is no speech, there are no words,/neither is their voice heard." The heavens express themselves to us not through their words, but through their very being. We marvel at the grandeur of the heavenly array. Imagine yourself outside on a cloudless night. The expanse of the heavens, the immensity of the cosmos and its beauty cannot help but leave a deep impression on you—and draw your thoughts to the One who created it all.

The subject shifts slightly in the last half of verse 5 and the next two verses. These are expressions of amazement at the sun. In Psalms, of course, the sun is not, in itself, the object of worship, as it was in so many other early civilizations. But it can be a proper object of our wonder. In Jewish tradition, the sun is often presented as a sign pointing to God, who created it, shaped it, and established its course through the heavens. Verse 6 looks for familiar images taken from human experience to capture the majesty of the sun as it makes its way daily through our sky. The power of the sun, the order and predictability—and its splendor—are appropriate sources of wonder, even awe.

Rabbinic literature is full of stories about a heathen who approaches one or another of the rabbis and argues that the God of the Jews is a fiction or an impossibility. In many of these stories, the rabbi tells the heathen, "Well then, look at the sun." The heathen says something like, "I cannot; it is too powerful," to which the rabbi replies, "Then imagine the power of the One who created it."

Without speaking, the heavens testify to their Creator, moving us to encounter the God who is the "maker and master" of the immense wonder of the world of nature that is our home.

If the message of Psalm 19:2–7 is presented allusively, it is put more directly in two verses in the midst of Psalm 8:

4 When I behold Thy heavens, the work of Thy fingers,
   The moon and the stars, which Thou hast established;
5 What is man, that Thou art mindful of him?
   And the son of man, that Thou thinkest of him?
(Psalm 8:4–5)

Here the psalmist puts into words what we might feel when standing in wonder before the heavens on a starry night or at the edge of the Grand Canyon. When we allow ourselves to feel the vastness of creation, we feel less than small—we feel truly insignificant. Robert Alter, in his *Art of Biblical Poetry*,[1] notes that the only verb ascribed to human beings in these verses is "behold" or "see," as if to suggest that people's role here is only to "see" the works of God. Verse 5 asserts that we are all the more overwhelmed when we let ourselves appreciate the implications of the fact that the One who created all this is still "mindful of us," still cares about us. The Chasidic Rabbi Nachman of Breslav told a parable based on Psalm 8:4.

There was a prince who lived far away from his father, the king, and he was very, very homesick for his father. Once he received a letter from his father, and he was overjoyed and treasured it. Yet, the joy and the delight that the letter gave him increased his longing even more. He would sit and complain, "Oh, oh, if I could only touch his hand! If he would extend his hand to me, how I would embrace it. I would kiss every finger in my great longing for my father, my teacher, my light. Merciful father, how I would love to touch at least your little finger." And while he was complaining, feeling sorry for himself, and longing for a touch of his father, a thought flashed in his mind: Don't I have my father's letter, written in his own hand! Is not the handwriting of the king comparable to his hand? And then a great joy burst forth for him. "When I look at the heavens, the work of Thy fingers."

The Yiddish poet Aaron Zeitlin reflects on this same theme and makes a daring assertion in his poem "If You Look at the Stars":

Praise Me, says God, and I will know that you love Me.
Curse Me, says God, and I will know that you love Me.
Praise Me or curse Me,
And I will know that you love Me.

Sing out My graces, says God.
Raise your fist against Me and revile, says God.
Sing out graces or revile,
Reviling is also a kind of praise, says God.

But if you sit fenced off in your apathy, says God,
If you sit entrenched in, "I don't give a hang," says God,
If you look at the stars and yawn,
If you see suffering and don't cry out,
If you don't praise and you don't revile
Then I created you in vain, says God.

(Aaron Zeitlin, "If You Look at the Stars")

The first half of Psalm 19 and the verses in Psalm 8 convey this same spirit. God's creative power overwhelms us when we truly understand what we are seeing.

## *Something More of This Earth*

On first reading, the message of Psalm 29 may be hard for us to find. As we look at it more closely, its real meaning becomes clearer:

1 A Psalm of David.
  Ascribe unto the Lord, O ye sons of might,
  Ascribe unto the Lord glory and strength.
2 Ascribe unto the Lord the glory due unto His name;
  Worship the Lord in the beauty of holiness.
3 The voice of the Lord is upon the waters;

The God of glory thundereth, even the Lord upon many
waters.
4 The voice of the Lord is powerful;
The voice of the Lord is full of majesty.
5 The voice of the Lord breaketh the cedars;
Yea, the Lord breaketh in pieces the cedars of Lebanon.
6 He maketh them also to skip like a calf;
Lebanon and Sirion like a young wild-ox.
7 The voice of the Lord heweth out flames of fire.
8 The voice of the Lord shaketh the wilderness;
The Lord shaketh the wilderness of Kadesh.
9 The voice of the Lord maketh the hinds to calve,
And strippeth the forests bare;
And in His temple all say: "Glory."
10 The Lord sat enthroned at the flood;
Yea, the Lord sitteth as King forever.
11 The Lord will give strength unto His people;
The Lord will bless His people with peace.

(Psalm 29:1–11)

Psalm 29 is a remarkable piece of religious poetry. It begins with an experience with which its first hearers—and we later ones, too—were well acquainted, and then goes on to reinterpret it for profound religious purposes. Here is a psalm whose very poetry is overwhelming, painting a compelling word picture and even capturing the force of its subject in the very sound of its verses. That subject—revealed in the reference to voices (repeated seven times); flames of fire; the shattering of trees; the shaking of even the most solid of mountains—is a powerful mountain thunderstorm. We can feel the intensity of that storm and sense its power in the composition of the poem itself. And yet the storm is not the real subject of the psalm. Ultimately, the purpose of the psalm is to help us experience the storm and then move beyond it. Psalm 24 wants us to see that storm as a metaphor for the power of God. After the unleashing of the storm's power, the psalm makes clear that it is but a reflection of the power of the One who is all-powerful. As the psalm comes to a close, it is God who "sits enthroned above the flood" and God who "rules forever" (verse 10).

And what of verse 11? It seems so inconsistent with the rest of the psalm. If it were not included, the psalm would end with the last word of verse 10, *l'olam*/forever, as do so many other psalms. In fact, this allusion to eternity is one of the sources of Psalms' ability to comfort us and give us a sense of security. So what is verse 11 doing here? Is it an afterthought, or an addition by a reader so overcome with terror at the power described in the psalm that he offered up a pious hope for tranquility? Or perhaps verse 11 is really part of the message of the psalm, teaching a profound and paradoxical truth: The God who is so powerful and can unleash such might is still the God who is concerned with God's people and can share some of that might with them. The psalmist reminds us that there are not two forces at work in this world. The God of power and force is also the God of tenderness, caring, and peace.

The readers of Psalm 29 are allowed an experience very much like that of Moses at the burning bush in Exodus 3. We stumble upon some element of the natural world, only to recognize that we are confronted with something more profound than we had first understood. That natural phenomenon—a bush for Moses, a storm for us—is a doorway into a deeper reality, an opportunity to find ourselves in the presence of God.

Perhaps the experience of Moses—and of those who enter into the spirit of Psalm 29—was best expressed by the patriarch Jacob. After coming upon some desolate spot during his flight from his home in Canaan to his ancestral home in Haran, Jacob has an unexpected encounter with God. When that revelation of the Divine is concluded, Jacob says, "Surely God was in this place and I did not know it ... how awesome is this place. This is nothing other than the house of God" (Genesis 28:16–17). As we search for God, we too can find in something as "mundane" as a thunderstorm a doorway into experiencing and appreciating the power of God.

Psalm 29 might hold even more levels of meaning for its earliest readers, and for us. There are times in the Bible when the world of nature becomes an instrument for God's breaking into human affairs. In Psalm 29 we see reference to two other occasions when God took control of natural phenomena for special purposes.

In verse 10, the Hebrew word that is used for flood is *mabul*. Although other words could have been employed to convey the concept, the author chose to use this one. As it happens, the word *mabul* is used in only one other place in the entire Bible: the chapters in Genesis that describe the events of Noah's ark. Through the use of this single word, verse 10 associates Psalm 29's description of God's power as experienced in nature with that earlier moment in the biblical narrative when God used nature as an instrument to shape human destiny.

In the second half of verse 8, we encounter a phrase that appears to be an interpretive addition by a later reader, and it has the effect of reframing the entire psalm. Some scholars dismiss this phrase as being simply the interpretive addition of someone who put it in after the original psalm was completed. But we can let it open still another layer of meaning for us. The wilderness that is mentioned without a name in the first half of verse 8 is given a name in the second half of the verse. There it is identified as the wilderness of Kadesh, through which Moses led the Israelites during the Exodus from Egypt. By drawing our attention to the Exodus event, the very nature of the thunderstorm described in Psalm 29 is given yet further significance. In this light we can now read the psalm as referring not just to any powerful meteorological phenomenon that we might happen to experience, but also to one particular historic event. The psalm, read this way, points us to the events described in Exodus 19. The thunder and lightning, the "voices," and the shaking earth can now be heard as an echo of what the Israelites experienced when they stood at Sinai, where "there was the voice of thunder and lightning ... and the whole mountain trembled violently" (Exodus 19:16, 18). Psalm 29 becomes less an example of how we can encounter God through the power of a natural phenomenon, and more about finding God in the collective history of the Jewish people. It becomes a poem not about seeing God behind a mountain thunderstorm, but about the giving of the Torah at Mount Sinai. You could say that that element of the psalm was added to the original intent of the psalmist. Or you can choose to say that this aspect of the psalm gives us the opportunity to see any thunderstorm as an occasion to return to Sinai and, through that journey, relive a profound encounter with God. Either way, thunderstorms become a doorway leading beyond that passing moment and into the presence of God.

Psalm 29 is included in the Sabbath liturgy. Perhaps it is included because of its association with the giving of the Torah by virtue of the reinterpretation of verse 8 that we have just discussed. This would be appropriate, because Shabbat is the day par excellence for the Torah to be read in synagogue. Or perhaps, as has been suggested in the Talmud (Berachot 29a), it is included because the seven-fold repetition of the word *voice* corresponds to the seven blessings that the central benediction of the liturgy has been abbreviated to on Shabbat (from the eighteen that are recited in the daily liturgy). Most likely, Psalm 29 is included in the Shabbat liturgy because, like Psalm 98, it enables us to use nature and the world of creation as a vehicle to experience and engage with God, who fashioned the entire natural world at the time of creation. In this psalm, we are encouraged to encounter God, whose work of creation is celebrated on the Sabbath.

## Nature as a Gateway to God

Two final psalms emphatically assert the role of nature as a gateway to the presence of God. Psalm 148 is an unrestrained and unalloyed expression of praise to God, as are the last six compositions in the Book of Psalms. In the midst of this poem of exaltation, we find a veritable catalog of the elements of creation that are called upon to join in the chorus of praise.

> ³ Praise ye Him, sun and moon;
>    Praise Him all ye stars of light ...
> ⁷ Praise the Lord from the earth,
>    Ye sea monsters, and all deeps;
> ⁸ Fire and hail, snow and vapor,
>    Stormy wind, fulfilling His word;
> ⁹ Mountains and all hills,
>    Fruitful trees and all cedars;
> ¹⁰ Beasts and all cattle;
>    Creeping things and winged fowl.
>
> (Psalm 148:3, 7–10)

In the ecstatic cataloging of elements from our natural world, we find a powerful expression of wonder at God's creative genius. It is as if the psalmist were saying, "Look at all the different things that God has created. The scope and diversity of this natural world offer reason enough for gratitude and celebration." The world of nature listed in these few verses evokes a sense of awe at the architect of the world we inhabit.

That sense of awe is the subject of Psalm 104, an expression of amazement at the complexity and beauty of the world we live in and wonder at the One who fashioned it all:

> ¹ Bless the Lord, O my soul.
>    O Lord my God, Thou art very great;

Thou art clothed with glory and majesty.
2 Who coverest Thyself with light as with a garment,
Who stretchest out the heavens like a curtain;
3 Who layest the beams of Thine upper chambers in the
waters,
Who makest the clouds Thy chariot,
Who walkest upon the wings of the wind;
4 Who makest winds Thy messengers,
The flaming fires Thy ministers.
5 Who didst establish the earth upon its foundations,
That it should not be moved forever and ever;
6 Thou didst cover it with the deep as with a vesture;
The waters stood above the mountains.
7 At Thy rebuke they fled,
At the voice of Thy thunder they hasted away—
8 The mountains rose, the valleys sank down—
Unto the place which Thou hadst founded for them;
9 Thou didst set a bound which they should not pass over,
That they might not return to cover the earth.
10 Who sendest forth springs into the valleys;
They run into the mountains;
11 They give drink to every beast of the field,
The wild asses quench their thirst.
12 Beside them dwell the fowl of the heavens,
From among the branches they sing.
13 Who waterest the mountains from Thine upper chambers;
The earth is full of the fruit of Thy works.
14 Who causest the grass to spring up for the cattle,
And herb for the service of man;
To bring forth bread out of the earth,
15 And wine that maketh glad the heart of man,
Making the face brighter than oil,
And bread that stayeth man's heart.

16 The trees of the Lord have their fill,
   The cedars of Lebanon, which He hath planted.
17 Wherein the birds make their nests;
   As for the stork, the fir-trees are her house.
18 The high mountains are for the wild goats;
   The rocks are a refuge for the rock badgers.
19 Who appointedst the moon for seasons;
   The sun knoweth his going down.
20 Thou makest darkness, and it is night,
   Wherein the beasts of the forest do creep forth....
24 How manifold are Thy works, O Lord!
   In wisdom hast Thou made them all;
   The earth is full of Thy creatures.
25 Yonder sea, great and wide,
   Therein are creeping things innumerable,
   Living creatures, both small and great.
26 There go the ships;
   There is leviathan, whom Thou hast formed to sport therein....
31 May the glory of the Lord endure forever;
   Let the Lord rejoice in His works!

(Psalm 104:1–20, 24–26, 31)

In the scope of its vision of creation, Psalm 104 is similar to the catalog of creation that we find in the Book of Job, chapters 38–41. In Job the wonder and intricacy of nature are enlisted as witnesses to the awesomeness and power of God. We find much the same thing from the prophet Amos (Amos 5:8), though Amos's list is not as extensive. In Psalm 104, too, this elaborate evocation of the natural world serves to remind us that if we are looking for testimony to God's power, we only have to look about us.

Psalm 104, as the chapters in Job, seems to suggest that we take the splendor of our surroundings for granted. The psalm calls on us to look at our world with eyes that are not clouded by the familiarity and indifference that come from routine. When we stop being jaded, when we let ourselves see—truly see—the wonder that is our home, we can rejoice in our good fortune. And as we rejoice, our hearts are directed beyond this or that particular expression of God's creative genius to reflect on God's power and God's generosity. Then our thoughts can turn toward the One who gave us all this—toward God, who created all this, created us, and placed us in the midst of such beauty and wonder.

No other psalm captures the sense of God as creator as powerfully as Psalm 104, and no other verses in Scripture express with such force and clarity the idea of finding God through God's handiwork. Psalm 104 serves almost as a poetic repetition of the events we find in the Book of Genesis. It follows the Genesis description in the order of creation, beginning with light and ascending through plants and trees to the animal world. Verse 31, in stating, "Let the Lord rejoice in His works," echoes the refrain of Genesis 1 that asserts "and God saw ... and it was good."

And yet with all its echoes of Genesis 1, Psalm 104 has a significant shift in verse 10. While all the previous verses were written in the past tense, this verse and the ones that follow it are in the present tense. Creation is presented as being not a one-time-only event. As reflected in this psalm, God did not create the world and then withdraw. God continues to tend the world. The work of creation continues. The psalm talks not only about what God did, but also about what God does. This reflects the same spirit as the prayer in the daily morning liturgy that asserts that God "renews every day, always the work of creation."

Verse 24 gives voice to the fundamental idea of Psalm 104, of Genesis 1, and of all who see creation as an expression of God's power: "In wisdom have You made them all." God creates with understanding, with purpose. Our universe is shaped by order and brought into being by design. The order and plan of the world about us are seen as tribute to the One who ordered and

planned it all. Because it puts into words a Jewish belief, this verse
has been incorporated into one of the prayers of the morning
liturgy, the *Yotzer Or,* which praises God for creating light. Indeed,
the entire psalm is customarily read on every *Rosh Chodesh*/new
lunar month, perhaps because of verse 19, which alludes to God
appointing "the moon for fixed seasons." Certainly, this psalm,
with its evocation of the orderliness and regularity of nature, is
most appropriate to be read on that occasion, which commemo-
rates orderly renewal.

Portions of several other psalms also are devoted to celebrating God's first act of creation:

1 A Psalm of David
The earth is the Lord's, and the fulness thereof;
The world, and they that dwell therein.
2 For He hath founded it upon the seas,
And established it upon the floods.

(Psalm 24:1–2)

6 Whatsoever the Lord pleased, that hath He done,
In heaven and in earth, in the seas and in all deeps;
7 Who causeth the vapors to ascend from the ends of the
earth;
He maketh lightnings for the rain;
He bringeth forth the wind out of His treasuries.

(Psalm 135:6–7)

12 Yet God is my King of old,
Working salvation in the midst of the earth.
13 Thou didst break the sea in pieces by Thy strength;
Thou didst shatter the heads of the sea monsters in the
waters.
14 Thou didst crush the heads of leviathan,

Thou gavest him to be food to the folk inhabiting the
   wilderness.
[15] Thou didst cleave fountain and brook;
   Thou driedest up ever-flowing rivers.
[16] Thine is the day, Thine also the night;
   Thou hast established luminary and sun.
[17] Thou hast set all the borders of the earth;
   Thou hast made summer and winter.

(Psalm 74:12–17)

[10] Thou rulest the proud swelling of the sea;
   When the waves thereof arise, Thou stillest them....
[12] Thine are the heavens, Thine also the earth;
   The world and the fulness thereof, Thou hast founded them.
[13] The north and the south, Thou hast created them;
   Tabor and Hermon rejoice in Thy name.

(Psalm 89:10, 12–13)

The sets of opposites in verses 16 and 17 of Psalm 74 underscore the point of this psalm. God is depicted as ruling over day
and night, summer and winter, the ends of the earth. In other
words, God is ruler over all.

Throughout the Book of Psalms we find words of praise for
God in the context of God's deeds "in the beginning." We hear the
creation account of Genesis 1:14–16 echoed in part of Psalm 136:

[5] To Him that by understanding made the heavens,
   For His mercy endureth forever.
[6] To Him that spread forth the earth above the waters,
   For His mercy endureth forever.
[7] To Him that made great lights,
   For His mercy endureth forever.
[8] The sun to rule by day,

For His mercy endureth forever.
9 The moon and the stars to rule by night,
For His mercy endureth forever.

(Psalm 136:5–9)

Another lengthy expression of praise for God as creator of the world is found in Psalm 147:

4 He counteth the number of the stars;
He giveth them all their names....
7 Sing unto the Lord with thanksgiving,
Sing praises upon the harp unto our God;
8 Who covereth the heaven with clouds,
Who prepareth rain for the earth,
Who maketh the mountains to spring with grass.
9 He giveth to the beast his food,
And to the young ravens which cry....
16 He giveth snow like wool;
He scattereth the hoar-frost like ashes.
17 He casteth forth His ice like crumbs;
Who can stand before His cold?
18 He sendeth forth His word, and melteth them;
He causeth His wind to blow, and the waters flow.

(Psalm 147:4, 7–9, 16–18)

Here we find God praised for the hosts of the heavens, and the wonder of winter (verses 16–17). Elsewhere we see God praised explicitly as creator of all that exists:

Who made heaven and earth,
The sea, and all that in them is;
Who keepeth truth forever.

(Psalm 146:6)

Similarly, Psalm 95 states:

4 In whose hand are the depths of the earth;
The heights of the mountains are His also.
5 The sea is His, and He made it;
And His hands formed the dry land.

(Psalm 95:4–5)

Psalm 65 praises God as creator of all:

6 With wondrous works dost Thou answer us in righteousness,
O God of our salvation;
Thou the confidence of all the ends of the earth,
And of the far distant seas;
7 Who by Thy strength settest fast the mountains,
Who art girded about with might;
8 Who stillest the roaring of the seas, the roaring of their
waves,
And the tumult of the peoples.

(Psalm 65:6–8)

Psalm 65 goes on to express gratitude for the specific way God's creative power affects us directly by yielding the rich and abundant harvest upon which we depend:

10 Thou hast remembered the earth,
and watered her, greatly enriching her,
With the river of God that is full of water;
Thou preparest them corn, for so preparest Thou her.
11 Watering her ridges abundantly,
Settling down the furrows thereof,
Thou makest her soft with showers;
Thou blessest the growth thereof.

¹² Thou crownest the year with Thy goodness;
   And Thy paths drop fatness.
¹³ The pastures of the wilderness do drop;
   And the hills are girded with joy.
¹⁴ The meadows are clothed with flocks;
   The valleys also are covered over with corn;
   They shout for joy, yea, they sing.

(Psalm 65:10–14)

## The "Normal Mysticism" of Everyday Life

What all the psalms in this chapter share is their sense of awe at the natural world around us. If we have become jaded to the splendor, or indifferent, these psalms call on us to see again through eyes of wonder. And then they steer our thinking beyond what we can experience with our senses to the realm of the invisible God who is the source of this awesome array. This is the spirit captured by the American poet John Berryman, when he addresses God as "master of beauty, craftsman of the snowflake, inimitable contriver, endower of Earth so gorgeous...."[2]

This way of thinking is also seen in the spiritual orientation of the Jewish tradition (and of other spiritual paths as well), which encourages us to move from the particulars of our daily experience to the reality of God who lies behind them. This has been called "the normal mysticism" of everyday life. We encounter God not in renouncing the world, or in moving out of it, but in entering into it with our spirit open to an appreciation of the One whose world this is. The elements of the natural world that we encounter in our daily lives are seen not as hindrances to our spiritual development, but as the very instruments for deepening our sense of gratitude to God. They are doorways into God's presence. This spirit is captured by the poet Leah Goldberg.

Teach us, O God, to praise and to pray
For the mystery of the withering leaf,
For the glow of the ripened fruit;
For the freedom to see, to feel,
To breathe, to know, to hope, to stumble.

Teach our lips a blessing, a hymn of praise,
As You renew each morning and each night;
Lest this day appear as yesterday
And the day before—
Lest our days become routine,
Lest our souls be blind to wonder.

(Leah Goldberg)

This "normal mysticism" is the same spiritual attitude that lies behind the practice of reciting blessings throughout the course of the day. According to one calculation, if we stopped and offered words of praise at each point Jewish tradition instructs us to, we would recite no less than 100 blessings each and every day. According to Jewish tradition, there are blessings to be recited for all the elements we encounter as part of our human experience: the wonders of the world around us; the workings of our own bodies; the cycle of the day, the week, the seasons. There are a variety of blessings to be recited over the different kinds of food we eat and beverages we drink, as well as over such occurrences as seeing a rainbow; experiencing an electrical storm; smelling fragrant spices; seeing the ocean or a tree blossoming; or anything unusually beautiful in the world of nature.

Jewish religiousness begins with an attitude of reverence for every aspect of the human experience. A story is told about the Chasidic Rabbi Zev Wolf of Zhitomer. To support his family, Zev Wolf worked as a village innkeeper. Once a wagon driver entered and asked him for a glass of brandy. As the driver was about to gulp

down the brandy without reciting a blessing, Zev Wolf stopped him
and asked, "Don't you realize all of the wondrous processes that
have to occur to the fruit of the vine for it to become the drink that
you are about to enjoy?" The wagon driver then recited the blessing and Zev Wolf answered, "Amen."

A prayerful life begins with, and intensifies, our awareness of
all the wondrous processes in the world around us. Among the
blessings we are instructed to recite each day is one called the
*Motzi.* Every time we eat bread we are instructed to say, "Blessed are
You O Lord our God, Ruler of the universe, who brings forth bread
from the earth." Of course, such a blessing can be recited mechan-
ically, without any true feeling of gratitude or without reflecting on
the true significance of the words spoken. But if the prayer is recited with *kavanah*—focused attention on what it means—the *Motzi*
can help us appreciate the miraculous quality of this seemingly
most ordinary of activities.

Instead, we can reflect on the amazing process that must take
place for us to have this piece of bread we are about to eat. How
miraculous that a tiny seed can grow into a grain of wheat. No less
wondrous that the wheat can be turned into flour. Still another
miracle enables the flour to be transformed into dough. Saying the
blessing directs our minds to reflect on the wonder of the process
through which fire transforms the dough into bread and the
processes within our bodies that enable the bread to nourish and
sustain us and give us strength to go about our daily lives.

Saying the blessing with *kavanah* takes the everyday act of eating bread and allows us to reflect on how it connects us to the wonders of the world of nature. It also allows us to see ourselves as
connected to an entire constellation of fellow human beings whom
we have probably never met. For us to have this piece of bread we
are about to eat (and which we might well have taken for granted),
we are indebted to the farmer who put the seed in the ground and
the harvester who gathered the wheat. A miller converted the

wheat to flour, and a baker turned the flour into dough. Someone baked the dough in the oven, and still another person transported the finished bread to the store. All of this human activity before we can say, "Blessed are You O Lord our God, Ruler of the universe, who brings forth bread from the earth."

Reciting the *Motzi* reflects in the same spirit as Psalm 34:9, which says, "Taste and see the Lord is good." We encounter God through our physical senses. The world around us becomes the place where we can meet God.

Of course, the blessing over bread is not the only one we recite before eating. There are other blessings to be recited before eating fruits, vegetables, non-bread baked goods, and sweets. Yet another blessing is prescribed for drinking anything made from fruit that grows on a vine.

Jewish tradition also instructs us to recite an extended blessing upon the completion of our meal. This reflects the spiritual sensibility expressed in Psalm 145:16, which is, in fact, quoted in the text of that blessing:

> Thou openest Thy hand,
> And satisfiest every living thing with favor.
>
> (Psalm 145:16)

The recognition that God provides food for all living creatures is found elsewhere in Psalms as well:

> 24 How manifold are Thy works, O Lord!
> In wisdom hast Thou made them all;
> The earth is full of Thy creatures.
> 25 Yonder sea, great and wide,
> Therein are creeping things innumerable,
> Living creatures, both small and great.
> 26 There go the ships;

> There is leviathan, whom Thou hast formed to sport therein.
> 27 All of them wait for Thee,
> That Thou mayest give them their food in due season.
> 28 Thou givest it unto them, they gather it;
> Thou openest Thy hand, they are satisfied with good.
>
> (Psalm 104:24–28)

> 1 O give thanks unto the Lord, for He is good,
> For His mercy endureth forever....
> 25 Who giveth food to all flesh,
> For His mercy endureth forever.
>
> (Psalm 136:1, 25)

> He giveth to the beast his food,
> And to the young ravens which cry.
>
> (Psalm 147:9)

So much of the Jewish calendar is a celebration of the world of nature. The weekly celebration of Shabbat is described as a "reminder of the work of creation." The monthly celebration of the new moon, which marks the beginning of each month on the Hebrew (lunar) calendar, attunes us to the heavens. The three major pilgrimage festivals—*Pesach*/Passover, *Shavuot*/the Feast of Weeks (Pentecost in the Christian calendar), and *Sukkot*/the Feast of Booths (Tabernacles)—all celebrate the cycle of vegetation, the harvest of different types of produce. Even Chanukah, which is usually thought of as being based exclusively on a historical event, is timed to coincide with the winter solstice. To live with real sensitivity to the Jewish calendar is to be attuned to the many different cycles of nature.

The events and activities of our daily lives are not distractions, or even hindrances in our quest for God. Rather, they are gateways through which we can enter into God's presence. Reciting the psalms, and feeling the words to be our own, can give us the experience of opening our eyes and saying, "Surely God was in this place, and I did not know it."

The poets with whose questions we began this chapter found answers through their capacity to see the miracles that constitute our everyday life. They shared in the spiritual vision that sees the world around us as gateways into the power and wonder of God. Rabindranath Tagore asked, "Lord, where shall I find you?" And he answered himself,

> Your glory fills the world.
> Behold, I find You
> Where the ploughman breaks the hard soil,
> Where the quarrier explodes stone
> Out of the hillside....
>
> Behold I find You
> When dawn comes up bearing golden gifts
> And in the fall of evening peace and rest
> from the Western sea.
>
> In the current of life flowing day and night
> through all things,
> Throbbing in my sinews and in the dust of the earth,
> In every leaf and flower....
>
> (Rabindranath Tagore, *Gitanjali*)

Almost 1,000 years earlier, Yehuda Halevi asked the same question, and answered it even more evocatively:

> O Lord where shall I find Thee
> Hid is Thy lofty place
> And where shall I not find Thee

Whose glory fills all space ...
Who saith he hath not seen Thee
The heavens refute his word
Their hosts declare Thy glory
Though never voice be heard.

1. Robert Alter, *The Art of Biblical Poetry* (New York: Basic Books, 1985), p. 119.
2. John Berryman, "Eleven Addresses to the Lord," *Love and Fame* (New York: Farrar, Straus, and Giroux, 1970), p. 85.

# 2

# FINDING GOD IN TORAH

... In the twin-scroll Torah
lie light and song
speaks the people's history
Behold your bride:
in gold-embroidered velvet gown and
coroneted headdress
your lips may kiss her
your arms may embrace her
as you dance with her
to the glory of the Lord....

(Rose Ausländer, "Hasidic Jew from Sadagora")

This I recall to mind, therefore I have hope.

(Lamentations 3:21)

R. Abba b. Kahana said: This may be likened to a king who married a lady and wrote her a large *ketubah*: "So many state-apartments I am preparing for you, so many jewels I am preparing for you, so much silver and gold I give you."

The king left her and went to a distant land for many years. Her neighbors used to vex her, saying, "Your husband has deserted you. Come and be married to another man."

She wept and sighed, but whenever she went into her room
and read her *ketubah* she would be consoled. After many
years the king returned and said to her, "I am astonished
that you waited for me all these years." She replied, "My
lord king, if it had not been for the generous *ketubah* you
wrote me then surely my neighbors would have won me
over." (Lamentations Rabbah)

Some people seriously misunderstand the Jewish tradition
regarding Torah. Countless generations of Christians—and not a
few Jews—have made the mistake of thinking that for Jews Torah
must be a burden. Even the familiar practice of translating the
Hebrew word *Torah* into English by using the word "law" makes it
sound oppressive. The fact is that in the eyes of Jewish tradition,
nothing could be farther off the mark. Torah is felt by the tradition
to be a gift, a delight. In the story at the beginning of this chapter,
Torah is understood as a sign of the Jewish people's enduring connection with God. Significantly, the prayers in the daily liturgy that
deal with the Torah describe it as an expression of God's eternal
love for the People of Israel. The association of God's word with
love is remarkable and one of the qualities that uniquely characterizes the Jewish religious tradition. Significantly, even the very
first psalm speaks of Torah in terms of delight:

But his delight is in the Torah of the Lord;
And in His law doth he meditate day and night.
(Psalm 1:2)

We see this same association frequently in Psalm 119, which is
a long composition in the form of an acrostic that contains many,
quite separate, teachings. The one theme it returns to consistently
is the power of the word of God. Torah is connected with love at
numerous points in Psalm 119. Indeed, we could create a litany:

Oh how I love Thy Torah!
It is my meditation all the day.

(Psalm 119:97)

I hate them that are of a double mind;
But Thy Torah I love.

(Psalm 119:113)

Therefore I love Thy commandments
Above gold, yea, above fine gold.

(Psalm 119:127)

I hate and abhor falsehood;
Thy Torah I do love.

(Psalm 119:163)

Torah is a beloved expression of God's love for us—and, most important, it is seen as a vehicle by which we can make our way to God.

If we are searching for ways to discover God, come into God's presence, or grow in the knowledge of God, Jewish tradition teaches us that one powerful way to do so is to become caught up in Torah. This attitude of reverence and devotion for the Torah itself finds expression in numerous places in the Book of Psalms.

Happy are they that are upright in the way,
Who walk in the Torah of the Lord.

(Psalm 119:1)

Unless Thy Torah had been my delight,
I should have then perished in mine affliction.

(Psalm 119:92)

Let Thy tender mercies come unto me, that I may live;
For Thy Torah is my delight.
(Psalm 119:77)

Great peace have they that love Thy Torah;
And there is no stumbling for them.
(Psalm 119:165)

I have longed for Thy salvation, O Lord;
And Thy Torah is my delight.
(Psalm 119:174)

Delight in Torah is contrasted with indifference to it. The good
and the wicked are differentiated by the way they regard Torah. The
wicked are, in the end, destined for destruction, "the way of the
wicked shall perish" (Psalm 1:6). Of such people Psalm 78 says:

They kept not the covenant of God,
And refused to walk in His Torah....
(Psalm 78:10)

We hear this same contrast again in Psalm 119:

Burning indignation hath taken hold upon me, because of
   the wicked
That forsake Thy Torah.
(Psalm 119:53)

Perhaps it is of these wicked ones, that Psalm 119 says:

It is time for the Lord to work;
They have made void Thy Torah.
(Psalm 119:126)

The good person, the one who delights in Torah, is compared to a tree:

And he shall be like a tree planted by streams of water,
That bringeth forth its fruit in its season,
And whose leaf doth not wither;
And in whatsoever he doeth he shall prosper.

(Psalm 1:3)

We see similar imagery in the words of Jeremiah 17:8, as well as in the *Pirkei Avot*/Sayings of the Fathers 3:22.

He shall be like a tree planted by waters, sending forth its roots by a stream: it does not sense the coming of heat, its leaves are ever fresh; it has no care in a year of drought, it does not cease to yield fruit. (Jeremiah 17:8)

Perhaps it is Psalm 1's tree imagery in such close conjunction with the delight in Torah of verse 2 that has caused Jewish tradition to identify Torah as a "Tree of Life." The liturgy surrounding the reading of the Torah in the synagogue borrows the language of Proverbs 3:17 and 18, which are a song of praise to wisdom, and reinterprets them as referring to Torah. Thus, as the Torah scroll is returned to the ark, we say:

She is a tree of life to those who grasp her, and whoever holds on to her is happy. Her ways are pleasant ways, and all her paths, peaceful. (Proverbs 3:18, 17)

Like a tree, Torah is firmly established, and yet grows ever upward. Torah nurtures and sustains, adds beauty and enhances our lives. Torah, like a tall tree, is a link between earth and heaven.

In the *midrash,* or rabbinic story, at the beginning of this chapter, the Torah is represented as a *ketubah,* a marriage contract, between God and the Jewish people. In this *midrash,* Torah is an expression of devotion, a source of fidelity and strength. The *ketubah* symbolizes the *brit,* the contract, between God and the Jewish People. In the *brit,* as in any contract, each side has its responsibilities. In the traditional understanding, God's role is to protect the Jewish people. The Jewish people's role is to remember God by observing God's *mitzvoth*/commandments as embodied in the Torah. That idea of faithfulness to God's words as a part of the covenant is expressed in Psalm 147:

> 19 He declareth His word unto Jacob,
>   His statutes and His ordinances unto Israel.
> 20 He hath not dealt so with any nation;
>   And as for His ordinances, they have not known them.
>   Hallelujah.
>
> (Psalm 147:19–20)

We hear this same idea also expressed in other psalms:

> 6 Moses and Aaron among His priests,
>   And Samuel among them that call upon His name,
>   Did call upon the Lord, and He answered them.
> 7 He spoke to them in the pillar of cloud;
>   They kept His testimonies, and the statute that He gave them.
>
> (Psalm 99:6–7)

> 2 I will open my mouth with a parable;
>   I will utter dark sayings concerning days of old.
> 3 That which we have heard and known,
>   And our fathers have told us,
> 4 We will not hide from their children,
>   Telling to the generation to come the praises of the Lord,
>   And His strength, and His wondrous works that He hath done.

5 For He established a testimony in Jacob,
And appointed a Torah in Israel,
Which He commanded our fathers,
That they should make them known to their children;
6 That the generation to come might know them, even the
    children that should be born;
Who should arise and tell them to their children,
7 That they might put their confidence in God,
And not forget the works of God,
But keep His commandments....

(Psalm 78:2–7)

The pillar of cloud in Psalm 99 is an allusion to the pillar of cloud that leads the Jewish people through the wilderness during the Exodus as described in Exodus 33:9. The psalmist seeks to show that the phenomenon of revelation has its roots in the historical experience of the Jewish people. It is significant that the verses of Psalm 147 that discuss revelation follow immediately after two verses that talk about God as being revealed in nature.

15 He sendeth out His commandment upon earth;
His word runneth very swiftly.
16 He giveth snow like wool;
He scattereth the hoar-frost like ashes.
17 He casteth forth His ice like crumbs;
Who can stand before His cold?
18 He sendeth forth His word, and melteth them;
He causeth the wind to blow, and the waters flow.

(Psalm 147:15–18)

What ties these two concepts together is that both are reflections about the power of God's word. It's as if the psalmist is saying God's word makes nature operate. Now God has chosen to reveal

God's word and God's will to the Jewish people. Taken together, the two sections remind us that the God who gives us the Torah is the same God who created and controls the world. One of the most important things Jewish tradition says about God is that God reveals God's will to human beings. And the primary ways we show that we are in covenant with God is by being faithful to those commandments. It is this relationship that explains how Psalm 119 can depict the author as crying out:

> O see mine affliction and rescue me;
> For I do not forget Thy Torah.
>
> (Psalm 119:153)

Psalm 105 gives us a summary of this traditional understanding:

> 42 For He remembered His holy word
> Unto Abraham His servant;
> 43 And He brought forth His people with joy,
> His chosen ones with singing.
> 44 And He gave them the lands of the nations,
> And they took labor of the peoples in possession;
> 45 That they might keep His statutes,
> And observe His laws.
> Hallelujah.
>
> (Psalm 105:42–45)

Torah becomes the Jewish people's part of their covenant with God. Rather than being imposed upon them, the covenant grows out of a reciprocal relationship. Rather than being a source of grudging fulfillment, it is the symbol of a bond that is a source of joy. The theme of delight is sounded again in Psalm 40, where we can reflect on the Torah in a very personal way:

6 Many things hast Thou done, O Lord my God,
Even Thy wondrous works, and Thy thoughts toward us;
There is none to be compared unto Thee!
If I would declare and speak of them,
They are more than can be told.
7 Sacrifice and meal-offering Thou hast no delight in;
Mine ears hast Thou opened;
Burnt-offering and sin-offering hast Thou not required.
8 Then said I: "Lo, I am come
With the roll of a book which is prescribed for me;
9 I delight to do Thy will, O my God;
Yea, Thy Torah is in my inmost parts."
10 I have preached righteousness in the great congregation,
Lo, I did not refrain my lips;
O Lord, Thou knowest.

(Psalm 40:6–10)

The Torah in verse 8 is an exact physical description of the *sefer Torah*—the Torah scroll—that we use today. Most pointedly, it is identified as a book prescribed—or written—"for me." The sense of personal identification with the Torah is compelling. Verse 7 echoes the message of the Prophets, who teach that God does not want sacrifice, but rather expects right behavior:

"What need have I of all your sacrifices?" says the Lord. "I am sated with burnt offerings of rams, and suets of fatlings, and blood of bulls; and I have no delight in lambs and he-goats. That you come to appear before Me—who asked that of you? Trample My courts no more; bringing oblations is futile, incense is offensive to Me. New moon and sabbath, proclaiming of solemnities, assemblies with iniquity, I cannot abide. Your new moons and fixed seasons fill Me with loathing; they are become a burden to Me, I cannot endure them. And when you lift up your hands I will turn My eyes away from you; though you pray at length, I will not listen. Your hands are stained with crime—wash yourselves clean; put your evil doings away from My sight. Cease to do evil; learn to do good. Devote yourselves to justice; aid the wronged. Uphold the rights of the orphan; defend the cause of the widow." (Isaiah 1:11–17)

I loathe, I spurn your festivals, I am not appeased by your solemn assemblies. If you offer Me burnt offerings—or your meal offerings—I will not accept them; I will pay no heed to your gifts of fatlings. Spare Me the sound of your hymns, and let Me not hear the music of your lutes. But let justice well up like water, righteousness like an unfailing stream. (Amos 5:21–24)

For I desire goodness, not sacrifice; obedience to God, rather than burnt offerings. (Hosea 6:6)

Like the Prophets, in place of sacrifice, the psalmist understands God as requiring us to do God's will and practice righteousness as embodied in Torah. Not only is Torah written "for me," but, in verse 9, it is described as literally having been internalized. This Torah is not "out there" somewhere, but "in my inmost parts." Torah becomes part of me. This sense of internalization sounds very much like the injunction of Deuteronomy 30:11–14:

Surely, this Instruction which I enjoin upon you this day is not too baffling for you, nor is it beyond reach. It is not in the heavens, that you should say, "Who among us can go up to the heavens and get it for us and impart it to us, that we may observe it?" Neither is it beyond the sea, that you should say, "Who among us can cross to the other side of the sea and get it for us and impart it to us, that we may observe it?" No, the thing is very close to you, in your mouth and in your heart, to observe it. (Deuteronomy 30:11–14)

We are pointedly reminded that the words are not outside of us, or far away from us. They are extremely close by. Indeed they are within us, and even more, they are in our hearts that we may "do them" (Deuteronomy 30:14). The teaching becomes part of who we are and directs our worldview and our conduct.

## Becoming Torah

Psalms reflects on the fundamental lesson of Torah—*tzedek*/righteousness. Psalm 40 participates in the stream of Jewish teaching that maintains that the essence of Torah is not ritual or practice, but the moral quality of our lives. When we become Torah, our way is *tzedakah*/righteousness, and we become *tzaddikim*/righteous ones. Torah is not something we study, it is something we take into ourselves. And when it is within us, Torah transforms us.

> 8 The Torah of the Lord is perfect, restoring the soul;
>   The testimony of the Lord is sure, making wise the simple.
> 9 The precepts of the Lord are right, rejoicing the heart;
>   The commandment of the Lord is pure, enlightening the eyes.
> 10 The fear of the Lord is clean, enduring forever;
>   The ordinances of the Lord are true, they are righteous
>     altogether;
> 11 More to be desired are they than gold, yea, than much fine gold;
>   Sweeter also than honey and the honeycomb.
> 12 Moreover by them is Thy servant warned;
>   In keeping of them there is great reward.
>
> (Psalm 19:8–12)

These words, too, have been incorporated into the liturgy for reading the Torah in the synagogue.

These verses, as they have come to be understood by the Jewish tradition, praise Torah and testify to its power. It is called perfect, sure, right, pure, true, righteous, enduring forever.

> Thy righteousness is an everlasting righteousness,
> And Thy Torah is truth.
>
> (Psalm 119:142)

Torah has the power to make us wise, and Torah "restores our soul" (Psalm 19:8). Significantly, Psalm 23:3 says that "restoring the soul" is something that God in God's own self does. Clearly there is a sense of Torah as having almost divine powers.

> Open Thou mine eyes, that I may behold
> Wondrous things out of Thy Torah.
>
> (Psalm 119:18)

## Torah as Life-Giver and Light

In Psalm 19:9 we are told that Torah rejoices the heart, once again emphasizing the idea that the Jewish tradition thinks of Torah in terms of joy. This verse also makes a claim for Torah that is more profound than might be apparent at first glance. Perhaps the phrase "enlightening the eyes" conveys the sense of serving as a guide on our way. After all, this is how we see God's word in Psalm 119:

> Thy word is lamp unto my feet,
> And a light unto my path.
>
> (Psalm 119:105)

Or perhaps the words may be understood as another way of suggesting that Torah makes us (even the simplest of us) wise. But this same phrase, "enlightening the eyes," is employed in Psalm 13 with a very different meaning:

Behold Thou, and answer me, O Lord my God;
Lighten mine eyes, lest I sleep the sleep of death....
(Psalm 13:4)

In Psalm 13 the phrase "enlightening the eyes" clearly has the sense of giving life. If we read Psalm 19:9 with this in mind, it is saying that Torah has the ability to give us life. This is a remarkable claim to make for any sacred text. And yet, the fact is that Torah has enlightened the eyes of the Jewish people in both senses of the phrase. For Torah is the ground of wisdom in the Jewish tradition, the source of knowledge and understanding. And Torah has also given the Jewish people life— and sustained our existence. Torah has given many of us life in the most profound way, giving meaning and direction to our lives, giving shape to the life we live. Torah creates the reality of our lives.

If the first half of Psalm 19 is about finding our way to God through the wonder of God's creation, and the last verses of Psalm 19 are about finding our way to God through Torah, how are we to understand the radical break between verses 1–7 and verses 8–12? Some scholars have suggested that these are simply two distinct compositions that became joined together—we can assume by an editor who did not pay too much attention to what the words were saying. It is more likely that the author of Psalm 19 is intentionally pointing to two of the royal roads for finding God: the wonder and order of the natural world, and the order and purpose that can fill our lives through Torah.

The medieval biblical commentator Rashi, too, argues that the psalm is one harmonious whole. Rashi teaches that the connection is the light with which Torah is associated in the literal understanding of verse 9, which connects the entire second section of the psalm to the heavenly lights that are the subject of the first seven verses. Rashi bolsters his argument by understanding verse 9 in relation to Proverbs 6:23, which states, "Torah is a light."

Another way to see Psalm 19 as an integrated unit is provided for us by the eleventh-century poet Solomon ibn Gabirol, while speaking of an entirely different subject:

> Three things conspire together in mine eyes.
> So that before me now Thy mem'ry lies.
> Thy heavens make me humbly speak Thy name,
> I find eternal witness in Thy skies.
> The world in which I dwell bestirs my thought
> To ponder Him who made my earthly ties.
> And that which in my heart I find is wrought
> Ceaselessly evokes my soulful cries.
>
> (Ibn Gabirol, "Shelosha Nosedu")

With these words, Ibn Gabirol expresses the same insight that was noted hundreds of years later by the philosopher Immanuel Kant: "Two things fill the mind with ever-increasing wonder and awe, the more often and the more intensely the mind the thought is drawn to them: the starry heavens above me and the moral law within me."

Ibn Gabirol and Immanuel Kant understand the logic of linking the two halves of Psalm 19. Nature and Torah are both pathways that lead from the world of our experience to the realm of the Divine. Both are like scrims used in theater, which appear to be scenery backdrops until the light is changed. Then, when they are lighted differently, they become transparent, allowing us to see the action taking place behind them. In the same way, both the world of nature and the Torah function like scrims, through which, if we look properly, we see God.

# 3

# FINDING GOD THROUGH THE HISTORICAL EXPERIENCE OF THE JEWISH PEOPLE

Without Jews there is no Jewish God.
If we leave this world
The light will go out in your tent.
Since Abraham knew you in a cloud,
You have burned in every Jewish face,
You have glowed in every Jewish eye,
And we made you in our image.
In each city, each land,
The Jewish God was also a stranger.
A broken Jewish head
Is a fragment of divinity.
We, your radiant vessel,
A palpable sign of your miracle.

Now the lifeless skulls
Add up into millions.
The stars are going out around you.
The memory of you is dimming,
Your kingdom will soon be over.

47

Jewish seed and flower
Are embers.
The dew cries in the dead grass!
The Jewish dream and reality are ravished,
They die together.
Your witnesses are sleeping:
Infants, women,
Young men, old.
Even the Thirty-six,
Your saints, Pillars of your World,
Have fallen into a dead, an everlasting sleep.

Who will dream you?
Who will remember you?
Who deny you?
Who yearn for you?
Who, on a lonely bridge,
Will leave you—in order to return?

The night is endless when a race is dead.
Earth and heaven are wiped bare.
The light is fading in your shabby tent.
The Jewish hour is guttering.
Jewish God!
You are almost gone.

(Jacob Glatstein, "Without Jews")

The searing words of the poem by Jacob Glatstein grow out of one of the most momentous—and tragic—events in the long history of the Jewish people. Glatstein speaks of the virtual destruction of the Jewish community of Europe; the murder of individual Jews millions of times over; the desecration of synagogues, Torah scrolls, and holy books; the almost total eradication of a Jewish cultural and religious presence from a continent on which it had flourished for almost 2,000 years. Glatstein symbolizes the totality of the destruction—and its deepest significance—in saying that "even the Thirty-six ... have fallen...." Who are the "Thirty-six"? Glatstein refers to a Jewish mythological belief in the existence of thirty-six righteous people in every generation. It is for the sake of these thirty-six anonymous and unknown just ones that God preserves the world from destruction. (This mythological belief is also the basis of the powerful novel *Last of the Just* by Andre Schwartz Bart.) To imagine that these thirty-six have been destroyed suggests that maybe the world itself is not worth preserving. It is an expression of complete loss of faith and hope.

One thing that stands out powerfully in Glatstein's poem is the audacity of implying that God's own fate is somehow bound up with the life of the Jewish people. What sense can we make of this bold suggestion? Christian theology includes an idea that is known as "the scandal of the cross," the central paradox of Christian belief: How could Jesus, understood as the third person of the divinity, be depicted as perishing on the cross? Glatstein's assumption rests on an idea that we could call the Jewish "scandal." And we might offer the same explanation for our "scandal" as Christian theologians do for theirs: It is a "mystery." That is, it is a central element of the faith tradition that is beyond the human capacity to comprehend or explain. Unexplainable, but fundamental to Jewish religious tradition, is the belief that a special relationship exists between the Jewish people and God—a relationship that existed from the beginning of the life of the Jewish people, when Abraham was called by God to leave everything that he had known and venture forth into the unknown. At that moment Abraham entered into a covenant with God. The covenant that Abraham accepted on his own behalf and on behalf of his descendants is understood as a relationship that continues to this day. Such a claim really does seem audacious. It is truly the "scandal" of the

Jewish religious tradition, a "mystery" we cannot understand or explain and yet which exerts such powerful force in Jewish faith.

Glatstein's poem rests on the idea of the interconnectedness of God and the Jewish people. Glatstein may well have assumed at the time he wrote the poem that the Jewish people truly had been utterly destroyed in the *Shoah*/Holocaust. In this he clearly was wrong. In terms of the mythological tradition of the thirty-six righteous ones, perhaps we may speculate that one or more of the thirty-six must have been among the survivors in Europe. Can we imagine that one of them may have been among the liberators of the death camps, or may already have found a home in America or made aliyah to Palestine, where a Jewish homeland was already being established? Glatstein is being sardonic when he refers to God as "the Jewish God." Still, we can note that the "Jewish God" need not have perished. There are other ways we can interpret the relationship on which Glatstein's poem seems to be based. As God continues to live, so do the Jewish people endure. Or to put it another way, as the Jewish people live on, so does the God to whom they serve as witness. Perhaps this is the true meaning of the words of the prophet Isaiah:

> You are My witnesses, says the Lord, My servant whom I have chosen, that you may know and believe Me, and understand that I am He.... I, truly I, am the Lord.... Therefore you are My witnesses, says the Lord, and I am God. (Isaiah 43:10–12)

One of the remarkable features of the Book of Psalms is the way it presents the historical experience of the Jewish people up to the time of its own composition. We can read its presentation of the history of Israel as a kind of national self-celebration. And if we did that, it would be significant enough. For the Book of Psalms does provide a powerful and moving saga of the nation's experience. We can turn to Psalms to learn how the Jewish people understood and depicted their collective experience. That alone might be of great value to us.

But the Book of Psalms, itself, does not seem content merely to provide a recitation of the history of the people that wrote it and read it, valuable as that might be. Instead it presents an account, sometimes joyous, sometimes filled with sadness, of the relationship between the Jewish people and their God. When we read the book in this light, the psalms become something even more compelling than an epic presentation of the life of the Jewish people. What the Book of Psalms offers us is yet another way of knowing God—through the ways that God has interacted with the Jewish people on their journey through history. This intent is made explicit in the opening verses of Psalm 78:

2 I will open my mouth with a parable;
   I will utter dark sayings concerning days of old.
3 That which we have heard and known,
   And our fathers have told us,
4 We will not hide from their children,
   Telling to the generation to come the praises of the Lord,
   And His strength, and His wondrous works that He hath done.
5 For He established a testimony in Jacob,
   And appointed a Torah in Israel,
   Which He commanded our fathers,
   That they should make them known to their children;
6 That the generation to come might know them, even the
      children that should be born;
   Who should arise and tell them to their children,
7 That they might put their confidence in God,
   And not forget the works of God,
   But keep His commandments;

(Psalm 78:2–7)

Psalm 78 reviews the Jewish people's history in order to know the people's God. By making the words of the psalm our own, we give voice to experiencing the presence of the hand of God intervening in the historic experience of our people.

The Book of Psalms' understanding of this subject, and all of the Bible, is put into words in Psalm 75:

> 5 I say unto the arrogant: "Deal not arrogantly";
>   And to the wicked: "Lift not up the horn."
> 6 Lift not up your horn on high;
>   Speak not insolence with a haughty neck.
> 7 For neither from the east, nor from the west,
>   Nor yet from the wilderness, cometh lifting up.
> 8 For God is judge;
>   He putteth down one, and lifteth up another.
> 9 For in the hand of the Lord there is a cup, with foaming
>     wine, full of mixture,
>   And He poureth out of the same;
>   Surely the dregs thereof, all the wicked of the earth shall
>     drain them, and drink them.
>
> (Psalm 75:5–9)

The message is clear enough: We cannot presume to control the events of our lives, and certainly we have no control over history itself. Behind everything that takes place in this world is God, the "judge … [who] putteth down one, and lifteth up another." The Book of Psalms is not the only book of the Bible that is clear on this subject. We see the same clarity in one of the few places in the Torah where God is discussed in a descriptive way. In Genesis 45 we read an extremely emotional scene in which Joseph reveals himself to his brothers, who had sold him into slavery in Egypt. Joseph, warmhearted and forgiving, actually engages in what we could call a theological discussion. He seeks to calm his brothers' fears by telling them:

Now, do not be distressed or reproach yourselves because you sold me hither; it was to save life that God sent me ahead of you. It is now two years that there has been famine in the land, and there are still five years to come in which there will be no yield from tilling. God has sent me ahead of you to ensure your survival on earth, and to save your lives in an extraordinary deliverance. So, it was not you who sent me here, but God; and He has made me a father to pharaoh, lord of all his household, and ruler over the whole land of Egypt. (Genesis 45:5–8)

Here we see the belief system that lies behind the teachings of the Prophets and the narratives of the Torah. It is clearly the belief system behind the urgent appeal of so many of the psalms for God to intervene on the author's behalf as well as the expression of gratitude on the occasions when the psalmist rejoices in God's saving power. It is the belief system that shapes Psalms' presentation of the historical experience of the Jewish people.

As noted in an earlier chapter, a number of psalms begin their review of history with the act of creation. The biblical understanding of history extends to the beginning of time, and Psalms clearly talks about the earliest stages of the human experience. But Jewish history, as such, does not begin until twenty generations after creation—with Abraham.

## The Exodus from Egypt

The narratives of the patriarchs begin the historical overview of the saga of the Jewish people in Psalm 105.

> 7 He is the Lord our God;
> His judgments are in all the earth.
> 8 He hath remembered His covenant forever,

The word which He commanded to a thousand generations;
9 [The covenant] which He made with Abraham,
    And His oath unto Isaac;
10 And He established it unto Jacob for a statute,
    To Israel for an everlasting covenant;
11 Saying: "Unto thee will I give the land of Canaan,
    The lot of your inheritance."
12 When they were but a few men in number,
    Yea, very few, and sojourners in it,
13 And when they went about from nation to nation,
    From one kingdom to another people,
14 He suffered no man to do them wrong,
    Yea, for their sake He reproved kings:
15 "Touch not Mine anointed ones,
    And do My prophets no harm."
16 And He called famine upon the land;
    He broke the whole staff of bread.
17 He sent a man before them;
    Joseph was sold for a servant;
18 His feet hurt with fetters,
    His person was laid in iron;
19 Until the time that his word came to pass,
    The word of the Lord tested him.
20 The king sent and loosed him;
    Even the ruler of the peoples, and set him free.
21 He made them lord of his house,
    And ruler of all of his possessions;
22 To bond his princes at his pleasure,
    And teach his elders wisdom.
23 Israel also came into Egypt;
    And Jacob sojourned in the land of Ham.
24 And He increased His people greatly,
    And made them too mighty for their adversaries.

25 He turned their heart to hate His people,
  To deal craftily with His servants.
26 He sent Moses His servant,
  And Aaron whom He had chosen.
27 They wrought among them His manifold signs,
  And the wonders in the land of Ham.
28 He sent darkness, and it was dark;
  And they rebelled not against His word.
29 He turned their waters into blood,
  And slew their fish.
30 Their land swarmed with frogs,
  In the chambers of their kings.
31 He spoke, and there came swarms of flies,
  And gnats in all their borders.
32 He gave them hail for rain.
  And flaming fire in their land.
33 He smote their vines also and their fig-trees;
  And broke the trees of their borders.
34 He spoke, and the locusts came,
  And the canker-worm without number,
35 And did eat up every herd in their land,
  And did eat up the fruit of their ground.
36 He smote also all the first-born in their land,
  The first fruits of all their strength.
37 And brought them forth with silver and gold;
  And there was none that stumbled among His tribes.
38 Egypt was glad when they departed;
  For the fear of them had fallen upon them.
39 He spread a cloud for a screen;
  And a fire to give light in the night.
40 They asked, and He brought quails,
  And gave them in plenty the bread of heaven.
41 He opened a rock, and waters gushed out;

They ran, a river in the dry places.
42 For He remembered His holy word
    Unto Abraham His servant;
43 And He brought forth His people with joy,
    His chosen ones with singing.
44 And He gave them the lands of the nations,
    And they took labor of the peoples in possession;
45 That they might keep His statutes,
    And observe His laws.
    Hallelujah.

(Psalm 105:7–45)


This remarkable summary of the Books of Genesis and Exodus weaves a poetic tapestry of the high points of biblical history. It is nothing less than a sweeping presentation of the saga of the People of Israel. Verse 9 presents the covenants with Abraham (Genesis 17:2) and Isaac (Genesis 26:3–4). Verses 10 and 11 allude to the reaffirmation of the covenant with Jacob (Genesis 28:13–15). Verses 12–16 recount the events in the careers of the earliest patriarchs: their wandering in the land, as told in Genesis 12, 13, 26, and 28, and the divine protection that God gave them, as told in Genesis 12:17ff., 20:3ff., and 26:9ff.. (Incidentally, in an earlier age this verse was frequently cited by people defending the idea of the divine right of kings in support of their cause.) Verses 16–22 are a summary of the story of Joseph. Verses 24 and 25 give a brief description of the enslavement of the Jewish people. In verses 26–36 we hear a retelling of the ten plagues that appear in Exodus chapters 7–11, presented in the same order. Verses 37–38 remind us of Exodus 12:33–36, where the departing slaves took advantage of the terror of the Egyptians to extract "reparations" for their 400 years of servitude. Verse 39 is a reference to the pillar of cloud by day and the pillar of fire by night, which Exodus 13:21–22 tells us accompanied the fleeing Israelites on their journey. Verse 40 refers to the quails of Exodus 16:13 and the manna of Exodus 16:4, which sustained the runaway slaves during their forty years of wandering. The rock that yielded water in Exodus 17:6 is the subject of verse 41. The psalm concludes by reminding listeners that what lies behind these events is the covenantal relationship that demands fidelity to God's Torah.

If Psalm 105 is a shining summary of the history of the People of Israel, Psalm 106, which in many ways is its complement, is an even grander panoramic view of the Jewish people's history, but depicted in dark tones. Here the story is of the people's constant unfaithfulness to the covenant, and of God's graciously forgiving them and taking them back. It is a painful perspective of biblical history that feels more appropriate to times of national peril, and yet the psalm ends on a note of hope and supplication.

6 We have sinned with our fathers,
    We have done iniquitously, we have dealt wickedly.
7 Our fathers in Egypt gave no heed unto Thy wonders;
    They remembered not the multitude of Thy mercies;
    But were rebellious at the sea, even at the Red Sea.
8 Nevertheless He saved them for His name's sake,
    That He might make His mighty power to be known.
9 And He rebuked the Red Sea, and it was dried up;
    And He led them through the depths, as through a wilderness.
10 And He saved them from the hand of him that hated them,
    And redeemed them from the hand of the enemy.
11 And the waters covered their adversaries;
    There was not one of them left.
12 Then they believed His words;
    They sang His praise.
13 They soon forgot His works;
    They waited not for His counsel;

14 But lusted exceedingly in the wilderness,
And tried God in the desert.

15 And He gave them their request;
But sent leanness into their soul.

16 They were jealous also of Moses in the camp,
And of Aaron the holy one of the Lord.

17 The earth opened and swallowed up Dathan,
And covered the company of Abiram.

18 And a fire was kindled in their company;
The flamed burned up the wicked.

19 They made a calf in Horeb,
And worshipped a molten image.

20 Thus they exchanged their glory
For the likeness of an ox that eateth grass.

21 They forgot God their savior,
Who had done great things in Egypt;

22 Wondrous works in the land of Ham,
Terrible things by the Red Sea.

23 Therefore He said that He would destroy them,
Had not Moses His chosen stood before Him in the breach,
To turn back His wrath, lest He should destroy them.

24 Moreover, they scorned the desirable land,
They believed not His word;

25 And they murmured in their tents,
They harkened not unto the voice of the Lord.

26 Therefore He swore concerning them,
That He would overthrow them in the wilderness;

27 And that He would cast out their seed among the nations,
And scatter them in the lands.

28 They joined themselves also unto Baal of Peor,
And ate the sacrifices of the dead.

29 Thus they provoked Him with their doings,
And the plague broke upon them.

30 Then stood up Phinehas, and wrought judgment,
  So the plague was stayed.
31 And that was counted unto him for righteousness,
  Unto all generations forever.
32 They angered Him also at the waters of Meribah,
  And it went ill with Moses because of them;
33 For they embittered his spirit,
  And he spoke rashly with his lips.
34 They did not destroy the people,
  As the Lord commanded them;
35 But mingled themselves with the nations,
  And learned their works;
36 And they served their idols,
  Which became a snare unto them;
37 Yea, they sacrificed their sons and daughters unto demons,
38 And shed innocent blood, even the blood of their sons and
    their daughters,
  Whom they sacrificed unto the idols of Canaan;
  And the land was polluted with blood.
39 Thus they were defiled with their works,
  And went astray in their doings.
40 Therefore was the wrath of the Lord kindled against His
    people,
  And He abhorred His inheritance.
41 And He gave them into the hand of the nations;
  And they that hated them ruled over them.
42 Their enemies also oppressed them,
  And they were subdued under their hand.
43 Many times did He deliver them;
  But they were rebellious in their counsel,
  And sank low through their iniquity.
44 Nevertheless He looked upon their distress,
  When He heard their cry;

⁴⁵ And He remembered for them His covenant,
And repented according to the multitude of His mercies.
(Psalm 106:6–45)

For all the light and joy of Psalm 105, this psalm is the opposite: dark and almost despairing. Where the great moments are evoked, it is almost always for the purpose of juxtaposing them to the people's infidelity that followed. Thus, in depicting the crossing of the Red Sea, Psalm 106 emphasizes the people's resistance to Moses' leadership as described in Exodus 14:12 (verse 7). Psalm 106 recounts how the fleeing slaves crossed the sea on dry land while their enemies drowned (verses 8–11) but goes on to assert that "soon" after singing God's praise (verse 12), they fell into disobedience.

In its account of the Exodus, Psalm 106 puts the emphasis on events such as the rebellion of Dathan and Abiram, which is described in Numbers 16 (verses 16–18); the incident of the golden calf of Exodus 32 (verses 19–23); the continual "murmuring" against Moses; the religious backsliding and its terrible aftermath described in Numbers 25 (verses 28–30); and the angry confrontation when the people demanded water at the place that came to be called Meribah—waters of contention—which is described in Exodus 17:6 and re-enacted in Numbers 25 (verses 32–33).

This accusatory reading of the Exodus experience is reminiscent of the account we find in Deuteronomy 32, which begins:

So Jeshurun grew fat and kicked—you grew fat and gross and coarse—he forsook the God who made him and spurned the Rock of his support. They incensed Him with alien things, vexed Him with abominations. They sacrificed to demons, no-gods, gods they had never known, new ones, who came but lately, who stirred not your father's fears.

You neglected the Rock that begot you, forgot the God who brought you forth. (Deuteronomy 32:15–18)

The Deuteronomy account continues in this vein for many verses. We can recognize this same reading of these events in many of the books of the Prophets as well. So Psalm 106 is part of a whole tradition of biblical writing about this central event in biblical history.

Psalm 106 begins its account of the people's history at a later stage than Psalm 105, and it continues its dark rendition of the collective story beyond the entry into the land of promise. Characteristically, the emphasis of its presentation is on the unfaithfulness of the people, such as their refusal, described in the Book of Judges chapter 1, to drive out the inhabitants of Canaan as they had been instructed (verse 34) or the times when they adopted the practices of their neighbors, such as engaging in the sacrifice of their children, which the prophet Jeremiah denounces in Jeremiah 32:35 (verses 35–39). The psalm appears to extend to the Babylonian Exile, with its description of the people being carried away captive (verse 46) and being scattered among the nations (verse 47). And yet for all its dark coloration, the point of Psalm 106 is not reprimand or reproach. Rather, its dominant message is God's faithfulness, God's eagerness to forgive the people for their backsliding and to reconcile with them. In this it reflects the same understanding of God as the words attributed to God by the prophet Isaiah:

> For a little while I forsook you, but with vast love I will bring you back. In slight anger, for a moment, I hid My face from you; but with kindness everlasting I will take you back in love—said the Lord your Redeemer. (Isaiah 54:7–8)

Psalm 106 is less about the people's infidelity than about God's desire for reconciliation with them and the restoration of covenantal union. The words of verse 45 echo the theme of the Book of Hosea, with its repeated insistence on God's need to reconcile with the people who have been unfaithful to the covenant.

Psalm 106 ends on a note of petition, calling on God to take the people back as God has done in the past. The psalmist pleads with God to end the dispersion of the people and, by implication, to restore them to their own land. The final verses allow us to see the psalm not as a harsh recapitulation of the history of the people but as a reflection on the complex and often tortured nature of their covenantal relationship with God. Above all, it underscores God's readiness, even eagerness, to forgive and God's capacity and willingness to save the people from distress, no matter how many times they have failed and disappointed God.

The Exodus figures in a number of other psalms as well. Psalm 136 is a poem of unalloyed praise and thanksgiving. Its history begins with the creation of the world, with which we have already dealt, and then moves directly to the events of Exodus.

> 1 O give thanks unto the Lord, for He is good …
>   For His mercy endureth forever.…
> 10 To Him that smote Egypt in their first-born,
>   For His mercy endureth forever.
> 11 And brought Israel out from among them,
>   For His mercy endureth forever.
> 12 With a strong hand, and with an outstretched arm,
>   For His mercy endureth forever.
> 13 To Him who divided the Red Sea in sunder,
>   For His mercy endureth forever.
> 14 And made Israel to pass through the midst of it,
>   For His mercy endureth forever.
> 15 But overthrew Pharaoh and his host in the Red Sea,
>   For His mercy endureth forever.
> 16 To Him that led His people through the wilderness.
>   For His mercy endureth forever.

¹⁷ To Him that smote great kings;
  For His mercy endureth forever;
¹⁸ And slew mighty kings,
  For His mercy endureth forever;
¹⁹ Sihon king of the Amorites,
  For His mercy endureth forever;
²⁰ And Og king of Bashan,
  For His mercy endureth forever;
²¹ And gave their land for heritage,
  For His mercy endureth forever;
²² Even a heritage unto Israel His servant,
  For His mercy endureth forever.

(Psalm 136:1, 10–22)

Psalm 136 is often called the Great *Hallel*—the great song of exaltation and gratitude. It is recited as part of the worship service on Chanukah, the three pilgrimage festivals—Passover, *Sukkot,* and *Shavuot*—and on every new moon. Verse 12 is a citation of the compelling image first used in Deuteronomy 4:34. In verse 15 the psalmist even uses the same word for *overthrow* as appears in the description of those events in Exodus 14:27. Sihon, king of the Amorites of verse 19, and Og, king of Bashan of verse 20, were leaders of two nations who were defeated by the Israelites during the Exodus as related in Numbers 21:21. Like Psalm 136, Psalm 135 begins with the events of creation and continues immediately with its presentation of the Exodus:

⁸ Who smote the first-born of Egypt,
  Both of man and beast.
⁹ He sent many signs and wonders into the midst of thee, O Egypt,
  Upon Pharaoh, and upon all his servants.
¹⁰ Who smote mighty nations,
  And slew mighty kings.

<sup>11</sup> Sihon king of the Amorites,
  And Og king of Bashan,
  And all the kingdoms of Canaan;
<sup>12</sup> And gave their land for a heritage,
  A heritage unto Israel His people.

(Psalm 135:8–12)

In this psalm, we might recognize a number of quotations and allusions to the text in the Torah. Thus, verse 8 echoes both Exodus 12:29 and 13:15. In verse 10 we hear an allusion to Deuteronomy 7:1. Sihon and Og occupy a prominent role in this telling, as they did in Psalm 136.

Another panoramic account of the people's history is found in Psalm 78. The psalm has something of a disjointed quality about it, treating events out of sequence, and has dramatic changes in tone. Parts of it are obscure in meaning and intention. Still others (verses 22, 31–34, 37, 40–41, 56–67) read like the powerful denunciation and warning of Psalm 126. Psalm 78, less structured than Psalm 106, seems to swing back and forth between straight narrative presentation and condemnation. The purely historical sections deal with the parting of the sea (verses 12–13, 53), the pillars of smoke and fire that accompanied the people (verse 14), the water that God made available to the people during their wandering (verses 15–16, 20), and the food with which they were provided (verses 20, 23–29). Read as a unit, these verses can give us a lovely summary of the Exodus event.

<sup>12</sup> Marvelous things did He in the sight of their fathers,
  In the land of Egypt, in the field of Zoan.
<sup>13</sup> He cleaved the sea, and caused them to pass through;
  And He made the waters to stand as a heap.
<sup>53</sup> And He led them safely, and they feared not;
  But the sea overwhelmed their enemies.

14 By day also He led them with a cloud,
  And all the night with a light of fire.
15 He cleaved rocks in the wilderness,
  And gave them drink abundantly as out of the great deep.
16 He brought streams also out of the rock,
  And caused waters to run down like rivers.
20 Behold, He smote the rock, that waters gushed out,
  And streams overflowed;
  Can He give bread also?
  Or will He provide flesh for His people?
23 And He commanded the skies above,
  And opened the doors of heaven;
24 And He caused manna to rain upon them for food,
  And gave them of the corn of heaven.
25 Man did eat the bread of the mighty;
  He sent them provisions to the full.
26 He caused the east wind to set forth in heaven;
  And by His power He brought on the south wind.
27 He caused flesh also to rain upon them as the dust,
  And winged fowl as the sand of the seas;
28 And He let it fall in the midst of their camp,
  Round about their dwellings.
29 So they did eat, and were well filled;
  And He gave them that which they craved.

(Psalm 78:12–13, 53, 14–16, 20, 23–29)

Psalm 78 also includes a recapitulation of the events of the ten plagues that God brought down on the Egyptians:

43 How He set His signs in Egypt,
  And His wonders in the field of Zoan;
44 And turned their rivers into blood,
  So that they could not drink their streams.

45 He sent among them swarms of flies, which devoured
   them;
And frogs, which destroyed them.
46 He gave also their increase unto the caterpillar,
And their labor unto the locust.
47 He destroyed their vines with hail,
And their sycamore-trees with frost.
48 He gave over their cattle also to the hail,
And their flocks to fiery bolts.
49 He sent forth upon them the fierceness of His anger,
Wrath, and indignation, and trouble,
A sending of messengers of evil.
50 He leveled a path for His anger;
He spared not their soul from death,
But gave their life over to the pestilence;
51 And smote all the first-born in Egypt,
The first-fruits of their strength in the tents of Ham;
52 But He made His own people to go forth like sheep,
And guided them in the wilderness like a flock.

(Psalm 78:43–52)

We saw a similar depiction of the plagues in Psalm 105, though
here, in Psalm 78, the list of plagues presented is incomplete, and the
order differs significantly from that of Psalm 105 and from the original account in the Book of Exodus. But, like all the other renditions
of this episode, it culminates with the death of the first-born and the
sparing of the Israelites. The psalm ends with the selection of Zion for
the site of the Temple, the building of the sanctuary (verses 67–69),
and the election of David as king (verses 70–72).

Of all the presentations of the events of the Exodus from Egypt,
perhaps the most poetically evocative is Psalm 114, also part of the
*Hallel:*

¹ When Israel came forth out of Egypt,
The house of Jacob from a people of strange language;
² Judah became His sanctuary,
Israel His dominion.
³ The sea saw it, and fled;
The Jordan turned backward.
⁴ The mountains skipped like rams,
The hills like young sheep.
⁵ What aileth thee O thou sea, that thou fleest?
Thou Jordan, that thou turnest backward?
⁶ Ye mountains, that ye skip like rams;
Ye hills, like young sheep?
⁷ Tremble, thou earth, at the presence of the Lord,
At the presence of the God of Jacob;
⁸ Who turned the rock into a pool of water,
The flint into a fountain of waters.

(Psalm 114:1–8)

The images in Psalm 114 are compelling and perhaps disturbing: rivers and seas reversing their normal course; hills and mountains moving about, appearing to skip; the earth trembling. Nothing is conveyed as much as a sense of the reversal of the natural order. Psalm 114, most likely intentionally, employs images in a way precisely opposite from how they are used elsewhere in the Book of Psalms. Rivers usually connote tranquility (as in Psalm 23:2) or even predictability (Psalm 1:3). Here there is a sense of turmoil, even chaos. Rivers run backward, seas "flee" (verses 3, 5) in contrast to their normal patterns. The image of the rock is normally used in Psalms to represent all that is solid and reliable (as in Psalms 31:3, 19:15, 89:27, and numerous other places). Here, rocks literally melt (verse 8). The image of mountains usually conveys a sense of eternity, consistency (as in Psalms 121:1, 125:1–2, and elsewhere). In Psalm 114, mountains move, so much so that they appear to be skipping (verses 4, 6). The earth is normally treated in Psalms as embodying unchangeableness and permanence, as stated explicitly in Psalm 93:1, "The earth is established, it cannot be moved." This same theme is expressed elsewhere in Psalms (Psalms 104:5, 119:90, 78:69). In this psalm, the earth is seen as trembling (verse 7). The total effect conveyed by Psalm 114 is fluidity and instability. Indeed, the effect of each one of these graphic images and the collective impression conveyed by the sum of those parts is what I have called reversal of fortune. Not merely the course of the river, but the very order of nature is made to run backward. We see something of the same imagery in Psalm 97:

> 4 His lightnings lighted up the world;
> The earth saw, and trembled.
> 5 The mountains melted like wax at the presence of the Lord,
> At the presence of the Lord of the whole earth.
>
> (Psalm 97:4–5)

When we look at them more closely, we see that the images employed in Psalm 114 are not random or arbitrary at all. Instead, they were chosen to evoke specific moments in the course of the Exodus from Egypt. The sea did indeed run backward when it parted, allowing the fleeing slaves to cross on dry land. Mount Sinai trembled and the very earth shook when the Torah was given, and the solid rock did yield a pool of water when the people clamored for drink at Meribah. In its brief eight verses, Psalm 114 calls to mind crucial episodes of the momentous event of the Exodus and reflects on their implications.

On yet a deeper level, Psalm 114 is conveying still one more message. It is not merely that nature reversed itself at several points during the Exodus event. Rather, the Exodus was, in itself, a profound reversal of fortune for the Jewish people and a reversal of the very order of things as conventionally understood. Seas and rivers are not supposed to turn backward. Mountains are not supposed to move. And slaves are not supposed to go free. The entire Exodus experience is a *tremendum:* a turning point in the history of the people who experienced it, and of all humanity.

Verse 7 says that the very earth shook. Significantly, very similar imagery appears two other times in the Book of Psalms:

> 9 Thou didst cause sentence to be heard from heaven;
> The earth feared, and was still,
> 10 When God arose to judgment,
> To save all the humble of the earth. Selah.
>
> (Psalm 76:9–10)

> 7 Nations were in tumult, kingdoms were moved;
> He uttered His voice, the earth melted.
> 8 The Lord of hosts is with us;
> The God of Jacob is our high tower. Selah.
>
> (Psalm 46:7–8)

In both of these psalms, as in Psalm 114, the very earth submits to the power of God. The earth and all the elements of the natural world yield before God the creator. What Psalm 114 reminds us is that the God who can cause the laws of nature to be reversed is the God who can also overturn the accepted patterns of history and society. The God of nature and the God of history are one. The message of Psalm 114 is that the God who controls the order of nature and the destiny of individuals and nations has worked an event of unprecedented magnitude in bringing the slaves out of Egypt.

## At the Red Sea

In Psalm 114, verse 2 and the second part of verse 7 remind us that the amazing events of the parting of the Red Sea, even beyond their importance in the history of Israel, serve as a symbol of the covenantal relationship that binds God and the People of Israel. The covenant assumes that God will work God's will on behalf of the people and for the sake of saving the people. The events of the Red Sea are the example *par excellence* of God's salvation—God breaking into the ordinary flow of history to execute God's saving power. The Exodus is celebrated for what it represents in itself and for the promise it represents for the Jewish people and for every individual. It is this sense of celebrating the particular events at the Red Sea, and the implication of those events for every individual life, that we hear sounded in two other psalms:

1 For the Leader. A Song, a Psalm.
  Shout unto God, all the earth;
2 Sing praises unto the glory of His name;
  Make His praise glorious.
3 Say unto God: "How tremendous is Thy work!
  Through the greatness of Thy power shall Thine enemies
    dwindle away before Thee.
4 All the earth shall worship Thee,
  And shall sing praises unto Thee;
  They shall sing praises to Thy name." Selah.
5 Come, and see the works of God;
  He is terrible in His doing toward the children of men.
6 He turned the sea into dry land;
  They went through the river on foot;
  There let us rejoice in Him!
7 Who ruleth by His might forever;
  His eyes keep watch upon the nations;
  Let not the rebellious exalt themselves. Selah.
8 Bless our God, ye peoples,
  And make the voice of His praise to be heard;
9 Who hath set our soul in life,

And suffered not our foot to be moved.

¹⁰ For Thou, O God, hast tried us;
Thou hast refined us, as silver is refined.

¹¹ Thou didst bring us into the hold;
Thou didst lay constraint upon our loins.

¹² Thou hast caused men to ride over our heads;
We went through fire and through water;
But Thou didst bring us out unto abundance.

¹³ I will come into Thy house with burnt-offerings,
I will perform unto Thee my vows,

¹⁴ Which my lips have uttered,
And my mouth hath spoken, when I was in distress.

¹⁵ I will offer unto Thee burnt-offerings of fatlings,
With the sweet smoke of rams;
I will offer bullocks with goats. Selah.

¹⁶ Come, and hearken, all ye that fear God,
And I will declare what He hath done for my soul.

¹⁷ I cried unto Him with my mouth,
And He was extolled with my tongue.

¹⁸ If I had regarded iniquity in my heart,
The Lord would not hear;

¹⁹ But verily God hath heard;
He hath attended to the voice of my prayer.

²⁰ Blessed be God,
Who hath not turned away my prayer, nor His mercy from me.

(Psalm 66)

² I will lift up my voice unto God, and cry;
I will lift up my voice unto God, that He may give ear
unto me.

³ In the day of my trouble I seek the Lord;
With my hand uplifted, [mine eye] streameth in the night
without ceasing;

My soul refuseth to be comforted....

12 I will make mention of the deeds of the Lord;
  Yea, I will remember Thy wonders of old.
13 I will meditate also upon all Thy work,
  And muse on Thy doings.
14 O God, Thy way is in holiness;
  Who is a great God like unto God?
15 Thou art the God that doest wonders;
  Thou hast made known Thy strength among the peoples.
16 Thou hast with Thine arm redeemed Thy people,
  The sons of Jacob and Joseph. Selah.
17 The waters saw Thee, O God;
  The waters saw Thee, they were in pain;
  The depths also trembled.
18 The clouds flooded forth waters;
  The skies sent out a sound;
  Thine arrows also went abroad.
19 The voice of Thy thunder was in the whirlwind;
  The lightnings lighted up the world;
  The earth trembled and shook.
20 Thy way was in the sea,
  And Thy path in the great waters,
  And Thy footsteps were not known.
21 Thou didst lead Thy people like a flock,
  By the hand of Moses and Aaron.

(Psalm 77:2–3, 12–21)

The tradition that the events of the Red Sea constitute the supreme example of God's power to save can be found in the Torah account itself. In what is perhaps one of the oldest examples of Hebrew poetry to be included in the biblical text we read:

I will sing to the Lord, for He has triumphed gloriously;
horse and driver He has hurled into the sea. The Lord is my
strength and might; he is become my deliverance. This is
my God and I will enshrine Him; the God of my father, and
I will exalt Him. The Lord, the Warrior—Lord is His name!
Pharaoh's chariots and his army he has cast into the sea;
and the pick of his officers are drowned in the Sea of
Reeds.... Who is like You, O Lord, among the celestials;
who is like You, majestic in holiness, awesome in splendor,
working wonders! You put out Your right hand, the earth
swallowed them.

In Your love You lead the people that You redeemed;
in Your strength You guide them to Your holy abode.

Sing to the Lord, for He has triumphed gloriously;
horse and driver He has hurled into the sea. (Exodus
15:1–4, 11–13, 21)

The opening words of this passage came to be included in the
liturgy of every Jewish worship service in a section called
*geulah*/redemption. The words of Exodus are introduced with a
section that says:

From Egypt, You redeemed us O Lord our God.... You
divided the Red Sea for us, drowning the arrogant ones
but making Your beloved ones ... pass through ... for
this the beloved ones offered hymns, songs, exaltation,
prayers, and expressions of thanks to the King, the living and enduring God, high and exalted, great and awesome who brings low the haughty and raises up the
lowly, frees the captive, delivering the meek, helping the
poor, and answering those who cry out to Him....
(Prayer book)

The Red Sea is memorialized in Psalms and throughout Jewish tradition as a great moment in the history of the people and as a symbol of the redemption that is possible at all times and in the life of every individual.

## At Mount Sinai

If we understand verses 4, 6, and 7 of Psalm 114 correctly, they speak about the specific moment when the fleeing slaves stood at the foot of Mount Sinai:

> On the third day, as morning dawned, there was a thunder and lightning, and a dense cloud upon the mountain, and a very loud blast of the horn; and all the people that were in the camp trembled.... Now Mount Sinai was all in smoke, for the Lord had come down upon it in fire; the smoke rose like the smoke of a kiln, and the whole mountain trembled violently. (Exodus 19:16, 18)

When we looked at Psalm 29 earlier we read it as the depiction of a mountain storm that can represent the power and force of God. But it could just as easily be a poetic allusion to this particular moment, when God's "voice" revealed not only God's power, but also God's word and will. The references to the sound of lightning, the fire, and the shaking of the wilderness allow us to understand this psalm as an evocation of the covenantal moment when the people renewed their commitment to God and took upon themselves obedience to God's word. Certainly Psalms 68 and 99 make clear reference to the moment when God appears at Sinai to give the people a "statute."

8 O God when Thou wentest forth before Thy people,
   when Thou didst march through the wilderness; Selah.

9 The earth trembled, the heavens
Also dropped at the presence of God;
Even yon Sinai trembled at the
Presence of God, the God of Israel.

(Psalm 68:8–9)

6 Moses and Aaron among His priests,
And Samuel among them that call upon His name,
Did call upon the Lord, and He answered them.
7 He spoke to them in the pillar of cloud;
They kept His testimonies, and the statute that He gave
them.

(Psalm 99:6–7)

# The Water of Meribah

One incident that occurred during the Exodus is singled out for special mention in a number of psalms. The episode of the waters of Meribah is mentioned twice in the biblical account—in Exodus 17:6 and again in Numbers 25. In our discussion of Psalms 105 and 106, we noted that this event, or really this pair of events, can be read in two distinct ways: either as epitomizing God's capacity to save graciously by overturning the normal laws of the workings of nature, or as representing the people's "stiff-necked" unwillingness to submit themselves to God despite being the beneficiaries of such miraculous redemption. This difference in understanding shows itself in two excerpts from those psalms:

He opened a rock, and waters gushed out;
They ran, a river in the dry places.

(Psalm 105:41)

32 They angered Him also at the waters of Meribah,
And it went ill with Moses because of them;
33 For they embittered his spirit,
And he spoke rashly with his lips.

(Psalm 106:32–33)

This same contrast is found in another pair of references to the waters of Meribah:

Thou didst call in trouble, and I rescued thee;
I answered thee in a secret place of thunder;
I proved thee at the waters of Meribah.

(Psalm 81:8)

8 Harden not your heart, as at Meribah,
As in the day of Massah in the wilderness;
9 When your fathers tried Me,
Proved Me, even though they saw My work.

(Psalm 95:8–9)

It is clear that by the time the Book of Psalms was written, the waters of Meribah had already assumed a specific symbolic significance.

# King David

Jewish tradition asserts that the entire Book of Psalms was composed by King David. A significant number of psalms bear the superscription *L'David*, which can carry the meaning "of David." Thus we are accustomed to calling the work "the Psalms of David." If we accept this understanding, then the entire book bears witness to the historical moment of David's career. Indeed, much of Jewish commentary on the text of Psalms involves identifying individual psalms with a particular moment in the life of King David. Or, if we

JEWISH LIGHTS PUBLISHING
SUNSET FARM OFFICES RTE 4
PO BOX 237
WOODSTOCK VT  05091-0237

*We hope that you will enjoy this book and find it useful in enriching your life.*

Book title: _____

Your comments: _____

How you learned of this book: _____

Reasons why you bought this book: (check all that apply)

❑ ATTRACTIVE INSIDE   ❑ RECOMMENDATION OF FRIEND   ❑ SUBJECT   ❑ AUTHOR   ❑ ATTRACTIVE COVER

If purchased: Bookseller _____   ❑ RECOMMENDATION OF REVIEWER   ❑ GIFT
City _____   State _____

**Please send me a JEWISH LIGHTS Publishing catalog. I am particularly interested in: (check all that apply)**

| | |
|---|---|
| 1. ❑ Spirituality | 5. ❑ Women's Issues | 9. ❑ Caregiving/Grieving |
| 2. ❑ Mysticism | 6. ❑ Environmental Issues | 10. ❑ Ideas for Adult Reading Groups |
| 3. ❑ Philosophy/Theology | 7. ❑ Healing/Recovery | 11. ❑ Religious Education Resources |
| 4. ❑ History/Politics | 8. ❑ Children's Books | 12. ❑ Audio Tapes of Author Lectures |

Name (PRINT) _____

Street _____

City _____   State _____   Phone _____

**Please send a JEWISH LIGHTS Publishing catalog to my friend:**

E-mail _____

City _____   State _____   Zip _____

Name (PRINT) _____

Street _____   Phone _____

Name (PRINT) _____

Street _____

City _____   State _____   Zip _____

**JEWISH LIGHTS PUBLISHING**

Sunset Farm Offices, Rte. 4 • P.O. Box 237 • Woodstock, VT 05091 • Tel: (802) 457-4000  Fax: (802) 457-4004

**Available at better booksellers. Visit us online at www.jewishlights.com**

choose, we can read many portions of the Book of Psalms as metaphorical presentations about the life of David.

On the other hand, modern scholarship, along with the way Jewish tradition treats Psalms in actual practice, does not embrace the idea that the entire Book of Psalms is the work of King David. As a result, the psalms that make explicit references to David and his legacy are all the more significant. For example, the city of Jerusalem, in its many and varied capacities, is a subject that is treated frequently in the Book of Psalms. Elsewhere in the Bible, we read about how David captured the city of Jerusalem, anticipated the Temple, and enlarged the city because "the Lord, the God of Hosts, was with him" (2 Samuel 5:9); about the time David brought the ark into Jerusalem (2 Samuel 6:12f.); and about when Solomon brought the ark into the completed Temple (1 Kings 8:1). The moment when Mount Zion was singled out to be the site of the Temple is celebrated at several points in the Book of Psalms:

[1] A song of Ascents.
Lord, remember unto David
All his affliction;
[2] How he swore unto the Lord,
And vowed unto the Mighty One of Jacob:
[3] "Surely I will not come into the tent of my house,
Nor go up into the bed that is spread for me;
[4] I will not give sleep to mine eyes,
Nor slumber to mine eyelids;
[5] Until I find out a place for the Lord.
A dwelling-place for the Mighty One of Jacob."
[6] Lo, we heard of it as being in Ephrath;
We found it in the field of the wood.
[7] Let us go into His dwelling-place;
Let us worship at His footstool.
[8] Arise, O Lord, unto Thy resting-place;

Thou, and the ark of Thy strength....
13 For the Lord hath chosen Zion;
He hath desired it for His habitation:
14 "This is My resting-place forever;
Here will I dwell; for I have desired it."

(Psalm 132:1–8, 13–14)

[God] ... chose the tribe of Judah,
The mount Zion which He loved.

(Psalm 78:68)

Why do you prance, you mountains of Gavnunim,
Toward the mountain which God has desired for His
    abode?

(Psalm 68:17)

No less significant to the history of the people was the selection of David as king. His early career is related in the Books of First Samuel and Second Samuel. We hear it summarized in Psalm 78:

70 He chose David also His servant,
And took him from the sheep-folds;
71 From following the ewes that give suck He brought him,
To be shepherd over Jacob His people, and Israel His inheritance.
72 So he shepherded them according to the integrity of his heart;
And led them by the skillfulness of his hands.

(Psalm 78:70–72)

In the Book of Second Samuel we read of God's promise to David to protect him and to establish his dynasty forever:

When your days are done and you lie with your fathers, I will raise up your offspring after you, one of your own issue, and I will establish his kingship.

He shall build a house for My name, and I will establish his royal throne forever. I will be a father to him, and he shall be a son to Me. When he does wrong, I shall chastise him with the rod of men and the affliction of mortals; but I will never withdraw my favor from him as I withdrew it from Saul, whom I removed to make room for you. Your house and your kingship shall ever be secure for you; your throne shall be established forever. (2 Samuel 7:12–16)

This critical moment in David's reign and the history of the Jewish people is recounted in the Book of Psalms:

10 For Thy servant David's sake
Turn not away the face of Thine anointed.
11 The Lord swore unto David in truth;
He will not turn back from it:
"Of the fruit of thy body will I set upon thy throne.
12 If thy children keep My covenant
And My testimony that I shall teach them,
Their children also forever shall sit upon thy throne."...
17 "There will I make a horn to shoot up unto David,
There have I ordered a lamp for Mine anointed.
18 His enemies will I clothe with shame;
But upon himself shall his crown shine."

(Psalm 132:10–12, 17–18)

He magnifies the victories of His king,
and does with His anointed,
to David and his seed, forever.

(Psalm 18:51)

⁴ I have made a covenant with My chosen,
  I have sworn unto David My servant:
⁵ Forever will I establish thy seed,
  And build up thy throne to all generations....
³⁷ His seed shall endure forever,
  And his throne as the sun before Me.
³⁸ It shall be established forever as the moon;
  And be steadfast as the witness in the sky.

(Psalm 89:4–5, 37–38)

# The Destruction of the Temple

Perhaps no moment in the history of the Jewish people until that time was as painful or traumatic as the destruction of the Temple and the exile of the people to Babylon. The human toll was devastating. In Psalms 79 and 74 we read what look like first-person accounts of the events.

¹ A Psalm of Asaph.
  O God, the heathen are come into Thine inheritance;
  They have defiled Thy holy temple;
  They have made Jerusalem into heaps.
² They have given the dead bodies of Thy servants to be food
    unto the fowls of the heaven,
  The flesh of Thy saints unto the beasts of the earth.
³ They have shed their blood like water
  Round about Jerusalem, with none to bury them.
⁴ We are become a taunt to our neighbors,
  A scorn and derision to them that are round about us.

(Psalm 79:1–4)

² Remember Thy congregation, which Thou hast gotten of old,
  Which Thou hast redeemed to be the tribe of Thine inheritance;

And Mount Zion, wherein Thou hast dwelt.
3 Lift up Thy steps because of the perpetual ruins,
Even all the evil that the enemy hath done in the sanctuary.
4 Thine adversaries have roared in the midst of Thy meeting-
place;
They have set up their own signs for signs.
5 It seemed as when men wield upwards
Axes in a thicket of trees.
6 And now all the carved work thereof together
They strike down with hatchet and hammers.
7 They have set Thy sanctuary on fire;
They have profaned the dwelling-place of Thy name even to
the ground.
8 They said in their heart: "Let us make havoc of them altogether";
They have burned up all the meeting-places of God in the land.
9 We see not our signs;
There is no more any prophet;
Neither is there among us any that knoweth how long.
10 How long, O God, shall the adversary reproach?
Shall the enemy blaspheme Thy name forever?

(Psalm 74:2–10)

We get a vivid sense of the scope of loss of human life and the destruction of the beloved sanctuary. We hear the human responses of fear, pain, rage, and desire for revenge in the rest of Psalm 79 and in portions of others, all of which sound as if they were written in the midst of the terrible events themselves:

5 How long, O Lord, wilt Thou be angry forever?
How long will Thy jealousy burn like fire?
6 Pour out Thy wrath upon the nations that know Thee not,
And upon the kingdoms that call not upon Thy name.

7 For they have devoured Jacob,
And laid waste his habitation.
8 Remember not against us the iniquities of our forefathers;
Let Thy compassions speedily come to meet us;
For we are brought very low.
9 Help us, O God of our salvation, for the sake of the glory of
Thy name;
And deliver us, and forgive our sins, for Thy name's sake.
10 Wherefore should the nations say: "Where is their God?"
Let the avenging of Thy servants' blood that is shed
Be made known among the nations in our sight.
11 Let the groaning of the prisoner come before Thee;
According to the greatness of Thy power set free those that
are appointed to death;
12 And render unto our neighbors sevenfold into their bosom
Their reproach, wherewith they have reproached Thee, O Lord.
13 So we that are Thy people and the flock of Thy pasture
Will give Thee thanks forever;
We will tell of Thy praise to all generations.

(Psalm 79:5–13)


Maschil of Asaph.
Why, O God, hast Thou cast us off forever?
Why doth Thine anger smoke against the flock of Thy pasture?

(Psalm 74:1)


8 "Will the Lord cast off forever?
And will He be favorable no more?
9 Is His mercy clean gone forever?
Is His promise come to an end forevermore?
10 Hath God forgotten to be gracious?
Hath He in anger shut up His compassions?" Selah.

(Psalm 77:8–10)

5 O Lord God of hosts,
How long wilt Thou be angry against the prayer of Thy
people?
6 Thou hast fed them with the bread of tears,
And given them tears to drink in large measure.
7 Thou makest us a strife unto our neighbors;
And our enemies mock as they please.
8 O God of hosts, restore us;
And cause Thy face to shine, and we shall be saved.

(Psalm 80:5–8)

6 Wilt Thou be angry with us forever?
Wilt Thou draw out Thine anger to all generations?
7 Wilt Thou not quicken with us again,
That Thy people may rejoice in Thee?
8 Show us Thy mercy, O Lord, and grant us Thy salvation.

(Psalm 85:6–8)

Beyond the toll in human life and suffering, and national shame and pain, the destruction of the Temple and the exile from their homeland had profound religious implications for the Israelites. To fully appreciate the importance of those events we must understand that the ideology of the Jewish people at that time was very much like the ideology of the neighboring peoples. Although the Israelites believed in one God, they shared the prevailing perception in that part of the world at that time that the power of their God was confined to their national borders, and that God was accessible only through the rites of sacrifice offered in one city—Jerusalem—and at only one place in that city—the Temple. The destruction of the Temple and their exile from their capital city and their land had profound implications for their ability to continue to exist as a people; it also represented a threat to their ability to maintain their unique religious identity. This is the

poignant dilemma at the heart of Psalm 137, a document that gives
painful testimony to that anguished moment:

> ¹ By the rivers of Babylon,
>   There we sat down, yea, we wept,
>   When we remembered Zion.
> ² Upon the willows in the midst thereof
>   We hanged up our harps.
> ³ For there they that led us captive asked of us words of song,
>   And our tormentors asked of us mirth:
>   "Sing us one of the songs of Zion."
> ⁴ How shall we sing the Lord's song
>   In a foreign land?
> ⁵ If I forget thee, O Jerusalem,
>   Let my right hand forget her cunning.
> ⁶ Let my tongue cleave to the roof of my mouth,
>   If I remember thee not;
>   If I set not Jerusalem
>   Above my chiefest joy.
> ⁷ Remember, O Lord, against the children of Edom
>   The day of Jerusalem;
>   Who said: "Raze it, raze it,
>   Even to the foundation thereof."
> ⁸ O daughter of Babylon, that art to be destroyed;
>   Happy shall he be, that repayeth thee
>   As thou hast served us.
> ⁹ Happy shall he be, that taketh and dasheth thy little ones
>   Against the rock.
>
> (Psalm 137:1–9)

Psalm 137 is included in the liturgy of *Tisha B'Av*/the ninth
day of the month of *Av*, the day on which, according to the Jewish
calendar, the Temple was destroyed, and on which that destruction

is commemorated every year. Verse 4 addresses the central religious dilemmas: What would become of the people's national identity as an exiled community, and what would become of their religious identity if the city and the shrine to which worship were confined were now in ruins? The final answer would be revealed after the passage of many years. At that moment, it was unknown. The nature of Jewish worship and religion were transformed forever by the experience of the Babylonian Exile.

In Babylonia, the institution that would ultimately join and then supplant the Temple in Jerusalem—the synagogue—was created. In Babylonia, in place of sacrifices, which were no longer possible, sung and spoken prayer and the study of sacred texts were introduced into the religious life of the Jewish people. There, the priesthood was replaced by a new class of religious leaders: the rabbis. But at the moment Psalm 137 was composed, the question posed in verse 4 was urgent and painful.

Verses 5 and 6 speak of the longing for Jerusalem and the devotion to that ruined city. The attachment to that place has become a consistent part of the Jewish experience. The words from Psalm 137 have given voice to that faithful devotion and yearning for all these thousands of years. At the moment of the composition of Psalm 137, that longing was a fresh reality and a new emotion in the collective life of the Jewish people.

The final verses of the psalm reflect the emotional reality of the exiles. We recognize that people who have suffered a loss experience several stages of grieving. They move from denial to pain and make their way through bitterness and rage before they can move on to acceptance and renewed wholeness. Verses 7–9 reflect the stage of rage at which the poet and the exiled community had arrived at this point in the collective experience. The emotions expressed may be shocking or uncomfortable for us. But they are disturbingly human. They are the immediate and unrefined experience of a newly exiled people. Who could not but feel—and give

voice to—such anger at having been uprooted from their homeland and resettled in the land of their conqueror? Reading these
words, who cannot but feel what such an emotional experience
must have been like? And who, whether he or she is comfortable
with that set of emotions or not, cannot but empathize with
what they reveal to us about that moment? Only by going
through—and acknowledging—the rage could the exile community begin to create the semblance of a normal life and
begin to dream of, and plan for, a return to the homeland they
left behind.

A lovely rabbinic *midrash*/commentative story on Psalm 137
is based on a word that seems to be unnecessary in verse 1.
Literally translated, the text says, "There we sat down, also we
wept." The Rabbis ask why the verse includes the word *gam*/also.
They teach that it conveys the idea that the weeping of the people
was so intense that it caused God to weep *gam*—also alongside
them. The sense of the *midrash* is that exile is not a condition of
the people alone; it affects God as well. God, too, as it were, is displaced. And God, too, is affected by the loss. The *midrash* reflects
an audacious and powerful Jewish idea that God and God's creatures are interdependent. God suffers alongside us. The exile is
not merely a fact of human history. It is part of the history of
God's own self.

The human sense of dislocation is searingly expressed in
another song of the exile, Psalm 102:

> 4 For my days are consumed like smoke,
>   And my bones are burned as a hearth.
> 5 My heart is smitten like grass, and withered;
>   For I forget to eat my bread.
> 6 By reason of the voice of my sighing
>   My bones cleave to my flesh.
> 7 I am like a pelican in the wilderness;

I am become as an owl of the waste places.
8 I watch, and I am become
Like a sparrow that is alone upon the housetop.
9 Mine enemies taunt me all the day;
They that are mad against me do curse by me.
10 For I have eaten ashes like bread,
And mingled my drink with weeping.
11 Because of Thine indignation and Thy wrath;
For Thou hast taken me up, and cast me away.
12 My days are like a lengthening shadow;
And I am withered like grass.

(Psalm 102:4–12)

We can feel the immediacy of the anguish in these verses. Especially poignant are the images of burning in verses 4 and 10, in light of the terrible conflagration that must have accompanied the conquest of Jerusalem and the destruction of its Temple. The repeated allusion to bread in several of the verses (5, 10) is rich in implications. We can imagine the terrible deprivation that the people must have endured during the siege and as captives in its aftermath. Could they have been forced to subsist on the "grass" that is mentioned in verses 5 and 12?

Of all the images in this compelling psalm, none convey the sense of dislocation and the pain of homelessness as much as the references to lost and wandering birds. These images give graphic expression to the sense of absolute dispossession that the people must have experienced in the first moments of their ordeal. This is in stark contrast to the birds who have found their home that we read about in Psalm 84:

Yea, the sparrow hath found a house, and the swallow a
nest for herself,
Where she may lay her young;

Thine altars, O Lord of hosts,
My King, and my God.

(Psalm 84:4)

All the images in Psalm 102 are burnt, dried up, parched—
or birds that have no home. The powerful poetry of the psalm
helps us experience the pain of the ordeal. Psalm 102 is as
wrenching as anything we read in the Book of Lamentations, the
dirge that bewails the same events of the destruction of the
Temple.

In the next verses of Psalm 102, the tone shifts from being
overcome by the tragedy to a realistic appraisal of the new situation—and then moving to resolve it.

13 But thou, O Lord, sittest enthroned forever;
    And Thy name is unto all generations.
14 Thou wilt arise, and have compassion upon Zion;
    For it is time to be gracious unto her, for the appointed
       time is come.
15 For Thy servants take pleasure in her stones,
    And love her dust.
16 So the nations will fear the name of the Lord,
    And all the kings of the earth Thy glory;
17 When the lord hath built up Zion.
    When He hath appeared in His glory;
18 When He hath regarded the prayer of the destitute,
    And hath not despised their prayer.
19 This shall be written for the generation to come;
    And a people which shall be created shall praise the Lord.
20 For He hath looked down from the height of His sanctuary;
    From heaven did the Lord behold the earth;
21 To hear the groaning of the prisoner;
    To loose those that are appointed to death;

22 That men may tell of the name of the Lord in Zion,
And His praise in Jerusalem;
23 When the peoples are gathered together,
And the kingdoms, to serve the Lord.

(Psalm 102:13–23)

In these verses the thoughts of the psalmist turn to Zion. But now the author thinks in new terms. Verse 15 reflects a realistic acceptance of the devastated condition in which Jerusalem must have languished in the years following its destruction. But even broken and destroyed, the city continues to be an object of affection. The overall tone of these verses reflects a new level of acceptance. The mood has shifted from sorrow and mourning to hope and resolve. Now the psalmist's thoughts are of return. We see a shift, as well, in the religious understanding of the Jewish people in very important ways. The psalmist speaks of God's eternity. God can "sit enthroned forever" (verse 13), even when the place that had been thought of as the location of God's seat has been reduced to ruin. Most significantly, the psalmist is now confident that God "wilt arise" and expresses certainty about God's "compassion upon Zion" and God's grace. In an even more insistent tone, the psalmist asserts that "the appointed time is come" (verse 14). The author experiences deepening confidence in God's saving power. Thus God looks, sees, hears, and acts to free those who might otherwise endure a dire fate. This progression of simple verbs reminds us of a similar progression of verbs at the moment God is about to intervene and liberate the same people from Egyptian bondage centuries earlier:

The Israelites were groaning under the bondage and cried out; and their cry for help ... rose up to God. God heard their moaning, and God remembered His covenant with

Abraham and Isaac and Jacob. God saw the Israelites and
God knew. (Exodus 2:23–25)

Similar to Psalm 102, the Book of Exodus says of God that
God heard, remembered, saw, and knew. And then God acted to
save the people.

In the final verses of Psalm 102, the psalmist looks forward to the
time of Zion's restoration. The author anticipates the day when this
amazing reversal of fortune shall be accomplished and people shall
speak of God's acts and sing God's praises—once again in Jerusalem.

These same sentiments are expressed even more forthrightly
in the concluding verses of Psalm 106, which earlier gave us a
description of the Exodus from Egypt. In the closing verses of the
psalm, the author turns to the true focus of the composition.

> 43 Many times did He deliver them;
> But they were rebellious in their counsel,
> And sank low through their iniquity.
> 44 Nevertheless He looked upon their distress,
> When He heard their cry;
> 45 And He remembered for them His covenant,
> And repented according to the multitude of His mercies.
> 46 He made them also to be pitied
> Of all those that carried them captive.
> 47 Save us, O Lord our God,
> And gather us from among the nations,
> That we may give thanks unto Thy holy name,
> That we may triumph in Thy praise.
>
> (Psalm 106:43–47)

Here the psalmist calls explicitly for God to save the people by
"gathering them" from among "those that carried them captive." In
these verses, the psalmist speaks not in tones of pain or rage, but

with a new measure of resolve. This psalm presents the people's condition dispassionately—and looks forward to their salvation. The focus of these verses is not the exile and dispersion, but the hope of being gathered back to their national home. The people have moved a long distance from the pain and anguish they felt when the exile was still new. In moving to a new emotional plane, they are now prepared to seek a realistic remedy to their condition.

Viewed from the perspective of those concluding verses, all the recounting of the ups and downs of the people's experience, all the dark recitation of the people's tumultuous relationship with God, was a preparation for the splendor of this great act of divine forgiveness and salvation. From the depths of exile, the psalmists now wait for God to bring them up to their own land, to restore and renew their national life.

The confidence that God would have compassion upon the people, save them, and restore them reflects the same perspective that is present in the concluding verse of the Book of Lamentations, another document of the Babylonian Exile. That work concludes:

Restore us, O God to You and let us come back; renew our days, as of old. (Lamentations 5:21)

The intent of the words in Lamentations is clear. The repetition of the verb *shuv,* which serves to convey the ideas of both "restore" and "return," or "come back," along with the phrase "renew" tells us that the petition is not for a return in the theological sense of repentance, but something far more concrete and tangible. The author is looking forward to being returned home. Psalm 80 repeats the same verb in several verses, among them:

O Lord God of hosts, restore us;
Cause Thy face to shine, and we shall be saved.
(Psalm 80:20)

O God of hosts, return, we beseech Thee;
Look from heaven and behold, and be mindful of this vine.
(Psalm 80:15)

This sense of confidence in God's ability and desire to save has become part of Jewish religious sensibilities. The words cited from Lamentations are included at a climatic moment of every service in which the Torah is read. As the scroll is replaced in the ark, these words are chanted in unusually plaintive and evocative tones.

In Psalms 13, 102, and 106 we have experienced the journey as the people must have lived it, from abject sorrow to rage to acceptance, and then to hope. And we have witnessed one of the most momentous transformations of religious understanding in human history, from "How shall we sing the Lord's song in a foreign land?" of Psalm 137 to "But Thou, O Lord sittest enthroned forever, and Thy name is unto all generations" of Psalm 102. We noted earlier that one rabbinic *midrash* suggests that God grieved along with the people. With the evolution of religious understanding, it was ensured that the God of Israel would continue to exist—along with God's people—even in exile.

The story of the Babylonian Exile is the story of a great national tragedy. It is also the story of the endurance of the profound relationship between God and the People of Israel, even in the midst of radically changed circumstances. It is the story of the transformation of the life of the people, and of the evolution in the way they understood God. But above all it is the story of how the people understood themselves as inextricably bound to God, and how they viewed their story as God's own. Even in the midst of what had been, until then, their darkest hour, they knew they must continue to hold fast to God, to find a new way to understand their relationship with God. And they found their way back to a confidence that God would "arise," have compassion upon them, and deliver them again.

# The Return Home

Just as suddenly as the Babylonian Exile befell the Jewish people, it ended. A change in the political power structure of Babylonia—now Persia—allowed the people to return home, restore their national life, and rebuild the Temple. Not all the people chose to return, but many did. The Book of Psalms gives a graphic account of the very difficult nature of the physical act of return:

1 "O give thanks unto the Lord, for He is good,
   For His mercy endureth forever."
2 So let the redeemed of the Lord say,
   Whom He hath redeemed from the hand of the adversary;
3 And gathered them out of the lands,
   From the east and from the west,
   From the north and from the sea.
4 They wandered in the wilderness in a desert way;
   They found no city of habitation.
5 Hungry and thirsty,
   Their soul fainted in them.
6 Then they cried unto the Lord in their trouble,
   And He delivered them out of their distresses.
7 And He led them by a straight way,
   That they might go to a city of habitation.
8 Let them give thanks unto the Lord for His mercy,
   And for His wonderful works to the children of men!
9 For He hath satisfied the longing soul,
   And the hungry soul He hath filled with good.
10 Such as sat in darkness and in the shadow of death,
   Being bound in affliction and iron—
11 Because they rebelled against the words of God,
   And condemned the counsel of the Most High.
12 Therefore He humbled their heart with travail,

They stumbled, and there was none to help—
13 They cried unto the Lord in their trouble,
   And He saved them out of their distresses.
14 He brought them out of darkness and the shadow of death,
   And broke their bands in sunder.
15 Let them give thanks unto the Lord for His mercy,
   And for His wonderful works to the children of men!
16 For He hath broken the gates of brass,
   And cut the bars of iron in sunder.

(Psalm 107:1–16)

The opening words of this psalm are echoed elsewhere in the Book of Psalms (106:1; 118:1; 136:1, 26). They appear as well in the Book of Ezra, which tells of the events of the return from exile (Ezra 3:10–13). That story is about the ingathering and the difficulties endured by those who returned home. Verses 2–9 present the experience of those who returned home as well. Verses 10–16 tell of what they had endured as captives. Once again the realities of the events are rendered graphically, and we are given the opportunity to experience those events ourselves and empathize with the people who lived through them. There is no escaping the realities of the historic moment out of which the words arose. Verses 17–22 of the psalm appear to be talking about people suffering the effects of illness. But we can understand them as being metaphorical in nature, a further reflection on the difficulties of the captives and the returning exiles.

17 Crazed because of the way of their transgression,
   And afflicted because of their iniquities—
18 Their soul abhorred all manner of food,
   And they drew near unto the gates of death—
19 They cried unto the Lord in their trouble,
   And He saved them out of their distresses;

20 He sent His word, and healed them,
   And delivered them from their graves.
21 Let them give thanks unto the Lord for His mercy,
   And for His wonderful works to the children of men!
22 And let them offer the sacrifices of thanksgiving,
   And declare His works with singing.

(Psalm 107:17–22)

Although verses 33–40 may not portray the historical events of the return as specifically as verses 2–9 do, they do grow out of those events. The psalmist repeatedly refers to the wilderness (verses 33, 34, 35, 40), and we read, too, of the tasks that the newly returned wanderers faced when they reached their destination: establishing cities where the (formerly) hungry could dwell (verse 36), sowing fields and planting vineyards (verse 37), and achieving abundance (verse 38).

The ideology reflected in these verses is consistent with what we have read in other psalms, particularly Psalm 114. The God who controls the forces of nature also controls the destiny of individuals and nations. The God who can turn a river into a wilderness (107:33) and a fruitful land into a salt waste (107:34) can also cause a prosperous nation to be defeated or enable a captive people to return home. The events of the return are celebrated not for themselves alone, but for what they affirm about the people's God.

33 He turneth rivers into a wilderness,
   And water springs into a thirsty ground;
34 A fruitful land into a salt waste,
   For the wickedness of them that dwell therein.
35 He turneth a wilderness into a pool of water,
   And a dry land into water springs.
36 And there he maketh the hungry to dwell,
   And they establish a city of habitation;

37 And sow fields, and plant vineyards,
   Which yield fruits of increase.
38 He blesseth them also, so that they are multiplied greatly,
   And suffereth not their cattle to decrease.
39 Again, they are diminished and dwindle away
   Through oppression of evil and sorrow.
40 He poureth contempt upon princes,
   And causeth them to wander in the waste, where there is
      no way.
41 Yet He setteth the needy on high from affliction,
   And maketh His families like a flock.
42 The upright see it, and are glad;
   And all iniquity stoppeth her mouth.
43 Who so is wise, let him observe these things,
   And let them consider the mercies of the Lord.

(Psalm 107:33–43)

Psalm 107 presents us with four life situations, at least two of which grew out of the historical setting of the end of the exile. What the psalm is really concerned about is not the particular human conditions it describes, but the affirmation of the religious reality the people serve to illustrate. That religious reality is expressed in the very first verse: "Give thanks to God for God is good, God's *chesed* is everlasting." The theme of Psalm 107 is God's *chesed*. *Chesed* is one of those words that is strikingly difficult to translate. It is conventionally translated as "mercy," and so, for the time being, we shall translate it as "mercy" here.

The next to last word of verse 1, *l'olam* (the text reads "God's *chesed* is *l'olam*"), is a word that signifies two ideas. As our translation indicates, *l'olam* can mean "forever" or "everlasting." But the word *olam* also has the meaning of "world." So the returning exiles could have been saying, "God's *chesed* is throughout the world." They could well have been giving voice to their new understanding that God's power and God's influence were not confined to their homeland, but extended throughout the world. They are, after all, celebrating the fact that God acted in Babylon, reaching out to them in that alien land, freeing them from their captivity, and enabling them to return home.

The event that lies behind Psalm 107 is the return of the exiles to their homeland, but the real theme of the psalm is God's *chesed:* God's mercy, or caring, or faithfulness, or steadfastness. We can see this clearly in a verse that is repeated four times and serves as a kind of refrain, running through the text (verses 8, 15, 21, 31). That "chorus" expresses the central message of the psalm:

> Let them give thanks unto the Lord for His mercy,
> And for His wonderful works to the children of men!
>
> (Psalm 107:8)

Indeed, the concluding verse of the psalm asserts:

> Who so is wise, let him observe these things,
> And let them consider the mercies of the Lord.
>
> (Psalm 107:43)

## Reestablishing Joy in Life

Psalm 126 represents a different moment in the history of the people. Now the people have completed their arduous journey. We are with them as they stand in wonder before the object of their longing all these years, the goal of their difficult trip across the wilderness. We hear the joy and exaltation in their return in the words of this psalm:

¹ A Song of Ascents
 When the Lord brought back those who returned to Zion,
 We were like unto them that dream.
² Then was our mouth filled with laughter,
 And our tongue with singing;
 Then said they among nations:
 "The Lord has done great things with these."
³ The Lord hath done great things with us;
 We are rejoiced.
⁴ Turn our captivity, O Lord,
 As the streams in the dry land.
⁵ They that sow in tears
 Shall reap in joy.
⁶ Though he goeth on his way weeping that beareth the
  measure of seed,
 He shall come home with joy, bearing his sheaves.

(Psalm 126:1–6)

This wonderful psalm has been incorporated in its entirety into the grace said after meals, which Jewish tradition calls on us to recite every time we eat. In its words, we can feel the delight of the returning exiles. So overcome were they with the wonder of what they had accomplished that it was all like a dream. The return was an event of such magnitude that even the other nations took note of it (verse 2). For those nations, and for the exiles, the return is understood as a great thing that has been done for them by God. The people who once were exiles recognize what the nations have said and echo their words with a subtle change. In verse 3 the former exiles say, "It is for *us* that God has done great things."

Psalm 126 pulsates with the human emotions of the people who have experienced this pivotal historical moment. Yet its lesson goes beyond celebrating that moment. The psalmist sees this event as another instance of God's ongoing relationship with the People of Israel: The very first verse does not say, "When we returned to Zion," but rather "When the Lord brought back those who returned to Zion." Clearly the people have encountered God in the wonder and joy of this moment of fulfillment overcoming adversity. As we make their words our own, we can do so as well.

The insistence on seeing great events not in terms of our own fulfillment but as testimony to God's saving power is surely the intent of the first verse in Psalm 115, which many scholars attribute to the time of the return from exile.

> Not unto us, O Lord, not unto us,
> But unto Thy name give glory,
> For Thy mercy, and for Thy truth's sake.
>
> (Psalm 115:1)

We see this same idea is stated at the beginning of Psalm 85:

> 2 Lord, Thou hast been favorable unto Thy land,
>    Thou hast turned the captivity of Jacob.
> 3 Thou hast forgiven the iniquity of Thy people
>    Thou hast pardoned all their sin. Selah.
> 4 Thou hast withdrawn all Thy wrath;
>    Thou hast turned from the fierceness of Thine anger.
>
> (Psalm 85:2–4)

But now the psalmist goes beyond the expression of joy at the return and moves to a petition that the people be restored fully to the level and quality of life they had known before the exile:

> 5 Restore us, O God of our salvation,
>    And cause Thine indignation toward us to cease.
> 6 Wilt Thou be angry with us forever?
>    Wilt Thou draw out Thine anger to all generations?

7 Wilt Thou not quicken with us again,
  That Thy people may rejoice in Thee?
8 Show us Thy mercy, O Lord,
  And grant us Thy salvation.

(Psalm 85:5–8)

We can read these verses as a plea for the full restoration of
the national honor. In verse 5 we again see the verb *shuv*, but in
this psalm its overtones have changed. Where in Psalm 126:1 and
in Lamentations 5:21 it spoke of the desire for "return"—return to
the national home—here it carries the sense of "restore"—restore
us to the status we had known before. The people have not only
returned home, but they are also looking to God for help in
reestablishing the quality of their national life.

Perhaps it was during this period in which individual families
were building homes, the people were rebuilding the house of
God, and the nation was reestablishing the city of Jerusalem that
this word of admonition was sounded:

A Song of Ascents; of Solomon.
Except the Lord build the house,
They labor in vain that build it;
Except the Lord keep the city,
The watchman waketh but in vain.

(Psalm 127:1)

In time, the work of rebuilding was complete and the people
could rejoice and give thanks:

1 Hallelujah;
  For it is good to sing praises unto our God;
  For it is pleasant, and praise is comely.
2 The Lord doth build up Jerusalem,

He gathereth together the dispersed of Israel;
3 Who healeth the broken in heart,
And bindeth up their wounds.
4 He counteth the number of the stars;
He giveth them all their names.
5 Great is our Lord, and mighty in power;
His understanding is infinite.
6 The Lord upholdeth the humble;
He bringeth the wicked down to the ground.
7 Sing unto the Lord with thanksgiving,
Sing praises upon the harp unto our God;
8 Who covereth the heaven with clouds,
Who prepareth rain for the earth,
Who maketh the mountains to spring with grass.
9 He giveth to the beast his food,
And the young ravens which cry.
10 He delighteth not in the strength of the horse;
He taketh no pleasure in the legs of a man.
11 The Lord taketh pleasure in them that fear Him,
In those that wait for His mercy.
12 Glorify the Lord, O Jerusalem;
Praise thy God, O Zion.
13 For He hath made strong the bars of thy gates;
He hath blessed thy children within thee.
14 He maketh thy borders peace;
He giveth thee in plenty the fat of wheat.
15 He sendeth out His commandment upon earth;
His word runneth very swiftly.
16 He giveth snow like wool;
He scattereth the hoar-frost like ashes.
17 He casteth forth His ice like crumbs;
Who can stand before His cold?
18 He sendeth forth His word, and melteth them;

He causeth the wind to blow, and the waters flow.
19 He declareth His word unto Jacob,
   His statutes and his ordinances unto Israel.
20 He hath not dealt so with any nation;
   And as for His ordinances, they have not known them.
   Hallelujah.

(Psalm 147:1–20)

The psalmist clearly rejoices in what has been accomplished in Jerusalem. Jerusalem has been reestablished and is at ease and comfortable. The former captives have begun to recover from their ordeal, and their psychic wounds have started to heal. This alone would be reason for thanksgiving.

But the psalmist chooses to put these events in context. The overarching theme of God's might is stated in verse 3. In verses 8 and 9 the psalmist reminds us of God's power in nature. In verses 16–17, the psalmist makes this abstract idea concrete by celebrating the power of God as displayed in the wonder of winter and in the transition to spring, when the ice melts and the water begins to flow again (verse 18). In verses 6 and 10–11 we see that God also exercises power in human history. Neither the strength of the warhorses nor the might of the warrior is of any importance to God (verse 10), who will reward those whom God chooses to reward and to whom God extends God's *chesed* (verse 11). As in other psalms, we are reminded that the God who is revealed in nature is also the God who determines the fate of nations. This is the background against which this psalm rejoices that God has chosen to return the people to their homeland and rebuild their beloved city.

The Book of Psalms is a remarkable testament to the history of the Jewish people. In some instances it serves as a compelling eyewitness to the events of its own times. Other psalms relate the events of what already happened; at the time of their composition, this was the distant past. Many of the psalms achieve a kind of epic retelling of the people's shared experience. Together these selections from the Book of Psalms make up a kind of epic poem of the Jewish people.

And yet Psalms does not aspire to the status of such a national epic. Instead what the Book of Psalms celebrates is the power of God to save a people from circumstances beyond their own abilities to rescue themselves. Psalms rejoices in God's steadfastness and saving power. The history of the People of Israel is a testimony to God as a redeemer. Implicit in all the tellings of our national story is the hope, indeed the certainty, that as God has redeemed the people in the past, so can God redeem the people again in a time of peril.

Psalms holds out hope for the individual as well. The God in the Book of Psalms is a God of *chesed,* steadfast and faithful—and a saving God. Psalms assures us that the God who has saved the people so consistently in the past, reversing the laws of nature and history, is a God who can reach out and save each of us in times of need. The reversal of fortune celebrated in Psalms, as the people moved from slavery to freedom, from exile to redemption, is a reversal of fortune that can occur for any of us. The Book of Psalms is all the more appreciated during times we feel ourselves to be exiled from good fortune or enslaved to despair.

The story of the people's redemption and salvation can be read as a metaphor of our own redemption. As we give voice to the songs of exaltation and rejoicing and allow ourselves to feel the words as our own, Psalms can truly be an anticipation of the liberation we can look forward to. The history of the people as recounted in Psalms is surely a gateway each one of us can enter to find ourselves in the presence of God.

Psalms expresses confidence that the Jewish people do not make their way through history alone. They were accompanied at each step, by the One with whom they were covenanted. On our journeys, we too can know ourselves to be in the presence of God. With the image of the people's journey, as related to us in Torah and in Psalms, we can make our way through our own, assured that the One who watched over and rescued them is there for us. We can experience the trials of life knowing that we live in the presence of the One who accompanied them, knowing that, in some way, the ones who went before us go with us now, as companions on our journey through life.

> Not sole was I born, but entire genesis:
> For to the fathers that begot me, this
> Body is residence. Corpuscular,
> They dwell in my veins, they eavesdrop at my ear,
> They circle as with Torahs round my skull,
> In exit and in entrance all day pull
> The latches of my heart, descent, and rise—
> And there look generations through my eyes.
>
> (A. M. Klein, "Psalm XXXVI: A Psalm Touching Genealogy")

The end of the matter, all having been heard: be filled with reverence for God. (*Koheleth*/Ecclesiastes 12:13)

We began this part of the book with a series of questions, all of which can be represented by the words quoted from Yehuda Halevi: "O God where shall I find You?" The pages since then have been devoted to exploring various answers to these questions. Which answers will ultimately be most useful for any one of us depends on a number of factors, including, perhaps most important, our own disposition, temperament, and life experience.

We have seen that Psalms points out three royal roads to knowledge of God. Evidence of God can be found in the world of nature: its awesome grandeur, power, and order. God can be intuited from the power of a mountain storm, in the more subtle beauty of winter, and in the wondrous fact that food is "provided for living creatures." God as creator, who acted during that first great feat of creation, and God whose creative power is manifest continually in the renewal of creation, can be present to us in our every encounter with the world of nature.

Elsewhere in Psalms, God's presence is felt most keenly in Torah—the record of God's self-disclosure—or in a sense of being commanded by God. God's presence during the great moments of revelation, or during our own grappling with the record of revelation, are ways in which we can experience God. Gratitude for Torah or engagement with Torah can be gateways through which we pass into the presence of the One from whom Torah came into the world.

Still other parts of Psalms talk about God in terms of God's ongoing presence in the history of the People of Israel. God is encountered as partner in a covenanted relationship. Psalms tells of God as redeemer and savior of the people in times of need and even mortal peril. God's ability and willingness to enter history as a saving presence is a moving and compelling memory from our collective past. It opens up, as well, the possibility of God's saving presence in our own lives.

Creation, revelation, and redemption. These are the routes open to us as we look for answers in Psalms to the question, "O God where shall I find You?" Significantly, they are also major categories of Jewish thought. The great twentieth-century philosopher of Judaism, Franz Rosenzweig, taught that for any learning to be considered authentically Jewish, it must incorporate these three elements. It is right, then, that we find them as the three roads that are laid out for us by the psalmist. These three ways—and their interaction and interpenetration—can form a path for us to find ourselves in the presence of the One who inspired the Book of Psalms.

Perhaps *Koheleth*/Ecclesiastes had it right all those thousands of years ago. Perhaps we can never fully "know" God, nor know how to know God. Perhaps the best we can do is find ourselves in relationship with God. And whether we understand that relationship or not, perhaps that may be enough.

# PART II
# THE QUEST FOR INSIGHT: USING THE PSALMS TO UNDERSTAND OUR FAITH

# 4

# THE PROBLEM OF EVIL IN OUR WORLD

O God of Mercy
For the time being
Choose another people.
We are tired of death, tired of corpses,
We have no more prayers.
For the time being
Choose another people
We have run out of blood
For victims,
Our houses have been turned into desert,
The earth lacks space for tombstones,
There are no more lamentations
Nor songs of woe
In the ancient texts.

God of mercy
Sanctify another land
Another Sinai.
We have covered every field and stone
With ashes and holiness.
With our crones
With our young

With our infants
We have paid for each letter of Your commandments

(Kadia Molodowsky, "God of Mercy")

The anger, even rage, in Kadia Molodowsky's poem—beginning with its bitterly ironic title—speaks to the most difficult issue that can challenge our faith. Each one of us, at some point in our spiritual development, must grapple with the issue characterized so succinctly by Rabbi Harold Kushner: "Why do bad things happen to good people?" If we believe that God is a good God, and also just and all powerful, or simply powerful—if we believe that God controls history, or shapes it—what sense can we make of the presence of evil in the world? Like Jacob Glatstein, whose poem was quoted at the beginning of chapter 3, Molodowsky's anger is forged by the experience of the *Shoah*/Holocaust, which cost her members of her family, her extended community, the very world and cultural universe in which she had been nurtured—the murder of six million Jews, one quarter of them children. How can we reconcile this cataclysm with a faith in a God who acts in this world? Molodowsky and Glatstein write in voices that challenge God directly. How can we worship You, they ask, when horrors of this magnitude befell people You call Your own? Better not to belong to the "people of God," says Molodowsky, than to be forced to endure the agony that Jews have known in her lifetime, and in earlier generations. In anguishing over the injustice and the evil we encounter in the world, we are entering one of the most profound issues of faith. It is called by the technical term *theodicy*—the problem of divine justice. No person can have whole-hearted faith in God and be sensitive to the suffering in the world around him or her without being forced to confront the painful issue of theodicy.

The generation of the *Shoah* was not the first generation to be troubled by this enigma. The problem has an ancient pedigree. The prophet Jeremiah depicts himself as putting the question directly to God: "Why does the way of the evil-doers prosper? Why are all those who behave treacherously secure?" (Jeremiah 12:1). The Book of Ecclesiastes notes:

> In my own brief life span, I have seen both things: Sometimes a good man perishes in spite of his goodness, and sometimes a wicked man endures in spite of his wickedness. (Ecclesiastes 7:15)

The well-known story in the Book of Job tells of a perfectly righteous man who suffers a series of anguishing calamities. Indeed, the very purpose of that book is to force us to confront the fact that in the world as we know it, people who appear to be upright are often forced to suffer unbearable pain.

Later generations wrestled with the same challenge. For the Rabbis, the dilemma was epitomized in an account of someone who dies in the process of scrupulously fulfilling a biblical injunction. In Deuteronomy 5:16 we are commanded to honor our parents. In Deuteronomy 22:6–7 we are enjoined:

> If, along a road, you chance upon a bird's nest, in any tree or on the ground, with fledglings or eggs and the mother sitting over the fledglings or on the eggs, do not take the mother together with her young. Let the mother go, and take only the young, in order that you may fare well and have a long life.

Both of these injunctions make mention of the promise of "length of days" for the person who fulfills them. The Rabbis tell of a boy whose father told him to climb up to the top of a tall tower to bring him some pigeon eggs that could be found there. In the course of fulfilling his father's wishes, the boy also made it a point to send away the mother bird before gathering the eggs. As he was climbing down from the tower, he slipped and fell to his death. "Where," the Rabbis ask, "is the well-being? Where is the length of days?" (B. Talmud Kiddushin 39b). Really what the Rabbis were asking is, "Where is the justice in this world?" Indeed, so contrary was this incident to the conventional way of thinking about good and evil that it is said to have caused one of the Rabbis, Elisha ben Abuyah, to lose his faith and become a heretic (B. Talmud Chagigah 77b).

In another rabbinic engagement with this question, the Rabbis tell a fable about Moses. In this story, when Moses enters heaven, he asks for the privilege of seeing how his Torah would be taught in the future. He is taken to the classroom of Rabbi Akiba and is amazed at his brilliance. Moses then asks God, "You have shown me [the depth of] his learning, now show me his reward." God instructs Moses, "Turn around." Moses then sees Akiba being tortured and put to death by the Romans for the "crime" of teaching Torah. Moses is depicted as asking indignantly, "Master of the universe, such is his learning and such is his reward?" And he is told to be silent (B. Talmud Menachot 29b). Many of the Rabbis whose teaching is found in the Talmud had themselves experienced the brutalities of Roman oppression—or had lived in the wake of the destruction of Jerusalem and the Temple, as well as the end of Jewish political independence after the victory of the Romans. In telling this story, they are confronting us with the dilemma of the defeat of the righteous and the triumph of the wicked. At the core of the story is the issue of justice in this world. How could God allow such things to happen?

## The Problem of Evil in the Psalms

In our own lives, our first awareness that things are not operating in the world as our understanding of faith tells us they should comes when we feel ourselves to be victims of injustice. Here, we believe, we are clearly innocent or in the right, and we did not prevail. Even worse, we know ourselves to be good people and yet, for no reason we can understand, something bad, maybe even something terrible, happened to us. We discover ourselves to be under attack by forces that can do us great harm. Many of the psalms speak of an "enemy." Perhaps the enemy is other people who have turned against us or threaten to injure us. Or perhaps the "enemy" that endangers us is illness or circumstances in our lives that can result in our harm. Whoever or whatever the enemy is, the idea of its triumph runs against everything we have expected. Suddenly the justice we had imagined prevailing in this world does not seem to be working at all.

We find many such personal encounters with the forces of destruction in the Book of Psalms. And we find many places where we can hear our own fears expressed by these ancient poems. Indeed, part of the power of Psalms is that we recognize our own life situations in them. They put into words what we ourselves are feeling. And, as we read them or recite them, the psalms help give voice to our own emotions and concerns. As we read the psalms, their words become our own. And as we make the psalms our own, the "I" or "me" we encounter in them becomes us, ourselves. So it is of great significance when we find psalms crying out to God as we encounter injustice—as many do—for the first, or most painful, time in our own lives:

2 Deliver me from mine enemies, O my God,
  Set me on high from them that rise up against me
3 Deliver me from the workers of iniquity,
  And save me from men of blood.
4 For, lo, they lie in wait for my soul;
  The impudent gather themselves together against me;
  Not for my transgression, nor for my sin, O Lord.
5 Without my fault, they run and prepare themselves;
  Awake Thou to help me, and behold.

6 Thou therefore, O Lord God of hosts, the God of Israel
Arouse Thyself to punish all nations;
Show no mercy to any iniquitous traitors. Selah.
7 They return at evening, they howl like a dog,
And go around about the city.
8 Behold, they belch out with their mouth;
Swords are in their lips:
"For who doth hear?"
9 But Thou, O Lord, shalt laugh at them;
Thou shalt have all the nations in derision.
10 Because of His strength, I will wait for Thee;
For God is my high tower.
11 The God of my mercy will come to meet me;
God will let me gaze upon my adversaries.
12 Slay them not, lest my people forget,
Make them wander to and fro by Thy power and bring
them down,
O Lord our shield.
13 For the sin of their mouth and the words of their lips,
Let them even be taken in their pride,
And for cursing and lying which they speak.
14 Consume them in wrath, consume them, that they are no
more;
And let them know that God ruleth in Jacob,
Unto the ends of the earth. Selah.
15 And they return at evening, they howl like a dog,
And go round about the city;
16 They wander up and down to devour,
And tarry all night if they have not their fill.
17 But as for me, I will sing of Thy strength;
Yea, I will sing aloud of Thy mercy in the morning;
For Thou hast been my high tower,
And a refuge in the day of my distress.

<sup></sup>18 O my strength, unto Thee will I sing praises;
For God is my high tower, the God of my mercy.

(Psalm 59:2–18)

2 How long, O Lord, wilt Thou forget me forever?
How long wilt Thou hide Thy face from me?
3 How long shall I take counsel in my soul,
Having sorrow in my heart by day?
How long shall my enemy be exalted over me?
4 Behold Thou, and answer me, O Lord my God;
Lighten mine eyes, lest I sleep the sleep of death;
5 Lest mine enemy say: "I have prevailed against him";
Lest mine adversaries rejoice when I am moved.
6 But as for me, in Thy mercy do I trust;
My heart shall rejoice in Thy salvation.
I will sing unto the Lord,
Because He hath dealt bountifully with me.

(Psalm 13:2–6)

10 How long, O God, shall the adversary reproach?
Shall the enemy blaspheme Thy name forever?
11 Why withdrawest Thou Thy hand, even Thy right hand?
Draw it out of Thy bosom and consume them.

(Psalm 74:10–11)

My soul is sore afflicted;
And Thou, O Lord, how long?

(Psalm 6:4)

We hear the urgency in these words, and, as we read them, the urgency becomes our own. There is evil in our world. And, with the psalmist, we call on God to rise up and put an end to it.

As we grow in understanding and compassion, we come to

recognize that not all the evil in the world is directed against us. We become sensitive to the injustice that afflicts so many people and is experienced in so many ways. Psalms, too, is sensitive to the presence of injustice and evil in the world. The words of Psalm 44 depict a situation of profound terror and injustice in a dramatic way:

10 Yet Thou hast cast off, and brought us to confusion;
   And goest not forth with our hosts.
11 Thou makest us to turn back from the adversary;
   And they that hate us spoil at their will.
12 Thou hast given us like sheep to be eaten;
   And hast scattered us among the nations.
13 Thou sellest Thy people for small gain,
   And hast not set their prices high.
14 Thou makest us as a taunt to our neighbors,
   A scorn and a derision to them that are round about us.
15 Thou makest us a byword among the nations,
   A shaking of the head among the peoples.
16 All the day is my confusion before me,
   And the shame of my face hath covered me,
17 For the voice of him that taunteth and blasphemeth;
   By reason of the enemy and the revengeful.

(Psalm 44:10–17)

The psalm seems to be about a great national catastrophe. Tragically, it reads as if it could be taken from accounts of the recent history of the Jewish people—indeed, more tragically still, from the chronicles of many peoples recently and in the past. Psalm 44 is filled with powerful, disturbing images. The people who had assumed they were safe in God's care suddenly find themselves cast off (verse 10). They feel themselves to be hated (verse 11), taunted, and derided by their enemies (verses 14, 17). Even more poignantly, they feel "sold" by the very God whom they had expected to protect them and despoiled by their foes (verse 11). In its most shocking image, the psalm speaks of the people being "eaten" by their adversaries (verse 12). (We find similar images of the enemy eating or consuming the just elsewhere in Psalms: 14:4, 27:2, 35:25, 53:5, and 119:87.) We do not know to which calamity Psalm 44 refers. Certainly the events sound so much like the description of the defeat and destruction of Jerusalem and the Temple in Psalms 74 and 79 that we read about in chapter 3. The events of Psalm 44 are echoed, as well, in Psalm 60:

> ³ O God, Thou hast cast us off, Thou hast broken us down;
> Thou hast been angry at us....
> ⁵ Thou hast made Thy people to see hard things;
> Thou hast made us drink the wine of staggering....
> ¹² Hast not Thou, O God, cast us off?
> And Thou goest not forth, O God, with our hosts.
> ¹³ Give us help against the adversary;
> For vain is the help of man.
>
> (Psalm 60:3, 5, 12–13)

Whatever the precise historical situation, the events raise a deep question for the psalmist—and for us. Significantly, Psalm 44 does not offer an answer to the question of why these catastrophes befell the people who felt themselves to be virtuous—and, more significantly, "under the wing" of God's protection. It merely raises the issue in stark, graphic, and poignant form for us to wrestle with.

The question of justice and the problem of evil in the world are raised forcefully as well in two other psalms, which try to supply answers to the questions they put before us. Before we look at their attempt to solve the problem, let us stay a little while longer in the dilemma with which they confront us. Psalm 73 speaks directly to the problem we have called *theodicy*. The psalmist—and those who give voice to the psalm—cannot understand how the wicked prosper:

<sup>1</sup> Surely God is good to Israel,
   Even to such as are pure in heart.
<sup>2</sup> But as for me, my feet were almost gone;
   My steps had well nigh slipped.
<sup>3</sup> For I was envious of the arrogant,
   When I saw the prosperity of the wicked.
<sup>4</sup> For there are no pangs at their death,
   And their body is sound.
<sup>5</sup> In the trouble of man they are not;
   Neither are they plagued like men.
<sup>6</sup> Therefore pride is as a chain about their neck;
   Violence covereth them as a garment.
<sup>7</sup> Their eyes stand forth from fatness;
   They are gone beyond the imaginations of their heart.
<sup>8</sup> They scoff, and in wickedness utter oppression;
   They speak as if there were none on high.
<sup>9</sup> They have set their mouths against the heavens,
   And their tongue walketh through the earth.
<sup>10</sup> Therefore His people return hither;
   And waters of fulness are drained out of them.
<sup>11</sup> And they say, "How doth God know?
   And is there knowledge in the Most High?"
<sup>12</sup> Behold, such are the wicked;
   And they that are always at ease increase riches.
<sup>13</sup> Surely in vain have I cleansed my heart,
   And washed my hands in innocency;
<sup>14</sup> For all the day have I been plagued,
   And my chastisement came every morning.
<sup>15</sup> If I had said, "I will speak thus,"
   Behold, I had been faithless to the generation of Thy children.
<sup>16</sup> And when I pondered how I might know this,
   It was wearisome in mine eyes.

(Psalm 73:1–16)

The description of the wicked and arrogant in Psalm 73 is vivid and lifelike. Perhaps they remind us of people we have encountered in our own lives. Sleek and self-satisfied, they seem to suffer no embarrassment or remorse. Indeed, they do not seem to suffer from anything. They are proud (verse 6), physically comfortable (verses 4, 7), and rich (verse 12). In fact, they are blessed with such ease and well-being that they do not seem human at all (verse 5). They seem almost superhuman in their security, despite the fact that they are wicked (verse 3) and violent (verse 6) and oppress others (verse 8). So convinced are they of their own superiority that they even deny the existence of God. This is the clear meaning of verse 11, and their blasphemy is most likely the subject of verses 8 and 9. Certainly we encounter this kind of denial of God and blasphemy by the wicked elsewhere in Psalms:

4 The wicked, in the pride of his countenance [saith]: "He will
  not require";
And his thoughts are: "There is no God." ...
11 He hath said in his heart: "God hath forgotten;
He hideth His face; He will never see." ...
13 Wherefore doth the wicked contemn God,
And say in his heart: "Thou wilt not require"?

(Psalm 10:4, 11, 13)


The fool hath said in his heart: "There is no God";
They have dealt corruptly, they have done abominably;
There is none that doeth good.

(Psalm 14:1)

The psalmist is so overcome by perplexity at the apparent prosperity of these wicked people that it becomes impossible to speak about it (Psalm 73: 14–16). So it must seem to us so often in our own experience. We can be literally struck mute at the apparent triumph of evil. The words of Psalm 94 will sound familiar to us. They speak in the same terms as Psalm 73 and echo the same concerns:

> ³ Lord, how long shall the wicked,
> How long shall the wicked exult?
> ⁴ They gush out, they speak arrogancy;
> All the workers of iniquity bear themselves loftily.
> ⁵ They crush Thy people, O Lord,
> And afflict Thy heritage.
> ⁶ They slay the widow and the stranger,
> And murder the fatherless.
> ⁷ And they say: "The Lord will not see,
> Neither will the God of Jacob give heed."
>
> (Psalm 94:3–7)

As in Psalm 73, the wicked are inflated and arrogant (verse 4) and self-satisfied (verse 3). The violence of their actions, however, is spelled out more specifically and graphically in Psalm 94. They crush the people (verse 5) and actually engage in the murder of the most powerless (verse 6). As in Psalm 73, their actions rest on a fundamental disbelief that there is a God to defend the help-less—or even to take note of their destructive acts (verse 7). How do we rectify the success of such people with a belief in a God who does take note, does care, and does protect the defenseless? This is the question of justice in the world to which the Book of Psalms offers a variety of answers.

## The Ambivalence of Psalm 94

Psalm 94 begins by presenting a vivid description of the apparent success of the wicked. Somehow we expect that it will conclude by proposing a solution to that enigma. But rather than satisfy that expectation, Psalm 94 appears to vacillate. It alternates between questioning God's justice and proposing several alternative solutions to the issue it has raised. We have already examined verses 3–7 of this psalm. In its entirety the psalm reads:

1 O Lord, Thou God to whom vengeance belongeth,
  Thou God to whom vengeance belongeth, shine forth.
2 Lift up Thyself, Thou Judge of the earth;
  Render to the proud their recompense.
3 Lord, how long shall the wicked,
  How long shall the wicked exult?
4 They gush out, they speak arrogancy;
  All the workers of iniquity bear themselves loftily.
5 They crush Thy people, O Lord,
  And afflict Thy heritage.
6 They slay the widow and the stranger,
  And murder the fatherless.
7 And they say: "The Lord will not see,
  Neither will the God of Jacob give heed."
8 Consider, ye brutish among the people;
  And ye fools, when will ye understand?
9 He that planted the ear, shall He not hear?
  And He that formed the eye, shall He not see?
10 He that instructeth nations, shall He not correct,
  Even He that teacheth man knowledge?
11 The Lord knoweth the thoughts of man,
  That they are vanity.
12 Happy is the man whom Thou instructest, O Lord,
  And teachest out of Thy Torah:
13 That Thou mayest give him rest from the days of evil,
  Until the pit be digged for the wicked.
14 For the Lord will not cast off His people,
  Neither will He forsake His inheritance.

<sup>15</sup> For right shall return unto justice,
And all the upright in heart shall follow it.
<sup>16</sup> Who will rise up for me against the evil-doers?
Who will stand up for me against the workers of iniquity?
<sup>17</sup> Unless the Lord had been my help,
My soul had soon dwelt in silence.
<sup>18</sup> If I say: "My foot slippeth,"
Thy mercy, O Lord, holdeth me up.
<sup>19</sup> When my cares are within me,
Thy comforts delight my soul.
<sup>20</sup> Shall the seat of wickedness have fellowship with Thee,
Which frameth mischief by statute?
<sup>21</sup> They gather themselves together against the soul of the
righteous,
And condemn innocent blood.
<sup>22</sup> But the Lord hath been my high tower,
And my God the rock of my refuge.
<sup>23</sup> And He hath brought upon them their own iniquity,
And will cut them off in their own evil;
The Lord our God will cut them off.

(Psalm 94:1–23)

The psalm begins on a note of addressing God in terms of God's expected role as avenging injustice and imposing fairness. Verse 1 sets the theme by repeating the phrase "God to whom vengeance belongeth." We are accustomed to thinking of the quality of vengeance with negative associations. Its sense in Psalm 94 is of one who avenges wrongs against those who cannot defend themselves, such as widows, strangers, and the fatherless in verse 6. Thus vengeance is understood to be a quality of God as protector. And the psalmist is virtually imploring, "Where is their protection?" Similarly, the notion of God as judge of the earth evokes the sense not of an impartial and disinterested adjudicator, but of a responsible administrator of justice among human beings. In the very opening verses of the psalm, the psalmist sets the tone for the work and makes clear the expectations—of God—that animate the work's concerns.

As we have seen, these concerns are presented dramatically and powerfully in verses 3–7. In verses 8–11, the psalmist pays special attention to responding to what I call "the functional atheism of the wicked." To their claims that God cannot know of their actions, the psalmist pointedly asserts that God, the creator of ears and eyes, is certainly able to hear and see. In this case, God can hear and see them and their destructive actions. In this understanding, verse 9 is reminiscent of the teaching of *Pirkei Avot*/the Sayings of the Fathers:

> Know what is above you: an eye that sees, an ear that hears,
> and all your deeds recorded in a book. (*Pirkei Avot* 2:1)

The image of God hearing and seeing, as stated in chapter 4, is not uncommon in the Book of Psalms. Less frequent is the image we encounter in verse 10, God as teacher—an image repeated in Psalm 94:12. This image is found elsewhere in Psalms as well:

> Teach me to do Thy will,
> For Thou art my God;
> Let Thy good spirit
> Lead me in an even land.
>
> (Psalm 143:10)

> 4 Show me Thy ways, O Lord;
> Teach me Thy paths.
> 5 Guide me in Thy truth, and teach me;
> For Thou art the God of my salvation;
> For Thee do I wait all the day.
>
> (Psalm 25:4–5)

Teach me Thy ways, O Lord;
And lead me in an even path,
Because of them that lie in wait for me.

(Psalm 27:11)

Teach me, O Lord, Thy way, that I may walk in Thy truth,
Make one my heart to fear Thy name.

(Psalm 86:11)

Cause me to know the way wherein I should walk.

(Psalm 143:8)

In itself it is quite a powerful image—the notion of God as a teacher who actually instructs us and directs us in the way God would have us live. It speaks of a different kind of relationship between us and God than we conventionally call to mind. It opens us up to the possibilities of a different kind of intimacy. Yet this is the idea that lies at the heart of the understanding of God as giver of revelation. The image of God as teacher carries a different resonance than the image that is usually associated with revelation: God as "lawgiver." There is something austere, distant, and perhaps even frightening in the image of lawgiver—often quite appropriate when we think of God. But it is equally appropriate to think of God in terms of the intimacy that one associates with teachers who have attentively shaped and guided us, especially teachers who were close to us when we were very young.

In the case of verses 10 and 12 of Psalm 94, there may be a specific purpose in the evocation of God as teacher. It is possible that the psalmist is suggesting one particular answer to the question of the suffering of the righteous that the psalm raises—an answer to which we will return shortly.

In contrast to the subjects of God's instructions are the thoughts of people, particularly, by implication, the thoughts of those who deny or disregard God. The psalmist characterizes these thoughts as *hevel*. Although we often translate this Hebrew word as "vanity," its literal sense is of something even more inconsequential. The word evokes the transitory quality of the frost that exists for an instant when we exhale on a cold day. *Hevel* is the same word that is employed in the well-known phrase of the Book of Ecclesiastes 1:2, "Vanity of vanities, all is vanity...." More properly it has the sense, "Frost of frosts, all is frost...." The psalmist would have us understand that such *hevel*, such frost, is the real character of the schemes devised by the workers of wickedness.

Psalm 94 continues to speak with assurance of God's protection and the triumph of the righteous in verses 13–15 and again in verses 17–19. The words of verses 13–15 are clear and powerful expressions of God's concern and protection. God will rule this world with justice (verse 15) and will not abandon the people the psalmist calls "God's people" (verse 14). When we read of God not permitting our foot to slip (verse 18), the image becomes more powerful when we associate it with some other verses from Psalms:

8 Bless our God, ye peoples,
  And make the voice of His praise to be heard;
9 Who hath set our soul in life,
  And suffered not our foot to be moved.

(Psalm 66:8–9)

36 Thou hast also given me Thy shield of salvation,
  And Thy right hand hath holden me up;
  And Thy condescension hath made me great.
37 Thou hast enlarged my steps under me,
  And my feet have not slipped.

(Psalm 18:36–37)

He will not suffer thy foot to be moved;
He that keepeth thee will not slumber.

(Psalm 121:3)

The words of 94:19 are among the most beautiful and reassuring of the entire Book of Psalms. As we read them, we understand the depths of the psalmist's confidence. And as we give voice to them, we can know what it feels like to have that confidence be our own.

The assurance of these verses, however, is undercut by the question posed in verse 16. The psalmist seems less than certain—and even anxious. In verse 20, the psalmist does not seem all that confident that God will be distanced from the wicked or will punish their violation of God's will. In verse 21, we see the wicked ones behaving with the same violence and impunity that we saw in verses 5 and 6.

Then, in the closing verses, the psalmist returns to the tone of confidence and security that we heard in verses 13–15 and 17–19. Here, God is evoked by some of the most powerful images in the Book of Psalms. God is a "high tower," the "rock of my refuge." The psalm closes with the dramatic image of God causing the intrigues of the wicked to rebound against them (verse 23). We can understand the full power of this image best in the context of similar sentiments that are found elsewhere in Psalms:

16 He hath digged a pit, and hollowed it,
And is fallen into the ditch which he made.
17 His mischief shall return upon his own head,
And his violence shall come down upon his own pate.

(Psalm 7:16–17)

They have prepared a net for my steps,
My soul is bowed down;

They have digged a pit for me,
They are fallen into the midst thereof themselves.

(Psalm 57:7)

Give them according to their deeds, and according to the
  evil of their endeavors;
Give them after the work of their hands;
Render to them their desert.

(Psalm 28:4)

Psalm 94 concludes on the note of the repeated assurance
that God will "cut off" the evil-doers. The repetition of the phrase
adds power to the sentiment, suggesting that this is the core affirmation of the psalm. This phrase also calls to mind the sense of
certainty expressed in Psalm 118:

10 All the nations compass me about;
  Verily, in the name of the Lord I will cut them off.
11 They compass me about, yea, they compass me about;
  Verily, in the name of the Lord I will cut them off.
12 They compass me about like bees;
  They are quenched as the fire of thorns;
  Verily, in the name of the Lord I will cut them off.

(Psalm 118:10–12)

We may see this as a powerful note of affirmation on which to
conclude this psalm. We may choose to see this vacillation between
certainty and insecurity as a rhetorical strategy employed by the
psalmist to lead up to what is ultimately a statement of confidence
in God's justice. Or we may see the alternation of moods as reflecting a true ambiguity. If the psalmist is, indeed, uncertain about the
existence of justice in the world, it would not be a situation very different from the one experienced by most human beings, including

people of faith. One day we are certain that there is justice in this life; the next day we see something that breaks our heart and we are not so confident again.

In Jewish practice, each day of the week has a specific psalm that is read during the worship services of that day (Psalm 24 on Sunday, Psalm 48 on Monday, Psalm 82 on Tuesday, Psalm 81 on Thursday, Psalm 93 on Friday, and Psalm 92 on Shabbat). In this arrangement, Psalm 94 is read on Wednesday, the exact middle of the week. Some commentators see a progression in the daily psalms from absolute certainty in God's justice in Psalm 24 at the start of the week to the apparent ambiguity and uncertainty of Psalm 94 in mid-week, back to confidence at the end of the week. If this is so, it is a reflection of the pendulum-like movement between faith and fear, hope and uncertainty, that characterizes our own response to the issue of justice in the world.

Perhaps Psalm 94 is arguing for a certain modesty in our con- fidence. At the very least, it is reminding us not to become so complacent in our certainty of God's judgment that we become insensitive to the suffering that takes place in the world around us. There is a story about the Chafetz Chayim, a saintly teacher who lived in the late nineteenth and early twentieth centuries. He once taught that everything in the world had a purpose. One of his stu- dents asked, "What is the purpose of atheism?" The Chafetz Chayim replied, "When you see a person in need, be an atheist: Do not tell them that 'God will provide.' Instead, you can rely only on yourself to take care of them." Perhaps such is the role of uncer- tainty, or at least modesty, in our faith when it comes to the ques- tion of justice in the world.

## A Note of Certainty

Like Psalm 94, Psalm 73 begins with a powerful outcry against injustice in the world. It raises the poignant issue of how God could permit the apparent success of the wicked. But Psalm 73 differs from Psalm 94 in arriving at a clear resolution to the dilemma. While Psalm 94 appears to vacillate between affirmation and continued questioning, Psalm 73 moves from a presentation of the problem to unwavering certainty:

17 Until I entered into the sanctuary of God,
And considered their end.
18 Surely Thou settest them in slippery places;
Thou hurlest them down to utter ruin.
19 How are they become a desolation in a moment!
They are wholly consumed by terrors.
20 As a dream when one awaketh,
So, O Lord, when Thou arousest Thyself, Thou wilt despise
their semblance.
21 For my heart was in a ferment,
And I was pricked in my reins.
22 But I was brutish and ignorant;
I was as a beast before Thee.
23 Nevertheless I am continually with Thee;
Thou holdest my right hand.
24 Thou wilt guide me with Thy counsel,
And afterward receive me with glory.
25 Whom have I in heaven but Thee?
And beside Thee I desire none upon earth.
26 My flesh and my heart faileth;
But God is the rock of my heart and my portion forever.
27 For, lo, they that go far from Thee shall perish;
Thou dost destroy them all that go astray from Thee.
28 But as for me, the nearness of God is my good;
I have made the Lord God my refuge,
That I may tell of all Thy works.

(Psalm 73:17–28)

There seems to be a clear break between the first half of the psalm, in which the question is asked, and the second half, in which an answer is presented. In a great number of psalms, the first part depicts the protagonist calling out in distress, pleading for help; the latter part consists of the protagonist rejoicing at being rescued from jeopardy and giving thanks and praise to God. So it is in Psalm 73, where the psalmist begins in a tone of profound perplexity and ends on a note of affirmation and in a mood of exaltation.

In many psalms, the transition is not gradual but involves an abrupt shift. In Psalm 73, the shift occurs after verse 16. In verse 17, the psalmist speaks of finding the answer upon going—perhaps to meditate on the issue—to what we can presume is the Temple in Jerusalem. There, the solution to the dilemma is disclosed. The change is not a change of events or conditions, but a change in perspective. While the reversal in many other psalms involves external circumstances, here the change is internal. Now the psalmist sees not the success of the wicked, but their destruction (verses 18–20). The psalmist bemoans the earlier unenlightenment that characterized his outlook (verses 21–22) and concludes on a note of affirmation and confidence in God (verses 23–28). Indeed, these last verses contain some of the most powerful expressions of trust in God found in the entire Book of Psalms. Verse 25 constitutes a beautiful expression of absolute trust. In verse 26, God is referred to, as in other psalms, as a rock: dependable, absolutely reliable, the proper object of our confidence.

At the funeral of Franz Rosenzweig, one of the giants of twentieth-century Jewish thought, Martin Buber—another giant—read Psalm 73. The choice was especially appropriate given the seven years of Rosenzweig's debilitating final illness. Verse 23 of this psalm, with its vigorous affirmation of God's nearness, was engraved on Rosenzweig's tombstone.

What is it that Psalm 73 affirms? Verse 27 tells us that all those who disobey God will perish. This is very much a reaffirmation of the conventional ideology found in many other psalms:

> The Lord preserveth all them that Love Him;
> But all the wicked will He destroy.
>
> (Psalm 145:20)

> All the horns of the wicked also will I cut off;
> But the horns of the righteous shall be lifted up.
>
> (Psalm 75:11)

> 11 The righteous shall rejoice when he seeth the vengeance;
> He shall wash his feet in the blood of the wicked.
> 12 And men shall say: "Verily there is a reward for the righteous;
> Verily there is a God that judgeth in the earth."
>
> (Psalm 58:11–12)

In the various depictions of the history of Israel in numerous psalms, the people were rewarded for obedience to God and punished for their backsliding. In Psalm 52, we find much the same idea:

> 3 Why boastest thou thyself of evil, O mighty man?
> The mercy of God endureth continually.
> 4 Thy tongue deviseth destruction;
> Like a sharp razor, working deceitfully.
> 5 Thou lovest evil more than good;
> Falsehood rather than speaking righteousness. Selah.
> 6 Thou lovest all devouring words,
> The deceitful tongue.
> 7 God will likewise break thee forever,
> He will take thee up, and pluck thee out of thy tent,
> And root thee out of the land of the living. Selah.
> 8 The righteous also shall see, and fear,

And shall laugh at him.
9 "Lo this is the man that made not God his stronghold;
But trusted in the abundance of his riches,
And strengthened himself in his wickedness."

(Psalm 52:3–9)

These verses provide a graphic description of the destruction of the wicked. Here is a man who was mighty and rich. But rather than trusting in God, he trusted in his own riches. In this, he was like other arrogant people we encounter in the Book of Psalms, who, in a sense, worshipped themselves.

6 Wherefore should I fear in the days of evil,
When the iniquity of my supplanters compasseth me about,
7 Of them that trust in their wealth,
And boast themselves in the multitude of their riches?

(Psalm 49:6–7)

Some trust in chariots, and some in horses;
But we will make mention of the name of the Lord our God.

(Psalm 20:8)

Even worse, he was wicked, deceitful, destructive, and a doer of evil. For this he would be broken and utterly destroyed. Much the same idea is expressed very succinctly in Psalm 55:

But Thou, O God, wilt bring them down into the nethermost pit;
Men of blood and deceit shall not live out half their days;
But as for me, I will trust in Thee.

(Psalm 55:24)

Here the wicked are not accorded even apparent success; they just die young. All these psalms express confidence in the cause-

and-effect relationship between good and reward, evil and punishment—an ideology that finds expression in the earlier sections of the Torah as well. At its heart, Psalms maintains that an inflexible law of the universe assures that the good are rewarded and the wicked are punished. In the same spirit of absolute faith in the almost automatic functioning of the moral process, we read a number of related verses from various psalms:

> 13 The righteous shall flourish like the palm-tree;
> He shall grow like a cedar in Lebanon.
> 14 Planted in the house of the Lord,
> They shall flourish in the courts of our God.
> 15 They shall bring forth fruit in old age;
> They shall be full of sap and richness;
> 16 To declare that the Lord is upright,
> My Rock, in whom there is no unrighteousness.
>
> (Psalm 92:13–16)

The man who "hath not walked in the counsel of the wicked" shall be happy (Psalm 1:1):

> And he shall be like the tree planted by streams of water,
> That bringeth forth its fruit in its season,
> And whose leaf doth not wither;
> And in whatsoever he doeth he shall prosper.
>
> (Psalm 1:3)

In Psalm 52 the wicked who "made God not his stronghold" (verse 9) is "broken" (verse 7):

> But as for me, I am like a leafy olive-tree in the house of God;
> I trust in the mercy of God forever and ever.
>
> (Psalm 52:10)

Here we have a veritable arboretum of certainty. In contrast is the
fate of the wicked:

> When the wicked spring up as the grass,
> And when all the workers of iniquity do flourish;
> It is that they may be destroyed forever.
>
> (Psalm 92:8)

> 2 For they shall soon wither like the grass,
> And fade as the green herb....
> 35 I have seen the wicked in great power,
> And spreading himself like a leafy tree in its native soil.
> 36 But one passed by, and lo, he was not;
> Yea, I sought him, but he could not be found.
>
> (Psalm 37:2, 35–36)

> God will likewise break thee forever,
> He will take thee up, and pluck thee from thy tent,
> And root thee out of the land of the living.
>
> (Psalm 52:7)

> Not so the wicked;
> But they are like the chaff which the wind driveth away.
>
> (Psalm 1:4)

Similar in spirit to these verses in Psalms is the statement by the
prophet Jeremiah:

> Thus saith the Lord: Cursed is the man that trusteth in
> man, and maketh flesh his arm, and whose heart departeth
> from the Lord. For he shall be like a tamarisk in the desert,
> and shall not see when good cometh; but shall inhabit the
> parched places in the wilderness, a salt land and not inhab-

ited. Blessed is the man that trusteth in the Lord, and whose trust the Lord is. For he shall be as a tree planted by the waters, and that spreadeth out its roots by the river, and shall not see when heat cometh, but its foliage shall be luxuriant; and shall not be anxious in the year of drought, neither shall cease from yielding fruit. (Jeremiah 17:5–8)

All these verses express an unwavering faith that the issue of evil is a straightforward one: The good are rewarded and the wicked are punished.

## The Success of the Wicked Is Only Apparent

It was the inconsistency between the idea that God rewards the righteous and punishes the wicked and the experiences of life that lay behind the revolution in understanding at the heart of the Book of Job. What are we to make of the wicked who seem to prosper and the good who suffer? That, after all, was the dilemma expressed at the beginning of Psalm 73 and throughout Psalm 94. Verses 18 and 20 of Psalm 73 offer a somewhat different answer than the unequivocal tone of verse 20. These verses do not deny the success of the wicked. But from the perspective of newly won enlightenment, the psalmist now understands that these are only apparent successes—and they are only for a moment. So when it looks like the wicked ones are on solid ground, it turns out to be a slippery place from which they topple to their destruction (verse 18). Their security evaporates in an instant (verse 19), as one waking from a dream (verse 20). This same solution to the problem of evil in the world is expressed in Psalm 92:

When the wicked spring up as the grass,
And when all the workers of iniquity do flourish;
It is that they may be destroyed forever.

(Psalm 92:8)

The transience of the apparent success of the wicked is contrasted with what a more literal translation of the final words would
render as the "everlasting eternity" of their destruction. The
wicked may seem to prosper, but the victory is ephemeral.

## Time Solves the Problem of Evil

We hear much the same lesson in Psalm 37, but with a rather different tone and with interesting new angles that sharpen its message:

> 1 Fret not thyself because of evil-doers,
>   Neither be thou envious against them that work unright-
>     eousness
> 2 For they shall soon wither like grass,
>   And fade as the green herb.
> 3 Trust in the Lord, and do good;
>   Dwell in the land, and cherish faithfulness
> 4 So shalt thou delight thyself in the Lord;
>   And He shall give thee the petitions of thy heart.
> 5 Commit thy ways unto the Lord;
>   Trust also in Him, and He will bring it to pass.
> 6 And He will make thy righteousness to go forth as the light,
>   And thy righteousness as the noonday.
> 7 Resign thyself unto the Lord, and wait patiently for Him;
>   Fret not thyself because of him who prospereth in his way,
>   Because of the man who bringeth wicked devices to pass.
> 8 Cease from anger, and forsake wrath;
>   Fret not thyself, it tendeth only to evil-doing.
> 9 For evil-doers shall be cut off;
>   But those that wait for the Lord they shall inherit the land.
> 10 And yet a little while, and the wicked is no more;
>   Yea, thou shalt look well at his place, and he is not.
> 11 But the humble shall inherit the land,

And delight themselves in the abundance of peace.
12 The wicked plotteth against the righteous,
And gnasheth at him with his teeth.
13 The Lord doth laugh at him;
For He seeth that his day is coming.
14 The wicked have drawn out the sword, and have bent their bow;
To cast down the poor and the needy,
To slay such as are upright in the way;
15 Their sword shall enter into their own heart,
And their bows shall be broken.
16 Better is a little that the righteous hath
Than the abundance of many wicked.
17 For the arms of the wicked shall be broken;
But the Lord upholdeth the righteous.
18 The Lord knoweth the days of them that are whole-hearted;
And their inheritance shall be forever.
19 They shall not be ashamed in the time of evil;
And in the days of famine they shall be satisfied.
20 For the wicked shall perish,
And the enemies of the Lord shall be as the fat of lambs—
They shall pass away in smoke, they shall pass away.
21 The wicked borroweth, and payeth not;
But the righteous dealeth graciously, and giveth.
22 For such as are blessed of Him shall inherit the land;
And they that are cursed of Him shall be cut off.
23 It is of the Lord that a man's goings are established;
And He delighted in his way.
24 Though he fall, he shall not be utterly cast down;
For the Lord upholdeth his hand.
25 I have been young, and now am old;
Yet have I not seen the righteous forsaken,
Nor his seed begging bread.
26 All the day long he dealeth graciously, and lendeth;

And his seed is blessed.
27 Depart from evil, and do good;
   And dwell forevermore
28 For the Lord loveth justice,
   And forsaketh not His saints;
   They are preserved forever;
   But the seed of the wicked shall be cut off.
29 The righteous shall inherit the land,
   And dwell therein forever.
30 The mouth of the righteous uttereth wisdom,
   And his tongue speaketh justice.
31 The Torah of his God is in his heart;
   None of his steps slide.
32 The wicked watcheth the righteous,
   And seeketh to slay him.
33 The Lord will not leave him in his hand,
   Nor suffer him to be condemned when he is judged.
34 Wait for the Lord, and keep His way,
   And He will exalt thee to inherit the land;
   When the wicked are cut off, thou shalt see it.
35 I have seen the wicked in great power,
   And spreading himself like a leafy tree in its native soil.
36 But one passed by, and lo, he was not;
   Yea, I sought him, but he could not be found.
37 Mark the man of integrity, and behold the upright;
   For there is a future for the man of peace.
38 But transgressors shall be destroyed together;
   The future of the wicked shall be cut off.
39 But the salvation of the righteous is of the Lord;
   He is their stronghold in the time of trouble.
40 And the Lord helpeth them, and delivereth them;
   He delivereth them from the wicked and saveth them,
   Because they have taken refuge in Him.

(Psalm 37:1–40)

Psalm 37, like a number of other psalms (25, 34, 111, 112, 119, and 145), is an alphabetic acrostic. The psalm follows the alphabet (omitting the letter *ayin*) for the first letter of every pair of verses. And, in a way, order, regularity, and predictability are its central theme. Psalm 37 lacks the anguished questioning that characterizes the beginning of Psalm 73 and Psalm 94. There is no reversal of mood or point of view here. Instead, this psalm is an affirmation from beginning to end. The mood of confidence of the psalm is articulated from the very first verse, "Fret not thyself...." The importance of this admonition is indicated in the fact that it is repeated in verses 7 and 8. The very tone allows us to feel the psalm is addressed directly to us. In place of any concern we might have about "evil-doers" and "them that work unrighteousness," we are counseled to trust (verses 3, 5). In both places the verb used is *betach,* one of the most frequently repeated words in all of Psalms. It signifies the absolute confidence in God upon which so many of the psalms would have us build our lives.

There is confidence aplenty in Psalm 37. The wicked may devise their schemes, but their plans are thwarted. They are cut off and they perish and pass away like smoke. Indeed, their own plans turn against them, and they are destroyed by the instruments of their own devising. But Psalm 37 does not simply reaffirm the more or less mechanical vision of the wicked being punished and the good rewarded. Its confidence comes from a different perspective.

The dominant mood of Psalm 37 is trust in God and not fretting about the wicked who inhabit the world. But Psalm 37 does not instruct us to accept passively whatever the world offers. Rather, its contribution to unraveling the riddle of evil is that the solution lies in time. Psalm 37 counsels us to "wait," even "wait patiently." It speaks of "yet a little while." We are assured that the wicked shall "soon"—or quickly—wither like grass and "fade" as speedily as the green herb. Verses 12–13 assert that God looks at the devisings of the wicked and "laughs" (who of us would not want to hear God laugh at the ones we see working evil?), adding ominously, "For He sees that his day is coming." What a wonderfully sardonic note. Several different interpretations of that future day are elaborated in the rest of the psalm. In reading of the promise of delayed justice, we might be reminded of another verse from Psalms:

For His anger is but for a moment,
His favor is for a life-time;
Weeping may tarry for the night,
But joy cometh in the morning.

(Psalm 30:6)

The great lesson of Psalm 37 is the contrast between the futures of the wicked and the righteous:

37 Mark the man of integrity, and behold the upright;
For there is a future for a man of peace.
38 But transgressors shall be destroyed together;
The future of the wicked shall be cut off.

(Psalm 37:37–38)

The wicked may prosper for a moment (verse 35), but their future is utter destruction (verse 38). In contrast, the future of the righteous is peace—tranquility (verse 37).

They shall not be ashamed in the time of evil;
And in the days of famine they shall be satisfied.

(Psalm 37:19)

The righteous's inheritance will be "forever" (verse 18). Indeed, they "dwell forevermore" (verse 27). These last two verses of assurance may speak of some sort of personal continuity, or they may indicate some kind of passing on of one's inheritance to one's descendants. It is true that in biblical society keeping the family land intact and in the family was of great importance. So, in the context of that society, this is no insignificant reward. If the verses are referring to personal continuity, we are hearing another version of delayed reward and punishment. If the verses speak about descendants, we are entering the realm of a slightly different solution to the dilemma posed by the problem of evil.

Taking a longer view than the lifetime of an individual, Psalm 37 contrasts the fate of the descendants of the righteous and the wicked. Verse 25 uses the medium of time to frame the argument it presents. From the perspective of a long lifetime, the psalmist asserts that he has never seen the righteous abandoned. Even if they have suffered for a while and endured privation, ultimately their descendants have not known want. This verse included by Jewish tradition in the grace after meals. So those who follow the practice of reciting grace after meals hear the lesson of verse 25 several times in the course of each day. Two other verses from Psalm 37 juxtapose the fate of the descendants of the righteous and the wicked:

All the day long he dealeth graciously and he lendeth;
And his seed is blessed.

(Psalm 37:26)

For the Lord loveth justice,
And forsaketh not His saints;
They are preserved forever;
But the seed of the wicked shall be cut off.

(Psalm 37:28)

Perhaps Psalm 37 is suggesting that one lifetime may not be enough to weigh the fruits of righteousness and wickedness. But, in the course of time, the consequences of people's deeds will be made evident in the lives of their descendants.

## The Ultimate Future

It is in the ultimate future, near or distant, that a number of verses of Psalm 37 seem to place their hope for a final reckoning where "all accounts are settled."

> But the humble shall inherit the land
> And delight themselves in the abundance of peace.
>
> (Psalm 37:11)

> For such as are blessed of Him shall inherit the land;
> And they that are cursed of Him shall be cut off.
>
> (Psalm 37:22)

> The righteous shall inherit the land,
> And dwell therein forever.
>
> (Psalm 37:29)

> Wait for the Lord, and keep His way,
> And He will exalt thee to inherit the land;
> When the wicked are cut off, thou shalt see it.
>
> (Psalm 37:34)

What a powerful phrase—to inherit the earth. Most Western readers may be surprised to find it in Psalms—or in the Hebrew Bible. We usually associate it with the Sermon on the Mount in the New Testament:

> Blessed are the meek, for they shall inherit the earth.
> (Matthew 5:5)

But it turns out that Matthew is really quoting from the Book of Psalms. Those verses promise us that the righteous will be rewarded by "inheriting the land"—or the earth. The same Hebrew word, *eretz*, means "land" (as in "plot of land"), or "country" (as in the "land of Israel"), or even the entire planet (as in "everyone on earth had the same language," Genesis 11:1). Here, again, the compensation for virtue is in the future. These verses lend themselves to a variety of interpretations. Do they tell us that we, ourselves, will come to take possession of our own (plot of) land or (piece of the) earth? Do they mean that in the course of time our possessions—unlike those of the wicked—will come to be inherited by our descendants who will possess them "forever"? That certainly is the meaning of this phrase as it is used elsewhere in Psalms:

12 What man is there that feareth the Lord?
   Him will He instruct in the way that he should choose.
13 His soul shall abide in prosperity;
   And his seed shall inherit the land.

(Psalm 25:12–13)

Here it is very clear that the reward for righteousness is that the family's holdings will remain in the hands of the righteous person's descendants in perpetuity. The prophet Isaiah makes use of the same phrase:

Thy people also shall all be righteous, they shall inherit the land forever; the branch of My planting, the work of My hands, wherein I glory. (Isaiah 60:21)

In Isaiah, the phrase "inherit the land" is intended to promise a reward for the entirety of the People of Israel. In due time, they shall all be considered righteous. When that occurs, they will dwell securely in their own land, without fear of being conquered or driven into exile. They will have permanent possession of the land of their people.

There is one other possible interpretation of the idea of "inheriting the earth." Perhaps these verses refer to the ultimate future, what the biblical Prophets call "that Day," the time of completeness and fulfillment. If this is the case, these verses are saying that in that ultimate time, whether it is close at hand or infinitely far off, all wickedness will be defeated and the humble, the righteous, will prevail over the earth. The reward for righteousness, says this strand of Psalm 37, may be delayed, perhaps delayed for an indeterminate time, but it will surely come.

## Living Better Is the Answer to the Problem of Evil

Psalm 37 tells us that reward and punishment are mediated by time. Justice waits. Maybe the wait is "a little while," or maybe a long time. Perhaps the wait extends beyond our lifetime to the world of our descendants. Perhaps the wait is into the ultimate future, whether that time is close or infinitely far away. Time, says Psalm 37, is the answer: "Don't fret yourself," "wait patiently." Justice will prevail. But in the meantime, what are the righteous to do until the reward comes to them—even if long delayed—or does not come to them at all, but is conferred on their descendants long after they have died? To the righteous who are waiting, Psalm 37 counsels:

> Better is a little that the righteous hath
> Than the abundance of many wicked.
> (Psalm 37:16)

This verse resonates with a number of similar statements in the Book of Proverbs, which speak to the same dilemma:

Better is little with fear of the Lord, than great treasure and turmoil therewith. Better is a dinner of vegetables where love is, than a fattened ox and hatred therewith. (Proverbs 15:16–17)

Better it is to be of a lowly spirit with the humble, than to divide the spoil with the proud. (Proverbs 16:19)

Better is a dry morsel and quietness therewith, than a house full of feasting with strife. (Proverbs 17:1)

Better is the poor that walketh in his integrity than he that is perverse in his lips and a fool at the same time. (Proverbs 19:1)

So says Psalm 37:16; even if the reward does not come in our lifetime, our life, lived righteously, is still "better." To this way of thinking, the answer to the problem of evil lies in our integrity. Maybe living "better" is an interim step until justice is finally done. Or, perhaps, living "better" is its own answer to the problem of evil around us.

## Suffering Makes Us Better People

In Psalm 119, we find a verse with a radically different understanding of the problem of human suffering from what we have examined thus far:

It is good for me that I have been afflicted,
In order that I might learn Thy statutes.
(Psalm 119:71)

In this verse, suffering is understood as serving a purpose—it is redemptive. We learn from our misfortunes; we are turned into better people in this life, because of what we have endured. This idea is stated explicitly earlier in the same psalm:

> Before I was afflicted, I did err;
> But now I observe Thy word.
>
> (Psalm 119:67)

We have already looked at Psalm 94, but one verse of that psalm takes on new meaning in light of this idea:

> Happy is the man whom Thou instructest, O Lord,
> And teachest out of Thy Torah.
>
> (Psalm 94:12)

Perhaps the suffering and privation we endure are not punishments at all, or even anomalies in a well-ordered system of reward and punishment. Perhaps, say these verses, they are God's way of instructing us, raising our aspirations, or deepening our understanding. Suffering, in this perspective, becomes not an affliction, but a gift. In a brief essay about his life, the Broadway theater producer and director Hal Prince reflects this same way of thinking. He refers to a nervous breakdown he experienced as a very young person and notes:

> People don't realize what a profound place luck plays in your life. My first piece of luck was having that breakdown and making something of it. I suspect there's a crucible in everyone's life, some emotional or traumatic confrontation, and I think if you come to grips with it, you emerge stronger on the other side.[3]

This same idea underlies two statements in Psalms that speak about God "trying" us, not as one tries a case in court, but as one tries metal in a furnace to make it stronger:

The Lord trieth the righteous;
But the wicked and him that loveth violence His soul
  hateth.

(Psalm 11:5)

10 For Thou, O God, hast tried us;
Thou hast refined us, as silver is refined.
11 Thou didst bring us into the hold;
Thou didst lay constraint upon our loins.
12 Thou hast caused men to ride over our heads;
We went through fire and through water;
But Thou didst bring us unto abundance.

(Psalm 66:10–12)

These verses have their counterpart in Isaiah:

> Behold, I have refined thee, but not as silver; I have tried
> thee in the furnace of affliction. (Isaiah 48:10)

The purpose, say these verses, of our suffering is to "try" us, to test us perhaps, certainly to make us stronger. Suffering, to this way of thinking, is not understood as a negative experience at all, but ultimately as a positive one.

The Rabbis, who had themselves certainly experienced the suffering of the Jewish people, elaborated on this theme when they commented on Psalm 11:5:

> R. Jonathan said: "The Lord tries the righteous (Psalm
> 11:5). The potter does not test cracked vessels; it is not
> worthwhile to tap them even once, because they would
> break; but he taps the good ones, because however many
> times he taps them, they do not break. Even so God tries,
> not the wicked, but the righteous."

R. Jose ben Chanina said: "The flax dealer who knows that his flax is good, pounds it, for it becomes more excellent by his pounding; and when he knocks it, it glistens the more. But when he knows his flax is bad, he does not knock it at all, for it would split. So God tries, not the wicked, but the righteous." (Genesis Rabbah 32)

With this understanding, our suffering is not seen as an indication of our distance from God, but as a mark of our intimacy.

## Suffering and Nearness to God

The Chasidic Rebbe Levi Yitzchak of Berditchev once said, "I do not want to know why it is that I suffer, only to know that I suffer for Your sake." Levi Yitzchak would have seen a deeper level of meaning in this psalm:

> Though he fall, he shall not be utterly cast down;
> For the Lord upholdeth his hand.
>
> (Psalm 37:24)

Levi Yitzchak would have heard this verse as teaching that our suffering offers us an opportunity to draw closer to God. Certainly the imagery of God upholding our hand is very graphic. It depicts real closeness and is very compelling. Who would not want God to uphold his or her hand, even at the price of "falling"? This solution to the problem of evil in the world is the least material, or tangible, that we have examined. It resolves the issue not in physical but in spiritual terms. It answers the dilemma not in relation to our place in the world but to our standing with God.

For all the certainty we saw in the second half of Psalm 73, perhaps there is one, deeper level of meaning. The psalm concludes by paralleling opposite ideas:

²⁷ For, lo, they that go far from Thee shall perish;
  Thou dost destroy all them that go astray from Thee.
²⁸ But as for me, the nearness of God is my good;
  I have made the Lord God my refuge,
  That I may tell of all Thy works.

(Psalm 73:27–28)

Perhaps, when read in the light of Levi Yitzchak's question and Psalm 37:24, this pair of verses is suggesting that the real reward for our righteousness *is* the suffering we endure and the nearness to God that comes from our struggle with the reality of our situation and with the meaning of our suffering. Like Jacob in Genesis 32, we cannot wrestle with God without drawing very close indeed. This understanding suggests that our suffering provides us with the opportunity to wrestle. For all the "goods" of Psalm 37:16 and the verses from Proverbs, perhaps the greatest "good" of all is our nearness to God.

# In the End the Answer Is Beyond Us

In life and in the Book of Psalms, there are many answers to the problem of evil. No doubt we sometimes find one argument convincing, sometimes another one. The truth is, we cannot truly know. The problem of evil in the world is one of the great mysteries of faith. In the Bible, the real subject of the Book of Job is the dissatisfaction with easy answers to this hard problem. The thrust of Job is to challenge what must have been accepted as the normative theology of its time. Job is a perfectly good man who has done no wrong. Yet he suffers one horrible affliction after another. The first hearers of the book—and those who read it today—know that Job is not being punished for anything he did. But the book presents us with three friends of Job who come to comfort him. The friends can only make sense of Job's afflictions by interpreting them in terms of the prevailing theology of that time. So they tell Job that some action of his must be the cause of all that has befallen him. Job forcefully maintains his innocence and even challenges God to reveal what he has done to deserve such terrible blows. (The Job of the Bible hardly has the "patience" with which he is endowed in the familiar cliché.) Finally, in the powerful account of chapter 38, God appears to Job and his friends and says, in effect, that Job is right and the friends are wrong. Job is guilty of no unrighteousness, but human beings cannot begin to understand what God does. God's deeds and God's ways are beyond our limited ability to comprehend. The problem of evil in the world, if understandable in God's infinite terms, is beyond the capacity of our finite minds. As we read in *Pirkei Avot*/the Sayings of the Fathers:

> Rabbi Yannai said, "[The reason why] the wicked prosper and the righteous suffer is not in our grasp." (*Pirkei Avot* 4:19)

---

3. Hal Prince, *Time Magazine*, January 20, 2003.

# 5

# FACING OUR MORTALITY

And if Moishe Leib the poet should tell
that he saw death in the waves,
as one sees oneself in the mirror,
in the morning, of all times, around ten o'clock,
would they believe Moishe Leib?

And if Moishe Leib greeted death from a distance
with his hand, and asked, How's it going?
precisely at the moment when thousands of people
were having the time of their life in the water,
would they believe Moishe Leib?

And if Moishe Leib, weeping, should swear
that he was drawn to death as much
as a fellow mooning around in the evening
at the window of a lady he's made holy,
would they believe Moishe Leib?

And if Moishe Leib should picture death for them,
not gray and dark, but gorgeously colorful,
just as it showed itself around ten o'clock,
there, far away, between sky and wave, alone,
would they believe Moishe Leib?

(Moishe Leib Halpern, "Memento Mori")

This poem by the Yiddish author Moishe Leib Halpern no doubt seems dissonant or disturbing to us. We are not accustomed to dealing with death, let alone finding it described as "not gray and dark, but gorgeously colorful." And we are not comfortable being confronted with it. But Halpern would have us understand that death is very much a part of life. We cannot be fully human unless we find some way to come to terms with it.

People in the United States tend to avoid dealing with the reality of death. We prefer to engage in what one another called "the denial of death." We avert our eyes from it, avoid speaking about it, resort to eupheism. In our society, people do not "die," they "pass away," "pass on," or even "go to a better place." We have been characterized as a sunny culture in which death takes place off-stage.

Of course, the reality of death cannot be as easily dismissed as all that, and it cannot be denied at all. The Protestant theologian Paul Tillich has written that the greatest challenge of the human condition is to come to terms with our "finitude," the limitations of our own powers and capacities—the greatest of which is our mortality. We can never know as much as we would like, understand as much as we would want, do as much as we would desire. And we do not live forever.

In the Buddhist tradition, the very first teaching that the Buddha spoke about after he attained enlightenment was called "the Four Noble Truths." The first of these involves acceptance of great expressions of "finitude" in our lives: sickness, decay, old age, and death.

Buddhism has been described by many as dark or pessimistic. Jewish teaching, in contrast, has been characterized as optimistic and life affirming, as if it participated in the American predilection for avoiding the kind of unpleasant subjects that the Buddha put front and center. And certainly many of the psalms radiate a powerful optimism. After all, what could be "sunnier" than the familiar words of Psalm 23:

¹ The Lord is my shepherd; I shall not want.
² He maketh me to lie down in green pastures;
He leadeth me beside the still waters.

(Psalm 23:1–2)

And yet there are very different voices and perspectives to be found in the Book of Psalms as well, instances where the writer of the psalm, and we who read it, do not avert our eyes from the reality of death and do not deny its power over us. Indeed, the psalms often hold our attention on that reality and help us learn lessons from our mortality, which have a bearing on how we conduct ourselves in life. We turn now to some selections from Psalms that help us address the riddle of death.

## To Be Human Is to Die

Death is, indeed, difficult to speak about because it is, for every one of us, such a painful reality. And yet it is woven into every one of our lives. It is part of what it means to be a human being.

What will remain after me?
A door standing ajar,
A shelf of books, old and dusty,
And an empty chair—
Where I dreamed forth my poems,
That I believed in.
Poems that lie hidden in a wooden drawer,
mute,
Like unfinished letters.

What will remain after me?
Shoes and socks,
A shirt that once covered

A terrified heart.
What will remain after me?
A sunbeam
Flickering at twilight
On a wall in a courtyard.

(Mendel Naigreshel, "What Will Remain after Me?")

The Yiddish poet Mendel Naigreshel is an example of someone trying to make sense of death. He writes from a poet's perspective. What will remain are poems, "lying mute" like unfinished letters. In this he sounds very much like his contemporary, the Hebrew poet Chaim Nachman Bialik:

After I am dead
Say this at my funeral:
There was a man who exists no more.

That man died before his time
And his life's song was broken off halfway.
O, he had one more poem
And that poem has been lost
Forever.

(Chaim Nachman Bialik, "After I Am Dead")

Bialik and Naigreshel see the world through poets' eyes. But their words reflect the concerns of all of us as we begin to wrestle with the issue of our mortality. Naigreshel begins his engagement with the subject of death in very simple human terms, asking, as all of us do at some point, a very tangible question. When death is the subject, perhaps questions are more appropriate than statements or assertions. Certainly that is what we find in Psalm 144:

3 Lord, what is man that Thou takest knowledge of him?
Or the son of man, that Thou makest account of him?
4 Man is like unto a vanity;
His days are as a shadow that passeth away.

(Psalm 144:3–4)

To the psalmist, our mortality is at the heart of the answer to the question of what it is to be human. A very similar question is posed and a very similar answer given in Psalm 39:

5 Lord, make me to know mine end,
And the measure of my days, what it is;
Let me know how short-lived I am.
6 Behold, Thou hast made my days as hand-breadths;
And mine age is as nothing before Thee;
Surely every man at his best estate is altogether vanity.

(Psalm 39:5–6)

The word translated as "vanity" in verse 4 of Psalm 144 and verse 6 of Psalm 39 is *hevel*, which, as mentioned earlier, more properly means "breath" or "frost"—the breath we see on a very cold day, which dissipates so quickly. We find this same image elsewhere in Psalm 39 and throughout Ecclesiastes:

With rebukes dost Thou chasten man for iniquity,
And like a moth Thou makest his beauty to consume away;
Surely every man is vanity.

(Psalm 39:12)

Vanity of vanities, saith Koheleth; vanity of vanities, all is vanity.
(Ecclesiastes 1:2)

The image of our days as a breath, or as the most transitory frost, captures very dramatically the sense that our life is fleeting. God may be a rock—permanent and unmovable—we are not.

This is the same message given in Psalm 89. In the midst of a plea to God about some national calamity, the psalmist includes the poignant petition:

> 48 O remember how short my time is;
> For what vanity hast Thou created all the children of men!
> 49 What man is he that liveth and shall not see death,
> That shall deliver his soul from the power of the grave?
>
> (Psalm 89:48–49)

In verse 49, the psalmist underscores the idea that death is the shared end of all who live. No one escapes its grasp.

## Death as a Solution to the Problem of Injustice

The inescapability of death seems to be the central message of Psalm 49:

> 2 Hear this, all ye peoples;
> Give ear, all ye inhabitants of the world,
> 3 Both low and high,
> Rich and poor together.
> 4 My mouth shall speak wisdom,
> And the meditation of my heart shall be understanding.
> 5 I will incline mine ear to a parable;
> I will open my dark saying upon the harp.
> 6 Wherefore should I fear in the days of evil,
> When the iniquity of my supplanters compasseth me
>     about,
> 7 Of them that trust in their wealth,

And boast themselves in the multitude of their riches?
8 No man can by any means redeem his brother,
  Nor give to God a ransom for him—
9 For too costly is the redemption of their soul,
  And must be let alone forever—
10 That he should still live always,
  That he should not see the pit.
11 For he seeth that wise men die,
  The fool and the brutish together perish,
  And leave their wealth to others.
12 Their inward thought is, that their houses shall continue
    forever,
  And their dwelling-places to all generations;
  They call their lands after their own names.
13 But man abideth not in honour;
  He is like the beasts that perish.
14 This is the way of them that are foolish,
  And of those who after them approve their sayings. Selah.
15 Like sheep they are appointed for the nether-world;
  Death shall be their shepherd;
  And the upright shall have dominion over them in the
    morning;
  And their form shall be for the nether-world to wear away,
  That there be no habitation for it.
16 But God will redeem my soul from the power of the nether-
    world;
  For He shall receive me. Selah.
17 Be not thou afraid when one waxeth rich,
  When the wealth of his house is increased;
18 For when he dieth he shall carry nothing away;
  His wealth shall not descend after him.
19 Though while he lived he blessed his soul;
  "Men will praise thee, when thou shalt do well to thyself";

20 It shall go to the generations of his fathers;
   They shall never see the light.
21 Man that is in honor understandeth not;
   He is like the beasts that perish.

(Psalm 49:2–21)

Psalm 49 is devoted to a specific concern: the inequality between the lives of the rich and the poor. For the psalmist, the situation is described as "evil." The wealthy are described as guilty of "iniquity"; their trust is in their riches. In this, they resemble other people described as guilty of wrongdoing elsewhere in the Book of Psalms:

Lo, this is the man that made not God his stronghold;
But trusted in the abundance of his riches,
And strengthened himself in his wickedness.

(Psalm 52:9)

Trust not in oppression,
And put not vain hope in robbery;
If riches increase, set not your heart thereon.

(Psalm 62:11)

Some trust in chariots, and some in horses;
But we will make mention of the name of the Lord our
   God.

(Psalm 20:8)

In each of these verses, trust in things of this world is juxtaposed to trust in God, the one reliable source of strength. But the great truth that the psalmist asserts is that riches cannot redeem us from death (Psalm 49:8). In the end, death is more powerful than anything of this world in which we put our trust. As Moishe Leib Halpern notes:

We deal in all that can be bought and sold …
It's amazing that we haven't cheated death
Of his death-tools with copper coins and schnapps!

(Moishe Leib Halpern, "Isaac Leybush Peretz")

Psalm 49 is, in its own way, very much a theodicy. The psalmist searches for an answer to the riddle of social inequality. The answer is found in the reality that everyone dies, rich and poor alike:

For he seeth that wise men die,
The fool and the brutish together perish,
And leave their wealth to others.

(Psalm 49:11)

Death claims us all. This same lesson is taught in the Book of Ecclesiastes:

For the wise man, even as the fool, there is no remembrance forever; seeing that in the days to come he will long ago have been forgotten. And how must the wise man die even as the fool! (Ecclesiastes 2:16)

In Psalm 49, "death the leveler" redresses the inequalities we experience in life. As noted in the last chapter, the reality of our mortality is one answer to the injustices we encounter on this side of the grave. In various ways, the psalmist reminds us that in the face of death, human beings, regardless of their station in life, are no different from animals. The reminder that we are "like the beasts that perish" is repeated twice—in verses 13 and 21. This is underscored by the poetically moving image "like sheep they are appointed for the nether-world; death shall be their shepherd" (verse 15). Because of our mortality, wealth is only a fleeting thing. No one can hold onto his or her possessions forever:

For when he dieth he shall carry nothing away;
His wealth shall not descend after him.

(Psalm 49:18)

The wealthy person might have been very self-satisfied, "bless-ing his soul" while he was alive. But that soul ultimately is destined to travel to another place—to leave life. We hear very much the same idea in Psalm 39:

Surely man walketh as a mere semblance;
Surely for vanity they are in turmoil;
He heapeth up riches, and knoweth not who shall gather
    them.

(Psalm 39:7)

However hard we struggle to acquire worldly goods, they can-not protect us from the reality of our death. When we die, our pos-sessions pass beyond our reach and we have no control over what will become of them. The rich are no different from anyone else. They will die just as their ancestors did before them (verse 20). The reference to the "fathers" makes the most sense when under-stood against the background of a phrase in Psalm 39:

For I am a stranger with Thee,
A sojourner, as all my fathers were.

(Psalm 39:13)

In light of this ultimate reality, the distinction between rich and poor is seen as trivial indeed. In Psalm 49, death teaches us a lesson about human equality and encourages us not to "be afraid" (verse 17) of the social distinctions we encounter.

# Death as a Teacher

There is another lesson about our mortality that can be learned from the Book of Psalms. This lesson finds expression in Psalm 90:

¹ A prayer of Moses the man of God.
Lord, Thou hast been our dwelling-place in all generations.
² Before the mountains were brought forth,
Or ever Thou hadst formed the earth and the world,
Even from everlasting to everlasting, Thou art God.
³ Thou turnest man to contrition;
And sayest: "Return ye children of men."
⁴ For a thousand years in Thy sight
Are but as yesterday when it is past,
And as a watch in the night.
⁵ Thou carriest them away as with a flood; they are as a sleep;
In the morning they are like the grass which groweth up.
⁶ In the morning it flourisheth, and groweth up;
In the evening it is cut down, and withereth.
⁷ For we are consumed in Thine anger,
And by Thy wrath are we hurried away.
⁸ Thou hast set our iniquities before Thee,
Our secret sins in the light of Thy countenance.
⁹ For all our days are passed away in Thy wrath;
We bring our years to an end as a tale that is told.
¹⁰ The days of our years are three-score years and ten,
Or even by reason of strength four-score years;
Yet is their pride but travail and vanity;
For it is speedily gone, and we fly away.
¹¹ Who knoweth the power of Thine anger,
And Thy wrath according to the fear that is due unto Thee?
¹² So teach us to number our days,
That we may get us a heart of wisdom.

<sup>13</sup> Return, O Lord; how long?
   And let it repent Thee concerning Thy servants.
<sup>14</sup> O satisfy us in the morning with Thy mercy;
   That we may rejoice and be glad all our days.
<sup>15</sup> Make us glad according to the days wherein Thou hast
      afflicted us
   According to the days wherein we have seen evil.
<sup>16</sup> Let Thy work appear unto Thy servants,
   And Thy glory upon their children.
<sup>17</sup> And let the graciousness of the Lord our God be upon us;
   Establish Thou also upon us the work of our hands;
   Yea, the work of our hands establish Thou it.

(Psalm 90:1–17)

There are parts of this psalm that are troubling to modern readers. All the talk of God's wrath and God's anger (verses 7, 9, 11) can be disturbing to us. Yet, these are not central or primary to the message of this psalm. The issue of sin (verse 8) and repentance (verse 13), similarly, are incidental to the lesson we can learn from the psalm. Far more significant than either of these ideas is the understanding conveyed about the human condition.

Psalm 90 frames its depiction of human mortality within a powerful evocation of God's immortality. Perhaps no verses in Scripture capture as compelling a sense of God's eternality as verses 2 and 4.

<sup>2</sup> Before the mountains were brought forth,
   Or ever Thou hadst formed the earth and the world,
   Even from everlasting to everlasting, Thou art God....
<sup>4</sup> For a thousand years in Thy sight
   Are but as yesterday when it is past,
   And as a watch in the night.

(Psalm 90:2, 4)

God existed before this world that we inhabit and the creation of which we are a part; and God will continue to exist for all eternity. The time we live by is irrelevant to God. This same idea is expressed in Psalm 102:

26 Of old Thou didst lay the foundation of the earth;
And the heavens are the work of Thy hands.
27 They shall perish, but Thou shalt endure;
Yea all of them shalt wax old like a garment;
As a vesture shalt Thou change them, and they shall pass
away;
28 But Thou art the selfsame,
And Thy years shall have no end.

(Psalm 102:26–28)

God endures in a way that the works of creation do not. We have encountered this same theme before, in Psalm 39:

5 Lord, make me to know mine end,
And the measure of my days, what it is;
Let me know how short-lived I am.
6 Behold, Thou hast made my days as hand-breadths;
And mine age is as nothing before Thee;
Surely every man at his best estate is altogether vanity.

(Psalm 39:5–6)

Here the psalmist contrasts the span of a human life with God's immortality, describing the length of our lives in terms of the smallest unit of measurement in the biblical world, a "hand-breadth" (verse 6).

In contrast to God's eternality is the condition of human beings. Our lives are presented in the most transitory terms:

⁵ Thou carriest them away as with a flood; they are as a
   sleep;
  In the morning they are like grass which groweth up.
⁶ In the morning it flourisheth and groweth up;
  In the evening it is cut down and withereth.

(Psalm 90:5–6)

Our lives are depicted as passing as quickly as sleep and as
being comparable to the life of a plant. We come into being, and
we pass away quickly. That same notion, and even some of the same
imagery, is found in Psalm 103:

¹⁴ For He knoweth our frame;
   He remembereth that we are dust.
¹⁵ As for man, his days are as grass;
   As a flower of the field, so he flourisheth.
¹⁶ For the wind passeth over it, and it is gone;
   And the place thereof knoweth it no more.

(Psalm 103:14–16)

Psalm 103 echoes Psalm 90 in viewing human beings within
the context of transitory creation. Likewise, Psalm 39 presents
human mortality in images derived from the world of nature, "like
a moth Thou makest [human] beauty to consume away" (Psalm
39:12). Like Psalm 49, which reminds us that we die "like beasts,"
these psalms leave us with the awareness that we are nothing other
than part of the order of creation, all of which exists for a finite
period of time. Everything that exists on earth—as the Book of
Ecclesiastes expresses it, "under the sun"—has the same quality of
impermanence and is subject to the same fate. The Yiddish poet
Aaron Zeitlin depicts our situation in this way:

We all—
Stones, people, little shards of glass in the sun,
Tin cans, cats and trees—
Are illustrations to a text.

In some places they don't need us.
In some places they only read the text—
The pictures fall off like shriveled parts.

When a death-wind blows in the deep grass
And clears off from the west all the pictures
That the clouds set up—then
Night comes and reads the stars.

(Aaron Zeitlin, "Text")

Psalm 90 gets even more specific about the reality of human mortality: We live for seventy years, or if we are fortunate enough to have a good constitution, perhaps eighty years. However many years we are allotted, they pass by quickly and in the end we perish.

## What Can We Learn from Our Mortality?

It is possible to read these words and become despondent. We can think of these psalms as depressing. But it is possible to understand the lesson of Psalms 103 and 90 in a very different way. Psalm 103 and Psalm 90 dwell on human fragility. But that is not the real thrust of their lesson. Each of these psalms evokes our mortality in the service of a particular purpose. Psalm 103 dwells on our mortality to contrast it with God's immortality and, in particular, with the everlasting quality of God's mercy:

16 For the wind passeth over it, and it is gone;
And the place thereof knoweth it no more.

17 But the mercy of the Lord is from everlasting to everlasting
    upon them that fear Him,
    And His righteousness unto children's children;
18 To such as keep His covenant,
    And to those that remember His precepts to do them.

(Psalm 103:16–18)

Psalm 103 encourages us to think about the passing of our years as an incentive to obey God's dictates and be faithful to our covenant with God.

Psalm 90 speaks a good deal about repentance. No doubt, part of the psalmist's intent was for the hearers of the psalm to reflect on the passing of their lives, turn from evil, and reconcile with God. There is, however, another note sounded in the midst of Psalm 90:

So teach us to number our days,
That we may get us a heart of wisdom.

(Psalm 90:12)

In verse 12, the passing of our years causes us to put our lives in perspective. Our days pass quickly, the psalm admonishes us, how are we using them? In his autobiography, Russell Baker, formerly a columnist for the *New York Times,* writes about a decisive moment in his life. He quotes from his diary: "Here I am 36 years old. When my father was 36, he had been dead for three years … given three years more than my father had, how have I used the time?" From the perspective of Psalm 90:12, the quick passing of time has an instructive purpose. Our mortality becomes the frame within which we do the work of our own acts of creation. Whatever we do that is worthy assumes a special urgency when viewed against the background of our finitude. Verse 12 urges us to be wise and use our time well. This idea is expressed powerfully by the twentieth-century teacher Rabbi Joshua Loth Liebman:

Actually, we could not have our sensitivity without fragility. Mortality is the tax that we pay for the privilege of love, thought, creative work—the toll we pay on the bridge of being from which clods of earth and snow-peaked mountain summits are exempt. Just because we are human, we are prisoners of the years. Yet that very prison is the room of discipline in which we, driven by time, create.

Although God is infinite and we are finite, although God is immortal and we are mortal, we can, nonetheless, be like God in that we can be creators too. Our very mortality adds a measure of urgency to our innate drive to create. The quick passing of our days serves to encourage us to value each one and use them well.

## Is This Life All There Is?

There is something in us that impels us to wonder whether this life is really all there is for us. Is there more to our journey than our experience in this life? The psalms we have examined certainly seem to sound a note of finality in death. They appear to suggest that there is nothing beyond this life. This is what is implied in Psalm 146:

> 3 Put not your trust in princes,
>   Nor in the son of man, in whom there is no help.
> 4 His breath goeth forth, he returneth to his dust;
>   In that very day his thoughts perish.
>
> (Psalm 146:3–4)

Psalm 88:13 refers to death by a poetically evocative name, "the land of forgetfulness." Psalm 39 seems to assert the finality of death explicitly:

168     KEEPING FAITH WITH THE PSALMS

Look away from me, that I may take comfort,
Before I go hence, and be no more.

(Psalm 39:14)

The phrase "be no more" clearly implies that with our death we are extinguished, like a candle when it is blown out. Perhaps we can hear echoes of that understanding in the poem "I Will Go Away" by the Yiddish author Zvi Shargel:

I will go away
And the table will remain bare, uncovered.
The chair in brown and green
Will await my eye, my hand.
I will go away
And the floor will remain behind ...

Dreams are guarding my departure.
My grief is being cut into beams
And the birds fly away.
But the great cloud
Obscures the sun for me,
And the night bites into the stars.
I follow in the steps of the sheep.
No one will see, no one will hear
Anything.

(Zvi Shargel, "I Will Go Away")

But this is not the only perspective we can find in the Book of Psalms. Perhaps we can hear some other voices in Psalms that speak of a life of some kind beyond the grave. Psalm 90 includes a reference to one kind of immortality:

And let the graciousness of the Lord our God be upon us;
Establish Thou also upon us the work of our hands;
Yea, the work of our hands establish Thou it.

(Psalm 90:17)

We remember this psalm as one that deals profoundly with the issue of human mortality. This psalm expresses the hope that we can learn from the reality of death something about how we should live our lives. And here, at the very end of the psalm, we find a plea that our work endure. Perhaps we can understand this verse as telling us that though we do not live on, whatever we accomplish survives beyond us. The medieval Jewish philosopher Bachya ibn Pakuda wrote, "Days are like scrolls: write on them what you want to be remembered."

Earlier in this chapter, we looked at the poem "What Will Remain after Me?" by Mendel Naigreshel. The poet lamented that he would leave unfinished works ... which is, of course, true. All of us leave in the middle of some chapter. But there is another reality that Naigreshel does not mention. He will leave behind all the poems he has completed, the body of his work, not "hidden in a wooden drawer" but out in the world. Whenever someone reads one of his poems, as we have read this one, the poet lives again for us, truly alive in some profound way that escapes our ability to put into words. Jacob Glatstein expresses this idea in his poetry:

But when a ... schoolboy will remember me
My name, a line of my poetry,
In a hundred years or more,
Wherever my spirit then may soar,
I shall say—honestly and thankfully
This is life, immortality....

(Jacob Glatstein, "Jew")

The work of our hands, whatever that may be—family, creations of our imagination or spirit, deeds of kindness that touched
the lives of others—is established and endures beyond our few years.
This is certainly the kind of immortality that would "teach us to number our days" (Psalm 90:12) and encourage us to use them wisely.

Some have heard intimations of yet another kind of immortality in Psalm 49:20 tells us that our soul "shall go to the generation of the fathers." Those words may be evocative of phrases we
find repeated frequently in the Bible, such as "to be gathered to ...
[the] fathers," as in "All that generation were gathered to their
fathers" (Judges 2:10); to "sleep with ... [the] fathers," as in "And
David slept with his fathers" (1 Kings 2:10); and to be "buried with
... [the] fathers," as in "And Rehoboam slept with his fathers and
was buried with his fathers ..." (1 Kings 14:31). These phrases may
simply be euphemisms for dying. Or they may have a more concrete reference to the act of burying the dead in family crypts,
which was common in the ancient Near East. Some choose to
understand such phrases as implying that there is some kind of
existence beyond this life, that our ancestors persist beyond the
grave, and that we join them after death.

There is a glimmer of one other possibility. In Psalm 121 we read:

4 Behold, He that keepeth Israel
  Doth neither slumber nor sleep.
5 The Lord is thy keeper;
  The Lord is thy shade upon thy right hand.
6 The sun shall not smite thee by day,
  Nor the moon by night.
7 The Lord shall keep thee from all evil;
  He shall keep thy soul.
8 The Lord shall guard thy going out and thy coming in,
  From this time forth and forever.

(Psalm 121:4–8)

Conventionally, this psalm is understood as praising God for watching over and protecting us in this life. But some readers find nuances of other meanings in these words—the emphasis is on the "soul" encountered in verse 7. For such readers, Psalm 121 is about God's protecting the soul as it leaves the body, about a journey beyond the realm of this earth. Verse 8 describes how God guards the soul when it "goes out" of the human body, which has contained it during its earthly career, and when it "comes in" to the realm of life eternal in which it will live "from this time forth and forever more." For those who read Psalm 121 in this fashion, these words represent a hope for eternal life.

There is a similar interpretation of Psalm 23, in which we read:

3 He restoreth my soul;
   He guideth me in straight paths for His name's sake.
4 Yea, though I walk through the valley of the shadow of
      death,
   I will fear no evil,
   For Thou art with me;
   Thy rod and Thy staff, they comfort me.
5 Thou preparest a table before me in the presence of mine
      enemies;
   Thou hast anointed my head with oil; my cup runneth over.
6 Surely goodness and mercy shall follow me all the days of
      my life;
   And I shall dwell in the house of the Lord forever.

(Psalm 23:3–6)

Some readers understand the protagonist of the psalm to be the "soul," which we encounter in verse 3. To such readers, Psalm 23 is about the journey of that soul, "through the valley of the shadow of death" to what lies beyond. To them, verse 6 is seen as a parallelism, not of repetition, but of contrast. Thus, the first line tells us that goodness and mercy follow the soul all the days of its life on earth, while the second line suggests that upon death, the soul will "dwell in the house of the Lord forever." Some people see this line as a promise that for all eternity our souls will know an existence beyond the one experienced in this life.

Such readings of Psalms 121 and 23 offer a glimpse of immortality. It is no wonder that both psalms are customarily read at Jewish funerals. To some they offer the promise of comfort. Others hear words of assurance that the soul of the one they mourn will continue on after it has left this life. Each set of hearers can draw hope and strength from the words.

Taken together with all the other selections we have examined in this chapter, Psalms 121 and 23 offer a glimpse—but not a promise—of immortality. Certainly these psalms help us come to terms with the reality of death as an inextricable part of life. And they help us use that understanding to live our lives with heightened awareness and deepened purpose.

# 6

# FINDING OUR
# RELATIONSHIP WITH GOD

Being a Jew means running forever to God
Even if you are His betrayer
Means expecting to hear any day,
Even if you are a nay-sayer
The blare of Messiah's horn;

Means, even if you wish to,
You cannot escape His snares,
You cannot cease to pray
Even after all the prayers,
Even after all the "evens."

(Aaron Zeitlin, "Being a Jew")

We have spent most of this book discussing how to understand God, how to think about God, and how to make sense of ideas we associate with God. And yet, in this chapter, I am going to suggest that what we think about God is less important than what we feel about God. Thinking, understanding, and making sense are all rational activities. Being in a relationship is an emotional one. In the end, our religious and spiritual life is lived on the emotional plane.

Martin Buber, the great twentieth-century philosopher, spoke about the importance of "I-Thou" relationships. These are relationships unclouded by ulterior motives or selfish purposes. They are pure mutual connectedness for its own sake. For Buber, no human life is fully lived without its share of I-Thou relationships. And of those, taught Buber, the most important one is the I-Thou relationship with God.

Like all relationships, our relationship with God has many dimensions. And, like other relationships, it requires work and our ongoing attention. Our relationship with God, even more than our understanding of God, gives our life direction and purpose. In this chapter, we will look at two aspects of what it means to feel ourselves in a living relationship with God.

## Trusting God

At God's command! Let Him lead
Wherever, however he wants ...
I will not stand against him, but
Walk after Him with confidence

On mountaintops, in deep ravines,
With my eyes open—and yet blind;
In wild beasts' lairs; the Father leads—
and the child softly treads behind.

(Joseph Rolnik, "At God's Command")

Rolnik's poem expresses what it means to have a relationship with God that radiates absolute trust and confidence. We hear this same sense of affirmation in a number of psalms. Psalm 62 begins with the word that will be its theme: the Hebrew word *ach*, which is translated as "only." The psalm is about relying exclusively on God:

2 Only for God doth my soul wait in stillness;
From Him cometh my salvation.

3 He only is my rock and my salvation;
My high tower, I shall not be greatly moved.
4 How long will ye set upon a man,
That ye may slay him, all of you,
As a leaning wall, a tottering fence?
5 They only devise to thrust him down from his height,
delighting in lies;
They bless with their mouth, but they curse inwardly.
Selah.
6 Only for God wait thou in stillness, my soul;
For from Him cometh my hope.
7 He only is my rock and my salvation,
My high tower, I shall not be moved.
8 Upon God resteth my salvation and my glory;
The rock of my strength, and my refuge, is in God.
9 Trust in Him at all times, ye people;
Pour out your heart before Him;
God is a refuge for us. Selah.
10 Men of low degree are vanity, and men of high degree are a lie;
If they be laid in the balances, they are altogether lighter
than vanity.
11 Trust not in oppression,
And put not vain hope in robbery;
If riches increase, set not your heart thereon.
12 God hath spoken once,
Twice have I heard this:
That strength belongeth unto God;
13 Also unto Thee, O Lord, belongeth mercy;
For Thou renderest to every man according to his work.
(Psalm 62:2–13)

Psalm 62 speaks about absolute and exclusive reliance on God. You could almost say that this is a poem about the "only-ness" of our relationship with God. The theme is stated by the very first word following Psalm 62's introduction: *ach*/only. That word runs like a leitmotif through the rest of the psalm, appearing five more times. This repetition underscores the idea that we are to put our trust *ach*/only in God. The psalm sings of absolute confidence in God. As we read the words we experience what it is like to have that kind of relationship with God for ourselves.

## Images of God's Protection

Psalm 62 underscores its major themes by repeating them. Thus, verse 2 is paraphrased in verse 6. God alone is worthy of our trust and dependence. The stillness in which the psalmist waits is not intended to convey timidity or resignation, but the inner stillness that comes from certainty. There is no need for agitation, says Psalm 62. Our trust in God will be proven to be justified. Above all, says the second line of this verse, God is the source of our redemption from whatever threatens us. In verse 2, this is spoken of as salvation, in verse 6, as hope. Both verses attest to the certainty that God can rescue us and is absolutely sure to do so.

Psalm 62 makes use of several significant images to depict graphically God's absolute, unshakable dependability. God is referred to as a rock in verses 3, 7, and 8. The image of God as a rock conveys both power and stability. Rocks are not easily affected by other elements of the natural world, or by human beings. Their force is virtually insurmountable. Large rocks—boulders, or larger rock formations—have a sense of permanence. They are unlike plants that spring up and then cease to exist, or animals that come into, and go out of, the world of our experience. Even trees change their appearance with the seasons. But rocks just are—ever the same, completely dependable. Thus is God called a rock. That same metaphor is employed frequently elsewhere in the Book of Psalms:

The Lord is my rock, and my fortress, and my deliverer;
My God, my rock, in Him I take refuge;
My shield, and my horn of salvation, my high tower.

(Psalm 18:3)

For who is God, save the Lord?
And who is a rock, except our God?

(Psalm 18:32)

The Lord liveth, and blessed be my Rock;
And exalted be the God of my salvation.

(Psalm 18:47)

Be Thou to me a sheltering rock, whereunto I may continu-
   ally resort,
Which Thou hast appointed to save me;
For Thou art my rock and my fortress.

(Psalm 71:3)

My flesh and my heart faileth;
But God is the rock of my heart and my portion forever.

(Psalm 73:26)

Let the words of my mouth and the meditation of my heart
   be acceptable before Thee,
O Lord, my Rock, and my Redeemer.

(Psalm 19:15)

Significantly, both Jewish and Christian traditions have hymns called "Rock of Ages." The reference in both hymns is to God as a reliable, ever-present shelter to which our ancestors have turned in the past and to which we can turn in our time of need.

In Psalm 62, verses 3 and 7 also speak of God as a *misgav*—a "high tower." The image is of a fortress to which we can flee from our enemies in times of danger. To think of God in this fashion is to understand God as offering us absolute protection. The meaning of this image is made clear in Psalm 59, in which the psalmist depicts God as rescuing us from surrounding enemies:

> ⁹ But Thou, O Lord, shalt laugh at them;
> Thou shalt have all the nations in derision.
> ¹⁰ Because of his strength, I will wait for Thee;
> For God is my high tower.
> ¹¹ The God of my mercy will come to meet me;
> God will let me gaze upon mine adversaries.
>
> (Psalm 59:9–11)

We find this image used in other psalms as well:

> The Lord also will be a high tower for the oppressed,
> A high tower in times of trouble.
>
> (Psalm 9:10)

> O my strength, unto Thee will I sing praises;
> For God is my high tower, the God of my mercy.
>
> (Psalm 59:18)

The verb from which the noun *misgav*/high tower is formed is also employed in a number of psalms:

> Deliver me from mine enemies, O my God;
> Set me on high from them that rise up against me.
>
> (Psalm 59:2)

> The Lord answer thee in the day of trouble;
> The name of the God of Jacob set thee up on high.
>
> (Psalm 20:2)

This imagery conveys the sense that when trouble is circling around you, God will lift you up to protect you from it.

In Psalm 62, verses 8 and 9 refer explicitly to God as a *machaseh*—a refuge. This word no longer functions as a metaphor. It has the clear meaning of a place we go to when we are in trouble. This affirmation of God's ability and desire to protect us, similarly, is found in many psalms:

God is our refuge and strength,
A very present help in trouble.

(Psalm 46:2)

For Thou hast been a refuge for me,
A tower of strength in the face of the enemy.

(Psalm 61:4)

But the Lord hath been my high tower,
And my God the rock of my refuge.

(Psalm 94:22)

But as for me, the nearness of God is my good;
I have made the Lord God my refuge,
That I may tell of all Thy works.

(Psalm 73:28)

Psalm 62, in many ways, depicts God as a consistent, reliable, ever-present source of protection and care for us. It also contrasts God's dependability with the unreliability, and even treachery, of human beings. Thus, while verse 9 states:

Trust in Him at all times, ye people;
Pour out your heart before Him;
God is a refuge for us.

(Psalm 62:9)

That affirmation is immediately followed by a contrasting vision:

> 10 Men of low degree are vanity, and men of high degree are
>   a lie;
>   If they be laid in the balances, they are together lighter
>   than vanity.
> 11 Trust not in oppression
>   And put not vain hope in robbery;
>   If riches increase, set not your heart thereon.
>
> (Psalm 62:10–11)

The dark depiction of human behavior is intended, by contrast, to underscore how absolutely we can depend upon God. In
making this contrast between God and human beings, Psalm 62
uses the word *betach*/trust in verses 9 and 11. We can truly trust
God. We would be foolish to put that same trust in human beings.
Psalm 62 is a hymn of praise to God as a rescuer and protector who
can be absolutely relied upon to come to our aid.

## Rejoicing in God's Care and Protection

We hear that same theme of praise of God the protector in Psalm 91:

> 1 O thou that dwellest in the covert of the Most High,
>   And abidest in the shadow of the Almighty;
> 2 I will say of the Lord, who is my refuge and fortress
>   My God, in whom I trust,
> 3 That He will deliver thee from the snare of the fowler,
>   And from the noisesome pestilence.
> 4 He will cover thee with His pinions,
>   And under His wings shalt thou take refuge;
>   His truth is a shield and a buckler.
> 5 Thou shalt not be afraid of the terror by night,

Nor of the arrow that flieth by day;
6 Of the pestilence that walketh in darkness,
 Nor of the destruction that wasteth at noonday.
7 A thousand may fall at thy side,
 And ten thousand at thy right hand;
 It shall not come nigh thee.
8 Only with thine eyes shalt thou behold,
 And see the recompense of the wicked.
9 For thou hast made the Lord who is my refuge,
 Even the Most High, thy habitation.
10 There shall no evil befall thee,
 Neither shall any plague come nigh thy tent.
11 For He will give His angels charge over thee,
 To keep thee in all thy ways.
12 They shall bear thee upon their hands,
 Lest thou dash thy foot against a stone.
13 Thou shalt tread upon the lion and asp;
 The young lion and the serpent shalt thou trample under
  feet.
14 "Because he hath set his love upon Me, therefore will I
  deliver him;
 I will set him on high, because he hath known My name.
15 He shall call upon Me, and I will answer him;
 I will be with him in trouble;
 I will rescue him, and bring him to honor.
16 With long life will I satisfy him,
 And make him to behold My salvation."

(Psalm 91:1–16)

Psalm 91 is a difficult psalm to understand, although its underlying meaning is absolutely clear. In the first place, we cannot be sure whether it was initially intended to refer to an individual or to the entire nation. Then there is the fact that the psalm alternates voices. The absence of a consistent sense of who the "he" or the "thou" is makes it harder to get a clear sense of the psalm's meaning. This difficulty accounts for why various traditional Jewish commentators have attributed the psalm to different authors—Moses, King David, or King Solomon—and located it in different historical circumstances.

If we look at Psalm 91 closely, we see that in the first thirteen verses the author addresses the hearer. Whoever that original audience was intended to be, the hearer came to be understood in later times as the individual reader. The final three verses clearly shift from the voice of the psalmist to a statement made by God about the audience of the psalm. As we read the psalm, we can understand it as being about ourselves, first as described by the psalmist and then as the recipients of God's promises.

Once the structural problems have been worked through, we can hear Psalm 91 as a straightforward exultant declaration of God's care and protection. The psalmist depicts us as living in God's covert—a hiding place or shelter (verse 1). This same image is found elsewhere in Psalms as well:

> For He concealeth me in His pavilion in the day of evil;
> He hideth me in the covert of His tent;
> He lifteth me up upon a rock.
>
> (Psalm 27:5)

> Thou hidest them in the covert of Thy presence from the
>     plottings of man;
> Thou concealest them in a pavilion from the strife of
>     tongues.
>
> (Psalm 31:21)

Psalm 32 even describes that hiding place as being God's own self:

Thou art my hiding-place; Thou will preserve me from the adversary;
With songs of deliverance Thou wilt compass me.

(Psalm 32:7)

Psalm 91 also portrays us as living in God's "shadow" (verse 1), having God as a refuge or fortress (verse 2), and being beneath God's "wings" (verse 4). The image of God's wings sheltering us evokes a sense of God as a mother bird, protecting her young. This image is found in a number of other psalms as well:

Keep me as the apple of the eye,
Hide me in the shadow of Thy wings.

(Psalm 17:8)

How precious is Thy lovingkindness, O God!
And the children of men take refuge in the shadow of Thy wings.

(Psalm 36:8)

Be gracious unto me, O God, be gracious unto me,
For in Thee hath my soul taken refuge;
Yea, in the shadow of Thy wings will I take refuge,
Until calamities be overpast.

(Psalm 57:2)

No image could more dramatically capture a sense of God watching over us, or attest to an attitude of absolute trust and confidence, than that of sheltering wings.

The psalm speaks of numerous instances of God's protecting help. Many of them can be understood as metaphors. Others have direct application to our own lives. God delivers us "from the fowler's snare and from noisome pestilence" (verse 3). We are delivered from the "terrors of the night" and from "arrows that fly by day" (verse 5) and from the pestilence that comes with dark and the destruction of noon (verse 6). Verses 5 and 6 together depict the totality of a day: darkness, night, daytime, and noon. Taken as a whole, they remind us that God is with us at all times, watching over us. Even if the situation is perilous for those around us, we can be confident in our safety, for our security comes from God. The final verses of Psalm 91 change perspective. In verses 14–16, we hear God speaking directly, offering assurance of God's ongoing care for us. Thus, God assures us that God will save us and set us on high—as in a *misgav*/high tower. God promises that when we cry out, God will answer us, be with us when we are in trouble and rescue us. God will see to it that we are blessed with long life and know that we will be saved by God.

The second line of verse 2 brings the central issue of Psalm 91 into clear focus. It speaks of "my God in whom I trust," using the word *betach*/trust. All the symbols and metaphors for God's protection, the instances of salvation, and the words of God's promises in the concluding verses serve to elicit a response from the initial audience of the psalm—and from those who read it now. To be the beneficiary of such steadfast concern evokes from us a profound sense of trust. This trust characterizes our side of the relationship described. Speaking in a number of voices, Psalm 91 is a dramatic testimony to God's protection. It is the testimony of one who has complete trust in God. As we read it, we enter into the experience of such confidence and can even begin to make this relationship of deep trust our own.

# A Very Present Help in Trouble

A similar expression of trust is found in Psalm 46:

2 God is our refuge and strength,
  A very present help in trouble.
3 Therefore will we not fear, though the earth do change,
  And though the mountains be moved into the heart of the seas;
4 Though the waters thereof roar and foam,
  Though the mountains shake at the swelling thereof. Selah.
5 There is a river, the streams whereof make glad the city of
    God,
  The holiest dwelling-place of the Most High.
6 God is in the midst of her, she shall not be moved;
  God shall help her, at the approach of morning.
7 Nations were in tumult, kingdoms were moved;
  He uttered His voice, the earth melted.
8 The Lord of hosts is with us;
  The God of Jacob is our high tower. Selah.
9 Come, behold the works of the Lord,
  Who hath made desolations in the earth.
10 He maketh wars to cease unto the end of the earth;
  He breaketh the bow, and cutteth the spear in sunder;
  He burneth the chariots in the fire.
11 "Let be, and know that I am God;
  I will be exalted among the nations, I will be exalted in the
    earth."
12 The Lord of hosts is with us;
  The God of Jacob is our high tower. Selah.

(Psalm 46:2–12)

Psalm 46 sounds as if it were intended to be a collective affirmation on behalf of the entire nation. Perhaps we hear echoes of an original national purpose in the reference to the "city of God" and the promise that "God will help her." Perhaps this psalm was created in the face of some national catastrophe. We can hear that in the references to nations in tumult and kingdoms that were moved (verse 7)—unlike the city of God, in verses 5 and 6, which was not moved. Indeed, we even hear intimations of battle with the references to wars, bows, spears, and chariots. The psalmist may have wanted to assure the nation as a whole of God's protection. Still, the sentiments that the psalm expresses can apply as readily to an individual. The words attest powerfully to the sense of security we can feel and to the relationship we can have with God whom we feel to be protecting us. In verse 11, we hear God's voice speaking, adding authority and assurance to the promises of the psalm. The central affirmation of the psalm is expressed in verses 2–4.

The meaning of these verses is very similar to what we encountered in Psalm 91:7. Whatever may be happening around us, we know that we will emerge safe and secure because of God's protection. The image of the *misgav*/high tower that is repeated in verses 8 and 12 is already familiar to us as a symbol of divine salvation from harm. The very language and imagery of Psalm 46 convey a sense of calm and certitude in the midst of chaos. Perhaps reading it as if it applied to us allows us to experience what such certitude could be like, and helps us understand the faith of someone who has it. Perhaps it allows us to begin to make such faith our own.

## Rejoicing in Absolute Confidence

The spirit of absolute confidence in God is sounded repeatedly in the Book of Psalms. A few more examples will suffice. Psalm 121 speaks of God's protection:

¹ A song of ascents.
I will lift up mine eyes unto the mountains;
From whence shall my help come?
² My help cometh from the Lord,
Who made heaven and earth.
³ He will not suffer thy foot to be moved;
He that keepeth thee will not slumber.
⁴ Behold, He that keepeth Israel
Doth neither slumber nor sleep.
⁵ The Lord is thy keeper;
The Lord is thy shade upon thy right hand.
⁶ The sun shall not smite thee by day,
Nor the moon by night.
⁷ The Lord shall keep thee from all evil;
He shall keep thy soul.
⁸ The Lord shall guard thy going out and thy coming in,
From this time forth and forever.

(Psalm 121:1–8)

Psalm 121 speaks explicitly of God as a helper. In an image that is echoed in virtually every verse of this psalm, God is spoken of as a *shomer*—a guard. The word is used to describe someone who stands watch. Not only does God watch over us, but, unlike human counterparts, we are assured that God will "neither slumber nor sleep." By employing a series of paired opposites, the psalmist conveys a sense that God's help and protection is constant and consistent. Thus, we are reminded that God made "heaven and earth," that God protects us by day and night, and that God guards us as we "go out and … come in," now and always.

Although Psalm 121 begins with a question, there is no questioning in the psalm itself. It depicts God as dedicated to our well-being and as utterly reliable. Its words of assurance in all times and circumstances provide a powerful depiction of a relationship of trust. That same relationship radiates through Psalm 23, probably the best known of the psalms.

In the first four verses of Psalm 23, God is depicted as a shepherd, watching over the flock. God, the shepherd, tends to the flock in a variety of ways and protects it in many circumstances. We, reading it, find ourselves asserting, "I will fear no evil, for Thou art with me." In chapter 6, I have noted how some people read Psalms 121 and 23 as alluding to God's protection after our death. Whether we find this dimension in these psalms, there is no way to read them without seeing how powerfully they depict God as watching over us, guarding and protecting us, in this life. They reflect complete and utter confidence in God; as we read them, they inspire that confidence in us.

# Betach: *Absolute Trust*

We have already seen God's protection as being compared to a mother bird protecting her young. Psalm 125 describes God's care with a metaphor drawn not from the animal world, but from geography:

> ¹ They that trust in the Lord
> Are as Mount Zion, which cannot be moved, but abideth
>     forever.
> ² As the mountains are round about Jerusalem,
> So the Lord is round about His people
> From this time forth and forever.
>
> (Psalm 125:1–2)

The psalmist employs the image of Jerusalem, surrounded by mountains, to depict God's presence, surrounding and protecting us. The assurance that we "cannot be moved" (verse 1) is a phrase that Psalms uses repeatedly to depict someone who is completely secure. We have seen it before in Psalms 62, 46, and 121. It occurs in a number of other psalms as well:

> Thou hast enlarged my steps under me,
> And my feet have not slipped.
>
> (Psalm 18:37)

> Cast thy burden upon the Lord, and He will sustain thee;
> He will never suffer the righteous to be moved.
>
> (Psalm 55:23)

> 8 Bless our God, ye peoples,
> And make the voice of His praise to be heard;
> 9 Who hath set our soul in life,
> And suffered not our foot to be moved.
>
> (Psalm 66:8–9)

In Psalm 125:1 we encounter again the word *betach*/trust, one of the most frequently repeated words in the Book of Psalms. Psalms resonates with the idea of trusting in God. As we read Psalms, we encounter the authors' profoundly trusting relationship with God. As we read Psalms performatively, we experience what such a relationship would feel like for ourselves.

In an earlier chapter, I mentioned briefly some references to the various "false gods" in which people put their trust. The Book of Psalms repeatedly contrasts putting our trust in things of this world with putting our trust where it properly belongs—in God:

> Some trust in chariots, and some in horses;
> But we will make mention of the name of the Lord our
>   God.
>
> (Psalm 20:8)

Put not your trust in princes,
Nor in the son of man, in whom there is no help.

(Psalm 146:3)

⁸ It is better to take refuge in the Lord
Than to trust in man.
⁹ It is better to take refuge in the Lord
Than to trust in princes.

(Psalm 118:8–9)

For I trust not in my bow,
Neither can my sword save me.

(Psalm 44:7)

⁸ The righteous also shall see, and fear,
And shall laugh at him:
⁹ "Lo, this is the man that made not God his stronghold;
But trusted in the abundance of his riches,
And strengthened himself in his wickedness."

(Psalm 52:8–9)

## Another Image for Trust in God

Psalm 33 contrasts misplaced trust with trust in God in explicit terms:

¹⁶ A king is not saved by the multitude of a host;
A mighty man is not delivered by great strength.
¹⁷ A horse is a vain thing for safety;
Neither doth it afford escape by its great strength.
¹⁸ Behold, the eye of the Lord is toward them that fear Him,
Toward them that wait for His mercy;
¹⁹ To deliver their soul from death,

And to keep them alive in famine.
20 Our soul hath waited for the Lord;
He is our help and our shield.
21 For in Him doth our heart rejoice,
Because we have trusted in His holy name.

(Psalm 33:16–21)

In verse 20, we encounter the word *magen*/shield. In addition to the metaphors of a rock, high tower, and secret hiding place, Psalms frequently depicts God's protection through the metaphor of a shield:

My shield is with God,
Who saveth the upright in heart.

(Psalm 7:11)

But Thou, O Lord, art a shield about me;
My glory, and the lifter up of my head.

(Psalm 3:4)

The Lord is my rock, and my fortress, and my deliverer;
My God, my rock, in Him I take refuge;
My shield, and my horn of salvation, my high tower.

(Psalm 18:3)

As for God, His ways are perfect;
The word of the Lord is tried;
He is a shield unto all them that take refuge in Him.

(Psalm 18:31)

Thou hast also given me a shield of salvation,
And Thy right hand hath holden me up;
And Thy condescension hath made me great.

(Psalm 18:36)

For of the Lord is our shield;
And of the Holy God of Israel is our king.

(Psalm 89:19)

The Lord is my strength and my shield,
In Him hath my heart trusted,
And I am helped;
Therefore my heart greatly rejoiceth,
And with my song will I praise Him.

(Psalm 28:7)

The image of God as a shield is a very tangible way of depicting God as our protector. It actually appears much earlier in the Bible, in the Book of Genesis, when God promises Abram—whose name has not yet been changed to Abraham—"Fear not Abram, I am a shield to you" (Genesis 15:1). From this reference, subsequent Jewish tradition included a reference to God as a shield in the liturgy. The *Avot* prayer, which is included in every service, concludes with the words, "Blessed are You, O Lord, shield of Abraham."

# My Trust Is in God

While things of this world cannot be the object of our absolute trust, the Book of Psalms repeatedly asserts that we can have complete trust in God. A number of psalms speak of the psalmist's trust and, by implication, encourage our own. In all of Pope John Paul II's precedent-shattering pilgrimage to the State of Israel, perhaps the most emotionally charged moment came when he visited Yad Vashem, the Holocaust memorial. At that place, so filled with significance for the world's Jews, the pope made a speech in which he repeatedly invoked words from Psalm 31 that bear witness to hope:

¹³ I am forgotten as a dead man out of mind;
  I am like a useless vessel.
¹⁴ For I have heard the whispering of many,
  Terror on every side;
  While they took counsel together against me,
  They devised to take away my life.
¹⁵ But as for me, I have trusted in Thee, O Lord;
  I have said: "Thou art my God."

(Psalm 31:13–15)

These words are an example of the refrain that repeats throughout the Book of Psalms, the affirmation of unshakable trust in God:

I hate them that regard lying vanities;
But I trust in the Lord.

(Psalm 31:7)

But as for me, in Thy mercy do I trust;
My heart shall rejoice in Thy salvation.
I will sing unto the Lord,
Because He hath dealt bountifully with me.

(Psalm 13:6)

But Thou, O God, wilt bring them down into the nethermost pit;
Men of blood and deceit shall not live out half their days;
But as for me, I will trust in Thee.

(Psalm 55:24)

In God—I will praise His word—
In God do I trust, I will not be afraid;
What can flesh do unto me?

(Psalm 56:5)

In God do I trust, I will not be afraid;
What can man do unto me?

(Psalm 56:12)

The Lord is for me; I will not fear;
What can man do unto me?

(Psalm 118:6)

In Psalm 22, the psalmist speaks of the trust in God that characterized earlier generations:

⁵ In Thee did our fathers trust;
They trusted, and Thou didst deliver them.
⁶ Unto Thee they cried, and escaped;
In Thee did they trust, and were not ashamed.

(Psalm 22:5–6)

In other verses, psalmists speak of the trust in God that was part of their own lifetime—indeed, starting at birth:

For Thou art He that took me out of the womb;
Thou madest me trust when I was upon my mother's breasts.

(Psalm 22:10)

⁵ For Thou art my hope;
O Lord God, my trust from my youth.
⁶ Upon Thee have I stayed myself from birth;
Thou art He that took me out of my mother's womb;
My praise is continually of Thee.

(Psalm 71:5–6)

In numerous places, Psalms asserts that trust in God brings happiness:

⁴ And He hath put a new song in my mouth, even praise unto
   our God;
Many shall see, and fear,
And shall trust in the Lord.
⁵ Happy is the man that hath made the Lord his trust,
   And hath not turned unto the arrogant, nor unto such as
   fall away treacherously.

(Psalm 40:4–5)


O Lord of hosts,
Happy is the man that trusteth in Thee.

(Psalm 84:13)


Trust in God is clearly one of the underlying messages of the
Book of Psalms. It speaks not only of trust that was representative
of the lives of earlier generations, but also of a trust that can come
to characterize our own lives. In a way, reading Psalms can allow us
to feel what it is like to have such trust and open us to the possibility of making that trust our own.

## Almost a Love Song

A number of psalms exalt in God's care. In Psalm 36 we read:

⁶ Thy loving kindness, O Lord, is in the heavens;
   Thy faithfulness reacheth unto the skies.
⁷ Thy righteousness is like the mighty mountains;
   Thy judgments are like the great deep;
   Man and beast, Thou preservest, O Lord.
⁸ How precious is Thy loving kindness, O God!
   And the children of men take refuge in the shadow of Thy
   wings.
⁹ They are abundantly satisfied with the fatness of Thy house;

And Thou makest them drink of the river of Thy pleasures.
10 For with Thee is the fountain of life;
In Thy light do we see light.

(Psalm 36:6–10)

In these verses, we hear the joy of living in relationship with God. We also find the psalmist praising God for various attributes, such as faithfulness and *chesed*/loving kindness, that make up God's protecting love. We note, also, the image in verse 8 of taking refuge in the shadow of God's wings.We hear the same exaltation in Psalm 146:

2 I will praise the Lord while I live;
I will sing praises unto my God while I have my being.
3 Put not your trust in princes,
Nor in the son of man, in whom there is no help.
4 His breath goeth forth, he returneth to his dust;
In that very day his thoughts perish.
5 Happy is he whose help is the God of Jacob,
Whose hope is in the Lord his God,
6 Who made heaven and earth,
The sea, and all that in them is;
Who keepeth truth forever....

(Psalm 146:1–6)

We recognize recurring admonitions not to trust human beings as we trust God. Verse 6 reminds us that the God who created our natural world is the God who looks after us. This same joy is heard in the words of Psalm 16:

1 Keep me, O God; for I have taken refuge in Thee.
2 I have said unto the Lord: "Thou art my Lord;
I have no good but in Thee"....

(Psalm 16:1–2)

In Psalm 16, the psalmist rejoices in God's closeness. The psalm is an exultant expression of knowing that we live in God's care. Traditional Jewish practice has taken Psalm 16:8 and given it concrete expression. Many Jewish homes have a *"shiviti"* plaque, which is named after the first words of this verse, *"shiviti Adonai l'negdi tamid*/I have set the Lord always before me." This plaque hangs on the wall as a constant reminder that we are living under God's protecting care. Psalm 16 concludes by portraying what it means to live in the presence of God. We experience more than trust and confidence—what we know is "joy" and "bliss forevermore." This is a powerful affirmation of living in relationship with God.

The sense of joy—even delight—at living in such intimacy with God is expressed in the first verses of Psalm 139:

1 O Lord, Thou hast searched me, and known me.
2 Thou knowest my downsitting and mine uprising,
Thou understandest my thought afar off.
3 Thou measurest my going about and my lying down,
And art acquainted with all my ways.
4 For there is not a word in my tongue,
But, lo, O Lord, Thou knowest it altogether.
5 Thou hast hemmed me in behind and before,
And laid Thy hand upon me.
6 Such knowledge is too wonderful for me;
Too high, I cannot attain to it.
7 Whither shall I go from Thy spirit?
Or wither shall I flee from Thy presence?
8 If I ascend up into heaven, Thou art there;
If I make my bed in the netherworld, behold, Thou art there.
9 If I take the wings of the morning,
And dwell in the uttermost parts of the sea;
10 Even there would Thy hand lead me,
And Thy right hand would hold me.

11 And if I say: "Surely the darkness shall envelop me,
   And the light about me shall be night";
12 Even the darkness is not too dark for Thee,
   But the night shineth as the day;
   The darkness is even as light.
13 For Thou hast made my reins;
   Thou hast knit me together in my mother's womb.
14 I will give thanks unto Thee, for I am fearfully and wonder-
      fully made:
   Wonderful are Thy works;
   And that my soul knoweth right well....

(Psalm 139:1–14)

In verses 1–6, the psalmist depicts what theologians refer to as God's omniscience and omnipresence: God knows everything and is everywhere. These are profound ideas, and important to the way Judaism, Christianity, and Islam understand God. But they can be very difficult to comprehend. As the psalmist says in verse 6:

Such knowledge is too wonderful for me;
Too high, I cannot attain unto it.

(Psalm 139:6)

In presenting these ideas, the psalmist does not speak in dry, abstract terms or in philosophical formulations. Rather, the psalmist speaks in very personal terms, in relation to our human lives and our ongoing encounter with God. Thus, God knows everything about us, and God is everywhere we are. These complex and lofty theological ideas are made very immediate and personal to our lives. They are stated in terms of our own relationship to God. This closeness is represented in verse 5, where God is depicted as virtually surrounding us and literally touching us. We cannot express a relationship in terms closer than this.

In verses 6–14, the psalmist gives voice to what sounds almost like a love song. The verses radiate with the nearly ecstatic sense of delight at God's nearness. The psalmist conveys the feeling that God is with us at all times and in all places. This same spirit is expressed by the eighteenth-century Chasidic Rebbe Levi Yitzchak of Berditchev in the "Dudele/You Song":

Almighty God, Lord of the Universe,
Almighty God, Lord of the Universe, Almighty God, I shall
    sing You a You-song,
You-You-You, You-You—
Where can I find You?
And where can I not find You?
You-You-You, You-You—

For wherever I go—You!
And wherever I stand—You
Always You, only You, again You, forever You—
You-You-You, You-You!

If things are good—You!
Alas, bad—You!
You-You-You-You-You-You!
You-You-You-You-You-You!

(Levi Yitzchak of Berditchev, "Dudele")


## The Other Face of the Relationship

Good morning to You, Master of the Universe
I, Levi Yitzchak, son of Sarah of Berditchev,
I come to You with a *Din Torah* from Your people Israel
What do You want of Your people Israel?

For everywhere I look it says, "Say to the children of Israel"
And every other verse says, "Speak to the children of Israel"
And over and over, "Command the children of Israel"
Father, sweet father in heaven,
How many nations are there in the world?
Persians, Babylonians, Edomites.

The Russians, what do they say?
That their Czar is the only ruler.
The Prussians, what do they say?
That their Kaiser is the only ruler.
And the English, what do they say?
That their King is the supreme ruler.
But I, Levi Yitzchak, son of Sarah of Berditchev, say
*Yisgadal v'yiskadash shmei raboh—*
Magnified and sanctified be thy great name

And I, Levi Yitzchak, son of Sarah of Berditchev, say,
I will not leave my place
Until there is an end to the exile and suffering of Your people.
*Yisgadal v'yiskadash shmei raboh—*
Magnified and sanctified be thy great name.

(Levi Yitzchak of Berditchev, "Kaddish")

The speaker/author of this poem is the same Levi Yitzchak who wrote the "Dudele/You Song," so filled with an ecstatic God-intoxication that it sounds like a love song. Levi Ytzchak was a beloved figure in his own lifetime and in subsequent generations because of his love for the Jewish people. He was especially loved for his willingness to argue on his people's behalf in disputations with God. This poem purports to be a record of Levi Yitzchak's variation on a practice then current in the Jewish community, a practice that is unfamiliar to many people today and that some may even consider sacrilegious. It was the custom to allow any member of the community who had a dispute with another member of the community to interrupt the worship service and call for a *Din Torah*—a court of arbitration in the presence of the Torah to assure that justice is done. In this account, Levi Yitzchak interrupts the service for the purpose of bringing a *Din Torah*—against God.

Levi Yitzchak is depicted as breaking into the Kaddish, a prayer of unalloyed praise and exaltation of God that is included in every service. The Kaddish begins with the words "*Yisgadal v'yiskadash shmei raboh/*Magnified and sanctified be Thy great name." Levi Yitzchak says that he will not allow the Kaddish to continue until God, "magnified and sanctified be Thy great name," puts an end to the exile and suffering of the Jewish people. To us this may appear like a breathtakingly audacious act. But it is not an isolated incident in Levi Yitzchak's life. He was known for berating and challenging the God he loved, and with some frequency. There is an account of a High Holy Day service at which Levi Yitzchak encouraged a member of his congregation—a poor tailor—to enter a *Din Torah* with God, and then added his own response to the event:

> The tailor said, "I told the Master of the universe, 'Today is the Day of Judgment. One must repent. But I didn't sin much. I took a little leftover cloth from the rich. Once I drank a glass of brandy and ate some bread without washing my hands. These are all my transgressions. But You, Master of the universe, how many are Your transgressions? You have taken away small children who have not sinned. From others You have taken away mothers of such children. But, Master of the universe, I will forgive Your transgressions and may You forgive mine....'" That year Levi Yitzchak proclaimed that it was the tailor's argument that prompted

God to spare the Jews. "Ah," Levi Yitzchak said, "but if it had been me in his place, I would not have forgiven the Master of the universe such great sins in exchange for a little leftover cloth. While I had Him, I would have demanded that He send us His messiah to redeem the world."

The sentiments in these accounts are very different from what Levi Yitzchak expressed in his "Dudele/You Song." We are reminded that no relationship plays in only one key. Every real relationship has many different, often contradictory, qualities. No one is as able to infuriate us as much as the ones we love. Our relationship with God is no different. Aaron Zeitlin certainly captured this in his poem, "If You Look at the Stars," which we read in chapter 1:

Praise Me, says God, and I will know that you love Me
Curse Me, says God, and I will know that you love Me
Praise Me or curse Me
And I will know that you love Me ...

(Aaron Zeitlin, "If You Look at the Stars")

Real relationships leave room for adoration and admiration, as well as their opposites: frustration and exasperation. Love and anger seem to be twins. If we are to have a real relationship with God, it needs to leave room for these other emotions as well as for the ones we associate with trust and praise.

The early twentieth-century author Joseph Roth wrote about the Jews of the *shtetel*/little Eastern European villages, "the *shtetel* Jews are not rare visitors of God, they live with him. In their prayers they inveigh against him, they complain at his severity, they go to God to accuse God. There is no other people that lives on such a footing with their God. They are an old people, and they have known him a long time!"

This capacity to disagree with God and take issue with God has a long history, extending back to the beginning of Jewish life. Abraham, the father of the Jewish people, the very first person, according to the Bible, to know God, nonetheless was willing to take issue with God. In Genesis 18 we read that when God decided to destroy the cities of Sodom and Gomorrah, God wondered, "Shall I hide from Abraham what I am about to do...?" (verse 17). We are left to infer that God did not reveal to Abraham what God intended to do. Somehow, despite this, Abraham learned of the plan. Then we read a remarkable indictment of God by Abraham:

> And Abraham drew near, and said: "Wilt Thou sweep indeed sweep away the righteous with the wicked? Peradventure there are fifty righteous within the city; wilt Thou indeed sweep away and not forgive the place for the fifty righteous that are therein? Far be it from Thee to do such a thing, to slay the righteous along with the wicked, so that the righteous should be as the wicked; far be it from Thee; shall not the Judge of all the earth do justly?" (Genesis 18:23–25)

In subsequent verses, Abraham engages in what might be characterized as an extended negotiation with God until he finally gets God to agree to spare the cities if ten righteous people can be found in them. Abraham is not humbly submissive before God. Indeed, Abraham does not appear to be intimidated by God. Instead, Abraham enjoys the type of relationship with God that allows him to challenge God. Those who trace their lineage to Abraham have continued to follow his example ever since.

Abraham's wife, Sarah, has by this time already challenged God by insisting that she "did not laugh," when she, the readers, and God know very well that she did (Genesis 18:15). Abraham's daughter-in-law, Rebecca, angrily confronts God in the midst of her pain during childbirth: "If it is going to be like this, how can I go on living?" (Genesis 25:22). Even Moses, the great exemplar of the Torah who is called "the servant of God" (Deuteronomy 34:5), begins his relationship with God by declining God's instructions to go back to Egypt and plead with the pharaoh:

> And Moses said unto God: "Who am I, that I should go unto Pharaoh, and that I should bring forth the children of Israel out of Egypt?" (Exodus 3:11)

> And Moses said unto the Lord: "Oh Lord, I am not a man of words, neither heretofore, nor since Thou hast spoken unto Thy servant; for I am slow of speech, and of a slow tongue." (Exodus 4:10)

When Moses finally does accept God's instructions and presents his case to the pharaoh, things got worse, rather than better, for the Hebrew slaves. Moses then demands angrily of God:

> And Moses returned unto the Lord, and said: "Lord, wherefore hast Thou dealt ill with this people? Why is it that Thou hast sent me? For since I came to Pharaoh to speak in Thy name, he hath dealt ill with this people; neither hast Thou delivered Thy people at all." (Exodus 5:22–23)

In the midst of the Exodus from Egypt, Moses had constantly to deal with the complaining of the people, interpreting their needs to God and God's demands to them. This burden must have been overwhelming. At one point, he demands of God:

> And Moses said unto the Lord: "Wherefore hast Thou dealt ill with Thy servant? And wherefore have I not found favor

in Thy sight, that Thou layest the burden of all this people upon me? Have I conceived all this people? Have I brought them forth, that Thou shouldest say unto me: Carry them in they bosom, as a nursing-father carrieth the sucking child, unto the land which Thou didst swear unto their fathers? Whence should I have flesh to give all this people? For they trouble me with their weeping, saying: Give us flesh, that we may eat. I am not able to bear all this people myself alone, because it is too heavy for me. And if Thou deal thus with me, kill me, I pray Thee, out of Thy hand, if I have found favor in Thy sight; and let me not look upon my wretchedness." (Numbers 11:11–15)

Clearly, this was not a relationship consisting exclusively of obedience and praise. In Moses' words to God, we hear frustration, even anger.

## Crying Out to God in the Psalms

Against such a background, it can come as no surprise that we hear these same very human emotions in the psalmists' relationship with God. As we read the psalms and put their words in our mouths, we experience what it is to have the kind of relationship with God that allows us to express our needs, frustration, and disappointment, as well as our gratitude and appreciation. We can find ourselves enacting a relationship that includes the dimension of arguing with God, just as that same dimension exists in all intimate relationships. Other relationships include expectations alongside of love. Why should our relationship with God be any different?

So many psalms include words that seem to resonate with frustration. The psalmists call on God in direct terms for God to come to our aid:

Arise, O Lord; save me, O my God.

(Psalm 3:8)

Arise, O Lord, in Thine anger,
Lift up Thyself in indignation against mine adversaries;
Yea, awake for me at the judgment which Thou hast com-
    manded.

(Psalm 7:7)

Arise, O Lord, let not man prevail;
Let the nations be judged in Thy sight.

(Psalm 9:20)

Arise, O Lord, O God, lift up Thy hand;
Forget not the humble.

(Psalm 10:12)

Arise, O Lord, confront him, cast him down;
Deliver my soul from the wicked, by Thy sword....

(Psalm 17:13)

1 Strive, O Lord, with them that strive with me;
Fight against them that fight against me.
2 Take hold of shield and buckler,
And rise to my help.

(Psalm 35:1–2)

Rouse Thee, and awake to my judgment,
Even unto my cause, my God and my Lord.

(Psalm 35:23)

There are many more verses in the same vein in Psalms.
Psalms can even reflect a more intense frustration and cross the

boundary of what, if addressed to a human counterpart, would be considered outright insulting:

> Awake, why sleepest Thou, O Lord?
> Arouse Thyself, cast not off forever.
>
> (Psalm 44:24)

Throughout the Book of Psalms, we encounter varying degrees of anger with God. Some of the psalms sound a plaintive note. The author feels abandoned by God and cries out to God asking why God seems to be far off:

> Why standest Thou afar off, O Lord?
> Why hidest Thou Thyself in times of trouble?
>
> (Psalm 10:1)

> Lord, why castest Thou off my soul?
> Why hidest Thou Thy face from me?
>
> (Psalm 88:15)

> For Thou art the God of my strength; why hast Thou cast me
>     off?
> Why go I mourning under the oppression of the enemy?
>
> (Psalm 43:2)

These verses are reminiscent of statements from the prophet Jeremiah, who remonstrated with God in very picturesque terms:

> Why shouldst Thou be as a man overcome, as a mighty man
> that cannot save? Yet Thou, O Lord, art in the midst of us, and
> Thy name is called upon us; leave us not. (Jeremiah 14:9)

We are familiar with the Prophets chastising the People of Israel. Here, Jeremiah reminds us, the people are equally capable of chastising God. Perhaps the best-known verses that speak in this tone are found in Psalm 22:

> 2 My God, my God, why hast Thou forsaken me,
>   And art far from my help at the word of my cry?
> 3 O my God, I call by day, but Thou answerest not;
>   And at night, and there is no surcease for me.
>
> (Psalm 22:2–3)

People familiar with the New Testament recognize the first words of these verses from the Gospel accounts of the crucifixion of Jesus. In both Matthew (27:46) and Mark (15:34), these words are presented as Jesus' last words. Early Christian commentators interpreted Psalm 22 as anticipating and predicting the events of the Passion. Contemporary Christian commentators teach that the accounts of Matthew and Mark depict Jesus quoting from the Book of Psalms in his moment of agony. In this, Jesus did what any Jew of that time would do, and what any of us can do—use Psalm 22 to express our sense of abandonment when we feel as if God is far away. The words express our need for God's presence, and our disappointment at God's absence. In our own day, these same thoughts were expressed by Jacob Friedman, who lived through the *Shoah:*

> Look, Father in heaven, how I say Kol Nidrei
> This Yom Kippur night!
> Lord God, Creator of the universe,
> A little Jew is calling to You.
> He cannot understand Your ways.
> Where is Your mercy, Your justice, where?
> Or do Your worlds revolve in darkness?
> Do You not care?
>
> (Jacob Friedman, "Kol Nidrei")

# Pleading with God to Respond to Us

There are times when it feels as if God has withdrawn from us. This feeling is given expression in Psalm 74:

> 10 How long, O God, shall the adversary reproach?
> Shall the enemy blaspheme Thy name forever?
> 11 Why withdrawest Thou Thy hand, even Thy right hand?
> Draw it out of Thy bosom and consume them.
>
> (Psalm 74:10–11)

A concern about God's unresponsiveness during our times of need is heard in other psalms as well:

> O Lord, God of hosts,
> How long wilt Thou be angry against the prayer of Thy
> people?
>
> (Psalm 80:5)

> How long, O Lord, wilt Thou be angry forever?
> How long will Thy jealousy burn like fire?
>
> (Psalm 79:5)

In some psalms this plea becomes even more urgent and takes on a more demanding tone:

> 2 How long, O Lord, wilt Thou forget me forever?
> How long wilt Thou hide Thy face from me?
> 3 How long shall I take counsel in my soul,
> Having sorrow in my heart by day?
> How long shall mine enemy be exalted over me?
> 4 Behold Thou, and answer me, O Lord, my God;
> Lighten mine eyes, lest I sleep the sleep of death....
>
> (Psalm 13:2–4)

Give ear, O Lord, unto my prayer;
And attend unto the voice of my supplications.

(Psalm 86:6)

2 Give ear, O God, to my prayer;
And hide not Thyself from my supplication.
3 Attend unto me, and answer me;
I am distraught in my complaint, and will moan....

(Psalm 55:2–3)

At times it must have seemed to the psalmist—and at times it may seem to us—that God has abandoned us altogether. In a number of psalms God is challenged, "Have You left us forever?"

8 Will the Lord cast off forever?
And will He be favorable no more?
9 Is His mercy clean gone forever?
Is His promise come to an end forevermore?
10 Hath God forgotten to be gracious?
Hath He in anger shut up His compassions?

(Psalm 77:8–10)

Why, O God, hast Thou cast us off forever?
Why doth Thine anger smoke against the flock of
     Thy pasture?

(Psalm 74:1)

These verses sound very much like the plea we hear at the very end of the Book of Lamentations:

Wherefore dost Thou forget us forever, and forsake us so long time? Turn Thou us unto Thee, O Lord, and we shall be turned; renew our days as of old. (Lamentations 5:20–21)

The words of Lamentations were composed in response to a great national catastrophe, the destruction of the first Temple. The people must have been utterly bereft. Among the emotions expressed in that book is the sense of being abandoned by the God who was supposed to protect them.

## Renew Us

In verse 21 of the selection from Lamentations, we come upon a new theme. We hear the plea to "renew" us, or make us new. We can understand these words to be a cry to return our lives to what they were before cataclysmic events befell us—to make us whole again. Or the words may have another, deeper meaning. They may be a petition to God to take us back. With these words, we call on God to "renew" the relationship we had with God before, which we feel has somehow been broken. "Make our days as before" can be a way of asking God to restore our relationship, make it what it was before the rupture, make *us*—we who read the words and God—whole. This plea has its counterparts in the Book of Psalms:

5 Restore us, O God of our salvation,
And cause Thine indignation toward us to cease.
6 Wilt Thou be angry with us forever?
Wilt Thou draw out Thine anger to all generations?

(Psalm 85:5–6)

Return, O Lord; how long?
And let it repent Thee concerning Thy servants.

(Psalm 90:13)

15 O God of hosts, return, we beseech Thee;
Look from heaven, and behold, and be mindful of this vine,

<sup>16</sup> And of the stock which Thy right hand hath planted,
And the branch that Thou madest strong for Thyself.
(Psalm 80:15–16)

The words of Lamentations 5:21 have been appropriated by the Jewish liturgy. As the Torah is returned to the ark, these words are chanted, often in plaintive tones. The same sense of beginning anew is captured by Jacob Glatstein:

Shall we perhaps begin anew, small and toddling,
With a small folk?
We two, homeless, wandering among the nations ...
Shall we perhaps go home now, You and I,
To begin again, small from the beginning?
Begin once more! Be the small God of a small people!
Go back, beloved God, go back to a small people!
You will become closer to us,
And together we shall spin new laws,
More suitable for you and for us.

Shall we perhaps begin anew,
Small and toddling,
To grow with the growing borders
Of a blessed land? ...
Shall we perhaps go home, You and I?
Shall we perhaps, unconquering, go home? ...

Save Yourself! Together with the pilgrims, return.
Return to a small land
Become once more the small God
Of a small people.

(Jacob Glatstein, "The Beginning")

The hope is not merely to "restore me" but to re-create the relationship that existed before we were driven apart.

## Reasoning with God

What we have examined so far have been emotional arguments—arguments from the heart, various forms of pleas, crying out to God, and expressing disappointment and the anger that can accompany it. There is another form of disagreeing with God: arguments of a more rational nature. The prophet Isaiah once depicted God as saying, "Come now, let us reason together" (Isaiah 1:18). There are times when we engage in a kind of reasoning with God. You can almost hear a resemblance, in some exchanges that we will examine, to exchanges between two people who know one another very well and know how to manipulate each other, seeking to bend each other to their way of understanding. We may attempt to use rational arguments to persuade God in this same way. Some have argued that such persuasion is what prayer is all about. Jewish tradition speaks about our efforts to influence God's decisions. In *Pirkei Avot*/the Sayings of the Fathers, we read, "[Rabban Gamliel] … used to say, 'Do … [God's] will as if it were your own will, so that … [God] may do your will as if it were … [God's] own will'" (*Pirkei Avot* 2:4).

In a number of psalms, we experience an even more direct kind of argumentative language. The psalmist—and we who make the psalmist's words our own—try to sway God's judgment. One part of Psalm 6 includes some verses that sound similar to verses we have already seen. But it adds to them a thought that moves in a very different direction:

> 4 My soul is sore affrighted;
>    And Thou, O Lord, how long?
> 5 Return, O Lord, deliver my soul;

Save me for Thy mercy's sake.
6 For in death there is no remembrance of Thee;
In the nether-world who will give Thee thanks?

(Psalm 6:4–6)

In verse 6 we encounter a profound and complex new idea, echoed elsewhere in Psalms:

What profit is there in my blood, when I go down to the pit?
Shall the dust praise Thee? Shall it declare Thy truth?

(Psalm 30:10)

11 Wilt Thou work wonders for the dead?
Or shall the shades arise and give Thee thanks?
12 Shall Thy mercy be declared in the grave?
Or Thy faithfulness in destruction?
13 Shall Thy wonders be known in the dark?
And Thy righteousness in the land of forgetfulness?

(Psalm 88:11–13)

What is the meaning of these references to death? Why does the psalmist, in the midst of calling out to God, describe the condition of those who are in "the land of forgetfulness"? The answer is provided by a pair of verses at the very end of Psalm 115:

17 The dead praise not the Lord,
Neither any that go down into silence;
18 But we will bless the Lord
From this time forth and forever.

(Psalm 115:17–18)

The rationale behind this line of argument is made explicit in Isaiah:

> For the nether-world cannot praise Thee, death cannot cel-
> ebrate Thee; they that go down into the pit cannot hope for
> Thy truth. The living, the living, he shall praise Thee, as I
> do this day; the father to the children shall make known
> Thy truth. (Isaiah 38:18–19)

The juxtaposition between the dead who cannot praise God and the living who can constitutes an argument that is intended to sway God's thinking. "Why let me die? I would be unable to praise You then. But if You spare me and let me live, I could go on worshipping You." The psalmist is not merely citing the difference between the living and the dead. Rather, the argument rests on the idea that it is in God's own self-interest to protect us and keep us alive, if for no other reason than that we can continue to offer our praises. Indeed, in Psalm 118 we find the same idea expressed in positive terms:

> I shall not die, but live,
> And declare the works of the Lord.
>
> (Psalm 118:17)

Jacob Glatstein echoes this strand of thinking in Psalms and relates it to the *Shoah*—the cataclysm that brought virtual extinction to his cultural universe:

> At Sinai we received the Torah
> At Lublin we gave it back
> Dead men don't praise God
> The Torah was given to the living.
>
> (Jacob Glatstein, "Dead Men Don't Praise God")

## Do It for Your Sake

With the psalmist's argument that our death is not in God's own interest, we are moved into a new mode of seeking to persuade God. In the Book of Exodus, we come upon a remarkable exchange between God and Moses. God is enraged at the people's unfaithfulness in creating the golden calf. In anger, God voices an intention to destroy the people. God even attempts to enlist Moses in this plan by promising to create a new people that will be descended from Moses. But Moses remains resolute and makes an argument that succeeds in dissuading God from destroying the people:

> And the Lord said unto Moses: "I have seen this people, and, behold, it is a stiff-necked people. Now therefore let Me alone, that My wrath may wax hot against them, and that I may consume them; and I will make of thee a great nation." And Moses besought the Lord his God, and said: "Lord, why doth Thy wrath wax hot against Thy people, that Thou hast brought forth out of the land of Egypt with great power and with a mighty hand? Wherefore should the Egyptians speak, saying: 'For evil did He bring them forth, to slay them in the mountains, and to consume them from the face of the earth?' Turn from Thy fierce wrath, and repent of this evil against Thy people. Remember Abraham, Isaac, and Israel, Thy servants, to whom Thou didst swear by Thine own self, and saidst unto them: 'I will multiply your seed as the stars of heaven, and all this land that I have spoken of will I give unto your seed, and they shall inherit it forever.'" And the Lord repented of the evil which He said He would do unto His people. (Exodus 32:9–14)

Moses' use of the phrase "Your people" throughout his statement is a subtle way of reminding God of God's responsibilities to the people God created. Moses reminds God of the promise that God had made to the people's ancestors to protect their descendants. Moses' entire argument rests on an appeal to God's own self-interest: If You go ahead and destroy the people, how will You look to the Egyptians who doubted You in the first place? This same sort of reasoning with God on the basis of God's own best interests is found in the Book of Psalms as well:

> 10 I will say unto God my Rock: "Why hast Thou forgotten me?
> Why go I mourning under the oppression of the enemy?"
> 11 As with a crushing in my bones, mine adversaries taunt me;
> While they say unto me all the day: "Where is thy God?"
>
> (Psalm 42:10–11)

Psalm 42 asks God to intervene on our behalf so that other nations will not question God's honor—God's keeping God's promises, or God's ability to save the people God had vowed to protect. In other words, God's own good name is on the line as much as our well-being. This is made explicit at the very beginning of another psalm:

> 1 Not unto us, O Lord, not unto us,
> But unto Thy name give glory,
> For Thy mercy and for Thy truth's sake.
> 2 Wherefore should the nations say:
> "Where is now their God?"
>
> (Psalm 115:1–2)

Here, too, the psalmist argues that we plead with God not just for our own interests, but also for God's interests, so that God will not be mocked by other peoples. This kind of argument attests to a very different state of mind from the one in the psalms that exalt and extol God. At the same time, it represents a relationship with God that is very deep and intense. Above all, it speaks of a connection with God, even with all its frustrations and disappointments, that can only be characterized as intimate.

## The Hidden Meaning of Anger at God

As we know from our personal lives, anger and arguing within a relationship can be complicated issues. We see a similar fluidity of emotions in the following poems by Jacob Glatstein. Glatstein begins in rage:

> Without Jews there is no Jewish God ...
> The light is fading in your shabby tent
> The Jewish hour is guttering.
> Jewish God!
> You are almost gone
>
> (Jacob Glatstein, "Without Jews")

In time, rage gives way to rejection:

> If I had now been Abraham, Terah's son,
> I would bow down to all sorts of idols,
> And I would not bow down to His dear great Name.
>
> I would think that the machine-gun is God,
> That the global death
> Annihilator of whole nations
> Is God.
>
> And at the edge of the undecided day
> I would prostrate myself, a bewildered lad.
> I would bow down to the last blade of grass,
> And pray:
> Dear pure holy name
> Reveal your dear awe to Abraham.

But I am Abraham, Isaac's son
And I know that over all the dead
Blues a clouded Truth, but I fear to look for it
Among the graves of millions.

Perplexed I shall leave
This world of chaos,
Where the seed of my people has been cut off
Without a voice from heaven, on a blood-drenched way.

Let my children's children
Unravel this tangle,
And I will lie among my own,
An unrecognized one.

No matter how much the scales justify
They will never exonerate for us the heavens....

(Jacob Glatstein, "Holy Name")

Ultimately, there comes a stirring of affection:

Like a little trap,
A shabby synagogue on Long Island.
Only a handful show up for prayer.
No one knows
If even God
Drops in there ...

Only a handful show up for prayer,
Plenty of room for God's glory
No one knows if God
Will sneak in for an hour.

(Jacob Glatstein, "Like a Mousetrap")

And then, somehow, Glatstein begins to feel compassion for the object of his anger. He evokes the legend of the man who was known as the Maharal, the great Rabbi Loewe of Prague, who created the Golem—a humanlike creature fashioned from clay—to protect his community, only to see the Golem run amok and wreak havoc on the Jews of Prague.

> God is a sad Maharal.
> A ray of His goodness
> Falls on a dark world.
> He broods beside the wellspring of His wonder.
> He tosses heavy stones in the water.
> Listen, He is miserable and alone.
> He has had too much of the Golem.
> He is overpowered.
> Every sigh is justified.
> Every outcry flashes in unattended skies.
> Eternity hurries to the crazy curtain call.
> God is a sad Maharal.

> God is a sad Maharal.
> The sound of the ram's horn
> Overtakes the Days of Awe quivering in the forest.
> The heart of the Great Reprover
> Is bitter and broken.
> Even He did not conceive such ruin.
> He is ashamed. He feels small.
> Like every frightened Jew.
> Quietly, He'll steal into the synagogue.
> He will stand in the anteroom
> Like a penitent wrapped in a prayer shawl.
> He will rip black skies with His lament.

The winds of autumn chill.
The trees sway
The leaves fall.
God is a sad Maharal.

(Jacob Glatstein, "God Is a Sad Maharal")


Glatstein, writing, of course, from the perspective of the events during his lifetime, sees God as very much like Rabbi Loewe, and he feels compassion for God's situation. In the end Glatstein expresses love as he speaks of God as a fellow exile, uprooted from home:

I love my sad God,
My brother refugee.
I love to sit down on a stone with him
And tell him everything wordlessly
Because when we sit like this, both perplexed,
Our thoughts flow together
In silence ...

My poor God
How many prayers I've profaned
How many nights I've
Blasphemed him
And warmed my frightened bones
At the furnace of the intellect
And here he sits, my friend, his arm around me,
Sharing his last crumb....

(Jacob Glatstein, "My Brother Refugee")


In his poem "I Believe," Aaron Zeitlin captures the complexity of our anger as we argue with God.

Thy would-be gods!
They—and those other shadows, ism and ism
More hollow than even their claims
After the all-destroying flames.
In whom can I believe if not in Him,
My living God of cataclysm,
God of naked revenge and secret consolation?
One is—what one is.
I am a Jew as He is God.
Can I even choose not to believe
in that living God whose purposes
when He destroys, seeming to forsake me,
I cannot conceive;
choose not to believe in Him
Who having turned my body to fine ash
begins once more to wake me? If I become a storm, or I
   blaze
in rebellion against Him,
is He not still the One who bleeding my wounds,
my cries still praise?
For even my pain confirms Him ...

(Aaron Zeitlin, "I Believe")

One cannot argue with God in the ways we have seen without
having a true and intense relationship with God. Trust in God and
expectations of God are really two sides of the same coin. Praising
God and making demands on God are two ways of acting out a
relationship with God that is alive and powerful. That kind of a
relationship can be the bedrock of our lives. Our lives can be rich-
er and more grounded for it. Whether praising or chastising,
extolling or demanding, our lives gain strength and purpose in
knowing that we live in "the shadow of God's wings."

# PART III

# THE QUEST FOR COMMITMENT: USING THE PSALMS TO LIVE OUR FAITH

# 7

# JERUSALEM AS SYMBOL AND REALITY

I never saw you, my city, but you were for me,
Reality seen in dream....
You stood, Jerusalem, so close to my heart
Where do you, wonderful city, start?

Later I know you from old collecting stamps
For the funds to help the pious pilgrims in Jerusalem,
Three trees weeping by the Wailing Wall
Weeping like my birch trees here
That sway in the autumn wind by the cross-roads

Is nothing more left, father dear,
Than this wall here,
And the trees that grow out of it?
Nothing more, my child, nothing more at all.

Yet when a book came
From Jerusalem
Because we stinted ourselves bread
And sent a few coins to the fund
For the pious pilgrims living in Jerusalem,
And he saw the words printed on

the title page—"Jerusalem, the holy city,"
His shrunken face with the bones showing through
Lighted up with an astonishing light,
And his old, dim eyes shone bright:
"Come here, my son, look at this,
A new book from Jerusalem,
come here and these pages kiss!"

(Israel Emmiot, "Jerusalem")


Everywhere I go, I am going to Jerusalem. (Rabbi Nachman
of Breslav)


There is a compass in the Jewish soul that points magnetically
toward Jerusalem. Part of being a Jew is to say, as did the medieval
Hebrew poet Yehudah Halevi, "My heart is in the East, but I am in
the West." The pull of Jerusalem sounds through all the generations of Jewish life. For all these thousands of years, wherever Jews
have lived, the Passover Seder concludes with the chant, "Next year
in Jerusalem." Part of the "cultural DNA" of the Jewish people is
the pull to that ancient city, a concept that has no real parallel in
Christianity. To be a Jew is to resonate to the words of Psalm 137:

5 If I forget thee, O Jerusalem,
  Let my right hand forget her cunning.
6 Let my tongue cleave to the roof of my mouth,
  If I remember thee not;
  If I set not Jerusalem
  Above my chiefest joy.

(Psalm 137:5–6)


In chapter 3, we witnessed the role of Jerusalem in the history
of the Jewish people. But even above and outside of history,
Jerusalem exercises a pull on the Jewish imagination. Remarkably,

it did so while the Temple still stood and the city served as the capital of the nation; it did so while the city was in ruins following the destruction of the first Temple in 586 B.C.E. It exercised its pull on Jews when the first exile was over and the Temple was rebuilt. And it has continued to do so in the 2,000 years since the second Temple was destroyed and Jews have lived in dispersion. In this chapter, we shall look at the loving ways Jerusalem has been described in the Book of Psalms, and the symbolic role it plays there.

## Through the Eyes of a Pilgrim

The absolute rapturous joy that a pilgrim to the Temple felt upon going up to Jerusalem is captured in Psalm 122:

> [1] A song of Ascents; of David
> I rejoiced when they said unto me:
> "Let us go unto the house of the Lord."
> [2] Our feet are standing
> Within thy gates, O Jerusalem;
> [3] Jerusalem that art builded
> As a city that is compact together;
> [4] Whither the tribes went up, even the tribes of the Lord,
> As a testimony unto Israel,
> To give thanks unto the name of the Lord.
> [5] For there were set thrones for judgment
> The thrones of the house of David.
> [6] Pray for the peace of Jerusalem;
> May they prosper that love thee.
> [7] Peace be within thy walls,
> And prosperity within thy palaces.
> [8] For my brethren and companions' sakes,
> I will now say: "Peace be within thee."

9 For the sake of the house of the Lord our God
I will seek thy good.

(Psalm 122:1–9)

The words of Psalm 122 sound almost like the stream of consciousness of a pilgrim making ascent to Jerusalem for the first time. We hear the invitation to make the pilgrimage and the joy of receiving it. Then we find ourselves in the city itself. We look around and take in the wonder of the physical surroundings and then reflect on what this city has meant in the history of our people. We offer a prayer for the city's well-being, and later words of blessing and leave-taking, before beginning the journey back home. In this reading, the concluding verses serve as a kind of loving farewell to Jerusalem before leaving it. We who have been privileged to be "within its walls" read the words of prayer with the same conviction and the same passion as we call to mind our time in Jerusalem and remember the city with longing.

One word in verse 3 presents a challenge for the translator and opportunities for the interpreter. The word *shechubrah* has been translated as "that is compact together." Certainly that is an evocative description of the physical reality of the city, where homes are built literally on top of one another. Or, maybe, during a time of pilgrimage, there were so many people in the city that they all felt "compacted together," just as Muslim pilgrims speak of feeling compacted together when they make the hajj to Mecca.

*Shechubrah* can have other associations as well. The letters that form the root of the word also form the word "friend" and convey the sense of "joined together," compacted in another sense. Historically it is true that the city of Jerusalem joined together the disparate tribes that formed the Hebrew kingdom. It may be, too, that the pilgrim's experience of being in Jerusalem created a sense of being joined to all the other pilgrims and to the entire people that a gathering of pilgrims represents, as Muslim pilgrims attest

the pilgrimage to Mecca makes them feel. That certainly may be
the sense of a verse from another psalm:

A song of Ascents; of David.
Behold, how good and how pleasant it is
For brethren to dwell together in unity!
(Psalm 133:1)

In both these cases, Jerusalem becomes a city that joins together.

The root letters that make up the word *shechubrah* are the
same letters found in the word *bachar*/to choose, which appears in
a string of references in the Book of Deuteronomy, such as "the
place which the Lord your God will choose" (Deuteronomy
12:16–18). The way these two words resonate with one another
serves to remind us that the place we are seeing through the eyes
of this pilgrim is the very place that God chose so many generations before for the people to gather in worship. Jerusalem is, thus,
not only a place of physical beauty and national importance but
also a city that occupies a special place in the divine plan.

In a literary sense, Psalm 122 is a beautifully constructed poem
with much alliteration and wordplay. The sound of the letter *shin*/sh
echoes throughout the psalm, a shimmering shower, as it were, shining through verses 2, 3, and 6. The name *Yerushalayim*/Jerusalem is
repeated in verses 2, 3, and 6. The word *shalom*/peace appears in
verses 6, 7, and 8. All these come together compellingly in verse 6:
*Shaalu shalom Yerushalayim*/Pray for the peace of Jerusalem.

The psalm ends on the note of a passionate prayer for the peace
and welfare of Jerusalem. Indeed, many find the word *shalom*/peace
to be the core of the name *Yerushalayim*/Jerusalem. How ironic,
then, and how tragic, that this city has known so little peace in its history. The history of Jerusalem, whose very name evokes peace, has
been one of war and bloodshed down to our times. The words of
verses 6–9, then, ring out all the more poignantly.

## Jerusalem, "The City of God"

Psalm 122 begins with the psalmist's delight in Jerusalem. Psalm 87 begins with the assertion of God's love for the city:

2 The Lord loveth the gates of Zion
   More than all the dwellings of Jacob.
3 Glorious things are spoken of thee,
   O city of God. Selah.
4 "I will make mention of Rahab and Babylon as among them
      that know Me
   Behold Philistia and Tyre, with Ethiopia;
   This one was born there."
5 But of Zion it shall be said: "This man and that was born in her;
   And the Most High Himself doth establish her."
6 The Lord shall count in the register of the peoples:
   "This one was born there." Selah.
7 And whether they sing or dance,
   All my thoughts are in thee.

(Psalm 87:2–7)

The words of Psalm 87 radiate with delight in the city—God's and the author's. The psalm asserts that God loves Jerusalem more than any other place in the land of the Hebrews, calling it "the city of God." The speaker of verse 4 is saying, in effect, "Let me tell you of some other great places." But the psalmist replies, in verse 5, that Jerusalem is superior to them all. God not only prefers Jerusalem to any other place in the Holy Land, but God also prefers it to any place in the world. So glorious is Jerusalem to the psalmist that the very fact of being born in it confers special status on its citizens.

The last verse poses a problem for translation. Some readers suggest that the very last line of verse 7 means "all my roots" or "all my sources" are in you. This translation continues the theme of being born in Jerusalem. Reading the reference to singers and dancers as forms of celebration, those who translate the verse this way would have verse 7 read, "singers and dancers [will celebrate] 'all my roots are in thee.'" I prefer to see the line as saying, "all my thoughts are *of* thee." Thus, the two lines of verse 7 can be seen as repeating the give and take pattern of verses 4 and 5. Thus, verse 7 would mean "let them celebrate other cities all they want, as for me, all *my* thoughts are of Jerusalem." In this reading, verse 7 resonates with the same sense as the closing lines of Psalm 137: "If I set not Jerusalem above my chiefest joy."

The psalmist begins Psalm 122 by speaking of God's love for Jerusalem. As we read it, we come to feel that the love for the city is the psalmist's own. And as we read ourselves into the psalm we are reciting, perhaps the words give voice to our love as well.

## Jerusalem, "The Joy of All the Earth"

In Psalm 87 we heard Jerusalem referred to as "the city of God." We find the city referred to in much the same way in verse 2 of Psalm 48:

2 Great is the Lord, and highly to be praised,
In the city of our God, His holy mountain,
3 Fair in situation, the joy of the whole earth;
Even Mount Zion, the uttermost parts of the north,
The city of the great King.
4 God in her palaces
Hath made Himself known for a stronghold.
5 For, lo, the kings assembled themselves,
They came onward together.
6 They saw, straightway they were amazed;
They were affrighted, they hasted away.

7 Trembling took hold of them there,
Pangs, as of a woman in travail.
8 With the east wind
Thou breakest the ships of Tarshish.
9 As we have heard, so have we seen
In the city of the Lord of hosts, in the city of our God—
God established it forever. Selah.
10 We have thought on Thy loving kindness, O God,
In the midst of Thy Temple.
11 As is Thy name, O God,
So is Thy praise unto the ends of the earth;
Thy right hand is full of righteousness.
12 Let Mount Zion be glad,
Let the daughters of Judah rejoice,
Because of Thy judgments.
13 Walk about Zion, and go round about her;
Count the towers thereof.
14 Mark ye well her ramparts,
Traverse her palaces;
That ye may tell it to the generations following.
15 For such is God, our God forever and ever;
He will guide us eternally.

(Psalm 48:2–15)

We could treat Psalm 48 as a historical document reflecting the deliverance of the city from attack by foreign kings. But the truth is that we cannot really be sure about the historical events that lay behind the composition of this psalm. Perhaps it was the invasion by Assyrian armies described in 2 Kings 16:9, Isaiah 10:9ff and 17:1, and Amos 1:4ff. But we really cannot be certain.

For sure, Psalm 48 is full of echoes of some historic victory over attackers, much like Psalms 46 and 47. The three were written in celebration of a national deliverance from calamity. We recognize the contrast between God, described as "the great King" (verse 3) and the assembled kings of verse 5. Verse 6 consists almost entirely of simple, straightforward verbs to describe the complete futility of the effort of those kings to conquer the city. Jerusalem is rescued by a supernatural event, an "east wind," just as the Hebrews were saved by an east wind at the Red Sea in Exodus 14:21. Indeed, verse 7 sounds very much like the Song of the Sea of Exodus 15:14, which celebrates that earlier salvation, thus drawing even more sharply the parallels between the two events. And we can hear the exultation in verses 13 and 14 as if the psalmist were saying, "Walk around the city, survey the damage, see how it has survived intact."

The last two verses of Psalm 48 use the event to teach its hearers a lesson about God. As mighty as the defenses of the city are, the city's Defender is all the more so. Verses 14 and 15 use the miraculous victory over the invaders as proof of God's protection and care. In this, the verses resemble other psalms:

O God, we have heard with our ears, our fathers have told us;
A work Thou didst in their days, in the days of old.

(Psalm 44:2)

3 That which we have heard and known,
And our fathers have told us,
4 We will not hide from their children,
Telling to the generation to come the praises of the Lord,
And His strength, and His wondrous works that He hath done.

(Psalm 78:3–4)

At the same time, by sounding this note, the psalmist introduces the theme that some special bond exists between God and this city.

We can readily see the historical origins of Psalm 48. But even more striking is the love of the city of Jerusalem that shines through its words. Even without the historical references, it is clear that Jerusalem occupies an honored place.

Verse 3 revels in the sheer physical beauty of the city, going so far as to call it "the joy of the whole earth." In verses 13–14, we hear more exultation, as if the psalmist were telling us, "Look at it. Isn't it remarkable? Really splendid." The delight in the city is palpable. All the exultation of Jerusalem's beauty is reminiscent of a verse in a Yiddish poem by Malke Locker. Here the poet alludes to a rabbinic axiom about the city:

All the centuries walk about in your streets, Jerusalem,
On all the faces shines Jerusalem's night-sky.
Ten measures of beauty descended on the world,
Nine were taken by Jerusalem,
And one by the whole world.

(Malke Locker, "Jerusalem")

But even beyond the city's beauty, Psalm 48 wants us to understand that Jerusalem is important. In verse 12, Jerusalem is described as a mother and the villages that surround it as her "daughters." This same imagery appears in Psalm 97:

Zion heard and was glad,
And the daughters of Judah rejoiced;
Because of Thy judgments, O Lord.

(Psalm 97:8)

The assertion of Jerusalem's superiority to the other cities of the people is similar to what we read in Psalm 87:2.

Most significantly, Psalm 48 makes clear why Jerusalem is so important. It asserts that Jerusalem is unique because it has a special relationship with God. It may sound audacious to our ears to depict God as having a special relationship with one particular city.

But, of course, it is no more audacious than the Jewish people's seeing itself as having a special relationship with God. The idea of Jerusalem occupying a special place in God's design clearly is the assumption throughout the Book of Psalms. That ancient attribution is part of the special hold that the city has exercised on generations of Jews ever since. These same themes are sounded in many other places throughout Psalms.

## God's Special Relationship with Jerusalem

In the psalms we have examined so far, we have heard undertones of the notion that Jerusalem enjoys a special measure of God's favor. That idea is stated explicitly and repeatedly throughout the Book of Psalms. When we discussed Psalm 122, we encountered the verb *bachar*/to choose in the Book of Deuteronomy. In Deuteronomy, this verb alludes to Jerusalem as the place God will choose at some future time. In several places in the Book of Psalms, the connection between that place which would be chosen and Mount Zion—a symbol of Jerusalem—is made clear. Psalm 132 and Psalm 78 use the word *bachar* to tell us that God chose Jerusalem:

> 13 For the Lord hath chosen Zion;
>     He hath desired it for His habitation
> 14 "This is My resting-place forever;
>     Here is where I dwell; for I have desired it.
> 15 I will abundantly bless her provision;
>     I will give her needy bread in plenty...."
>
> (Psalm 132:13–15)

> 68 But He chose the tribe of Judah,
>     The Mount Zion which He loved.
> 69 And He built His sanctuary like the heights,
>     Like the earth which He hath founded forever.
>
> (Psalm 78:68–69)

This is the same verb used in the Bible to express how God chose the Israelites from among all nations. In Psalm 68 we read that God desired Mount Zion for a habitation:

> 16 A mountain of God is the mountain of Bashan;
> A mountain of peaks is the mountain of Bashan.
> 17 Why look ye askance, ye mountain of peaks,
> At the mountain which God hath desired for His abode?
> Yea, the Lord will dwell therein forever.
>
> (Psalm 68:16–17)

These verses acknowledge that there are other, more lofty, mountain peaks—"mountains of God," if you will—but that God has desired this particular mountain as a permanent home.

Psalm 78:69 reminds us that God not only chose Jerusalem as a home but also built it, in the very same way God "built" the heavens and the earth. This idea is also expressed in Psalm 147:

> 2 The Lord doth build up Jerusalem,
> He gathereth together the dispersed of Israel....
> 12 Glorify the Lord, O Jerusalem;
> Praise thy God, O Zion.
> 13 For He hath made strong the bars of thy gates;
> He hath blessed thy children within thee.
> 14 He maketh thy borders peace;
> He giveth thee in plenty the fat of wheat.
>
> (Psalm 147:2, 12–14)

As with Psalm 48, these words might be associated with a particular historical event—in this case the rebuilding of Jerusalem after the Babylonian Exile—but the emotion that shines through them is love for the city. Psalm 78 and Psalm 147 express the powerful idea that God actually created the city of Jerusalem, as well as the sacred mountain associated with it.

Other psalms go on to assert that God actually lives in Jerusalem or on Mount Zion:

Blessed be the Lord out of Zion,
Who dwelleth at Jerusalem.

(Psalm 135:21)

Sing praises to the Lord, who dwelleth in Zion;
Declare among the nations His doings.

(Psalm 9:12)

Remember Thy congregation, which Thou hast gotten of old,
Which Thou hast redeemed to be the tribe of Thine inheritance;
And Mount Zion wherein Thou hast dwelt.

(Psalm 74:2)

2 In Judah is God known;
His name is great in Israel.
3 In Salem also is set His tabernacle,
And His dwelling-place in Zion.

(Psalm 76:2–3)

This idea seems to be implied as well in Psalms 20:3 and 50:2; and perhaps in Psalm 14:7.

## Jerusalem Is Special Because of the Temple

The city of Jerusalem was considered to be special to God because at the time the psalms were composed, Jerusalem was the site of the Temple. In chapter 3, we noted that many psalms are about the Temple's construction, destruction, and reconstruction. While the Temple was standing, the religious life of the Israelites centered on it. People were expected to "go up" to Jerusalem at least three times a year—on the major festivals—to bring first fruits and make sacrifices. Indeed, we can hear a foreshadowing of the role of Jerusalem in various places in the Torah, such as this injunction in the Book of Deuteronomy:

> Thou mayest not sacrifice the passover-offering within any of thy gates, which the Lord thy God giveth thee; but at the place which the Lord thy God shall choose to cause His name to dwell in, there thou shalt sacrifice the passover-offering.... And thou shalt rejoice before the Lord thy God, thou, and thy son, and thy daughter, and thy man-servant, and thy maid-servant, and the Levite that is within thy gates, and the stranger, and the fatherless, and the widow that are in the midst of thee, in the place which the Lord thy God shall choose to cause His name to dwell there.... Three times in a year shall all thy males appear before the Lord thy God in the place which He shall choose: on the feast of unleavened bread, and on the feast of weeks, and on the feast of tabernacles; and they shall not appear before the Lord empty-handed.... (Deuteronomy 16:5–6, 11, 16)

Several other psalms mention the Temple as part of the people's everyday life:

> 17 I will offer to Thee the sacrifice of thanksgiving,
>    And will call upon the name of the Lord.
> 18 I will pay my own vows unto the Lord,
>    Yea, in the presence of all His people;
> 19 In the courts of the Lord's house,
>    In the midst of thee, O Jerusalem.
>
> (Psalm 116:17–19)

²⁹ Thy God hath commanded thy strength;
   Be strong, O God, Thou that hast wrought for us
³⁰ Out of Thy temple at Jerusalem,
   Whither kings shall bring presents unto Thee.

(Psalm 68:29–30)

We have already seen a similar reference in Psalm 48:10. Delight in the Temple animates Psalm 84:

² How lovely are Thy tabernacles, O Lord of hosts!
³ My soul yearneth, even pineth for the courts of the Lord;
   My heart and my flesh sing for joy unto the living God.
⁴ Yea, the sparrow hath found a house, and the swallow a
     nest for herself,
   Where she may lay her young;
   Thine altars, O Lord of hosts,
   My King and my God—
⁵ Happy are they that dwell in Thy house,
   They are ever praising Thee. Selah.
⁶ Happy is the man whose strength is in Thee;
   In whose heart are the highways,
⁷ Passing through the valley of Baca
   They make it a place of springs;
   Yea, the early rain clotheth it with blessings.
⁸ They go from strength to strength,
   Every one of them appeareth before God in Zion.
⁹ O Lord God of hosts, hear my prayer;
   Give ear, O God of Jacob. Selah.
¹⁰ Behold, O God our shield,
   And look upon the face of Thine anointed.
¹¹ For a day in Thy courts is better than a thousand;
   I had rather stand at the threshold of the house of my God,
   Than to dwell in the tents of wickedness.

<sup>12</sup> For the Lord God is a sun and a shield;
The Lord giveth grace and glory;
No good thing will He withhold from them that walk
    uprightly.
<sup>13</sup> O Lord of hosts,
Happy is the man that trusteth in Thee.

(Psalm 84:2–13)

The pilgrim in Psalm 122 rejoiced in coming up to Jerusalem; in Psalm 84 we hear the wonder and joy of the person who has come to the Temple. Running through the psalm are words such as lovely, joy, and happy. Verse 3 speaks of yearning for the Temple when we are away from it. The sense of feeling truly at home in the Temple is captured powerfully by the imagery of the sparrow building a nest to lay her eggs. The image of the sparrow is in stark contrast to the images of displaced and endangered birds in Psalm 102, which captures the people's emotions regarding the destruction of the Temple:

<sup>7</sup> I am like a pelican of the wilderness;
I am become an owl of the waste places.
<sup>8</sup> I watch, and am become
Like a sparrow that is alone upon the housetop.

(Psalm 102:7–8)

The words of Psalm 84:5 have been incorporated into the worship service, recited twice during the morning service and at the begin-ning of the afternoon service. By including these words, the liturgy attests to the transfer of our devotion from the Temple to the synagogue, which succeeded it as the place of worship when the Temple was destroyed.

We cannot help but feel a paradox in the idea of God living in the Temple in Jerusalem. After all, is the God who created heaven and earth, whose "glory fills all space," to be confined to a physical structure? We have already heard this paradox hinted at in Psalm 78:69:

> And He built His sanctuary like the heights,
> Like the earth which He hath founded forever.
>
> (Psalm 78:69)

That paradox seems to stand out even more starkly in Psalm 134:

> 1 A Song of Ascents.
> Behold, bless ye the Lord, all ye servants of the Lord,
> That stand in the house of the Lord in the night seasons.
> 2 Lift up your hands to the sanctuary,
> And bless ye the Lord.
> 3 The Lord bless thee out of Zion;
> Even He that made heaven and earth.
>
> (Psalm 134:1–3)

It is difficult to know precisely what is being described in this psalm. Some commentators suggest that the psalmist is "blessing," or praising, the officiating priests who, in turn, bless those in attendance. We can also understand this scene as one in which the pilgrims gathered at the Temple to bless God and lift up their hands—and God reciprocated by blessing the pilgrims. In either case, the blessing in verse 3 highlights our paradox. The first line of verse 3 repeats the first line of a blessing found in Psalm 128:5. The second line repeats the words of Psalm 115:

> Blessed be ye of the Lord,
> Who made heaven and earth.
>
> (Psalm 115:15)

This last line is also the last line of Psalm 124.

By repeating the lines from each of these verses, the psalmist underscores the paradox of thinking of the infinite God as confined to a finite, physical structure. This same paradox seems to have troubled King Solomon, who was considered "wiser than all men" (1 Kings 5:11). In Solomon's blessing at the Temple's dedication, he put this paradox boldly:

> Then spoke Solomon: "The Lord hath said that He would dwell in the thick darkness. I have surely built Thee a house of habitation, a place for Thee to dwell in forever.... But will God in very truth dwell on the earth? Behold, heaven and the heaven of heavens cannot contain Thee; how much less this house that I have builded!" (1 Kings 8:12–13, 27)

Solomon seems to have both made the affirmation that God would dwell in the Temple and been sensitive to the incongruity of that idea. He embraced the paradox. So, perhaps, did those who wrote and those who recited the psalms in praise of the Temple.

## God's Holy Mountain

This same description of Jerusalem and Mount Zion appears in other places in the Bible as well. The prophets Isaiah and Micah both make use of the same phrase:

> It shall come to pass in the end of days, that the mountain of the Lord's house shall be established at the top of the mountains and shall be exalted above the hills; and all nations shall flow unto it.
>
> And many peoples, shall go and say: "Come let us go up to the mountain of the Lord, to the house of the God of Jacob; and He will teach us of His ways, and we will walk in His paths." For out of Zion shall go forth Torah, and the

word of the Lord from Jerusalem. (Both Isaiah 2:2–3 and Micah 4:1–2)

Because Jerusalem was the site of the Temple, and was understood to be chosen by God, its association with God came to define its very character. When Psalm 2 seeks to represent God as establishing the line of the kings of Israel, it identifies Mount Zion in a specific way:

> Truly it is said I have established My king
> Upon Zion, My holy mountain.
>
> (Psalm 2:6)

This same designation appears repeatedly in the Book of Psalms:

> With my voice I call unto the Lord,
> And He answereth me out of His holy mountain.
>
> (Psalm 3:5)

> O send out Thy light and Thy truth; let them lead me;
> Let them bring me unto Thy holy mountain, and to Thy
>     dwelling-places....
>
> (Psalm 43:3)

> Lord, who shall sojourn in Thy tabernacle?
> Who shall dwell upon Thy holy mountain?
>
> (Psalm 15:1)

> Exalt ye the Lord our God,
> And worship at His holy mountain;
> For the Lord our God is holy.
>
> (Psalm 99:9)

In Psalm 24, we find a further reference to the "mountain of the Lord":

> Who shall ascend into the mountain of the Lord?
> And who shall stand in His holy place?
>
> (Psalm 24:3)

Just as Mount Zion came to be identified with God, so too did the entire city of Jerusalem. In Psalm 48:3, Jerusalem is referred to as "the city of the great King," a designation that clearly refers to God. We have already explored references to Jerusalem as the city of God in Psalms 87:3, 46:5, and 48:2. In Psalm 48:9 we also saw the city referred to as "the city of the Lord." Jerusalem is referred to in this way as well in Psalm 101:8.

Zion and Jerusalem came to be so identified with God's presence that reference to them seems to have served as some sort of shorthand for reference to God. Thus, in two psalms we have already explored, a plea for divine help was expressed in terms of Zion and the Temple:

> Send forth thy help from the sanctuary,
> And support thee out of Zion.
>
> (Psalm 20:3)

> [29] Thy God hath commanded thy strength;
> Be strong O God, Thou that hast wrought for us
> [30] Out of Thy Temple at Jerusalem....
>
> (Psalm 68:29–30)

God and the place where God dwelled had become completely identified with one another. We see this in more contemporary times in a charming Hebrew poem by the Israeli poet Yehudah Amichai:

Jerusalem a port on the shore of eternity
The Temple Mount a huge ship, a luxury cruise liner.
From the portholes of her Western Wall peer jolly
Saints, the passengers. Hasids on the platform wave
Goodbye, shout hurray see you. The ship
Always arrives, always sails. And the fences and piers
And the police and the banners and the tall masts of
   churches
And mosques and the smokestacks of synagogues and the boats
Of praise and the waves of mountains. Voice of the Shofar
   is heard: one
More sailed. Yom Kippur sailors in white uniforms
Scale ladders and ropes of tested prayers.

And the give and take and the gates and the golden domes:
Jerusalem is the Venice of God.

(Yehuda Amichai, "Poems of Jerusalem #21")

## Jerusalem Becomes a Metaphor

In the Book of Psalms, Jerusalem became completely identified with God. God chose it and God built it. God could send deliverance from there. God lived there. It was the city of God. It is no wonder that Jerusalem came to have a certain holiness of its own. Thus, in a number of places we see the city of Jerusalem or the Temple associated with the ability to confer special blessing:

Blessed be he that cometh in the name of the Lord;
We bless you out of the house of the Lord.

(Psalm 118:26)

The Lord bless thee out of Zion....

(Psalm 134:3a)

The Lord bless thee out of Zion;
And see thou the good of Jerusalem all the days of thy life.

(Psalm 128:5)

Jerusalem came to possess such sanctity in its own right that even in the Book of Psalms there are times when it seems to be treated less like a physical reality than as a metaphor for God's protection and care. Thus we read in Psalm 125:

¹ A Song of Ascents.
They that trust in the Lord
Are as Mount Zion, which cannot be moved, but abideth
   forever.
² As the mountains are round about Jerusalem,
So the Lord is round about His people,
From this time forth and forever.

(Psalm 125:1–2)

Here Jerusalem is not presented as an actual city or geographical entity. Jerusalem is treated as a tribute to God's utter dependability and concern for us. We see the same idea in Psalm 133:

¹ A Song of Ascents; of David.
Behold, how good and how pleasant it is
For brethren to dwell together in unity!
² It is like the precious oil upon the head,
Coming down upon the beard;
Even Aaron's beard,
That cometh down upon the collar of his garments;
³ Like the dew of Hermon,

That cometh down upon the mountains of Zion;
For there the Lord commanded the blessing,
Even life forever.

(Psalm 133:1–3)

Some readers understand this psalm, like Psalm 122, in terms of a pilgrim's experience upon visiting the Temple. Verse 1 would be an expression of joy at the unity the pilgrim feels with all the others who have made the pilgrimage to dwell together for that period of time. Then, using the sights and experiences of that pilgrimage, the pilgrim would celebrate those ties. In the final verse, the pilgrim would elaborate upon that experience and see Zion as a symbol of God's greatest bounties. Whether or not Psalm 133 is a representation of the pilgrim's experience, it clearly shows Zion as being seen not in terms of its own tangible reality, but as a symbol for what is beyond it. In Psalms 125 and 133, we almost catch a glimpse of "the eternal Jerusalem"—a city that exists beyond time and space. Can we, perhaps, hear that reflected in the very last words of Psalm 133, "Even life forever"?

## Jerusalem as the Object of Longing

Of course Jerusalem was a physical, earthly reality. And that real city experienced the devastation of conquest and destruction. In chapter 3, we discussed the devastation of the city by the Babylonians in 586 B.C.E. and saw how the Book of Psalms treated the rebuilding of the Temple and the city. Centuries later, in 72 C.E., the Romans destroyed the Temple and razed Jerusalem again. In the millennia that followed, Jews continued to remember Jerusalem and long for her. In that longing, the earthly and the eternal Jerusalem became fused in the hearts and minds of those who were devoted to her, and Jerusalem became an object of the most passionate longing. Wherever they lived, Jews said their prayers facing toward Jerusalem.

Jewish homes had a special marker on their walls indicating the direction of Jerusalem. For all those years, Jews fasted and prayed on the ninth day of the Hebrew month of *Av*, as a remembrance of the day on which both the first and second Temples were destroyed. The Rabbis ordained that on that day, called *Tisha b'Av*, Jews were to recite Psalm 79 and Psalm 137. Some selected verses give us a sense of the depth of the longing felt by hundreds of generations:

> 1 By the rivers of Babylon,
> There we sat down, yea, we wept,
> When we remembered Zion.
> 2 Upon the willows in the midst thereof
> We hanged up our harps.
> 3 For there they that led us captive asked of us words of song,
> And our tormentors asked of us mirth:
> "Sing us one of the songs of Zion...."
> 4 How shall we sing the Lord's song
> In a strange land?
> 5 If I forget thee, O Jerusalem,
> Let my right hand forget her cunning.
> 6 Let my tongue cleave to the roof of my mouth,
> If I remember thee not;
> If I set not Jerusalem
> Above my chiefest joy.
>
> (Psalm 137:1–6)

> 1 O God, the heathen are come into Thine inheritance;
> They have defiled Thy holy Temple;
> They have made Jerusalem into heaps....
> 4 We are become a taunt to our neighbors,
> A scorn and derision to them that are round about us.
> 5 How long, O Lord, wilt Thou be angry forever?
> How long will Thy jealousy burn like fire?

6 Pour out Thy wrath upon the nations that know Thee not,
And upon the kingdoms that call not upon Thy name....

(Psalm 79:1, 4–6)

Countless generations felt those words deeply and personally
as they recited them. As they read those words, the pleas and supplications became their own. Jerusalem became the object of the
profoundest longing. Remarkably, we can hear that same longing
expressed within the Book of Psalms:

20 Do good in Thy favor unto Zion;
Build Thou the walls of Jerusalem.
21 Then wilt Thou delight in the sacrifices of righteousness, in
burnt-offering and whole-offering;
Then will they offer bullocks upon Thine altar.

(Psalm 51:20–21)

Perhaps the Jerusalem we would have God rebuild is not the
center of sacrifices and burnt offerings. But the longing and desire
that the psalmist put into words were felt as personally compelling
emotions by Jews for thousands of years. As we give voice to these
words of love and longing for Jerusalem—Jerusalem the earthly
city and the Jerusalem of eternity—perhaps we can experience
those emotions as our own as well.

This feeling of ongoing connection—the personal sense of
waiting, longing, and hoping—is captured, two and a half millennia
after the psalms were written, by the Yiddish poet J. Manik
Lederman:

Your young proud streets
Smile to the day that is new
Like your wounded uprising,
How beautiful are you!

How much envy you have met,
How much hate
Till your redeemer comes
You stand and wait.

When your redeemer comes
All will see.
Who will compare then with you,
In your majesty?

He will bless you,
With hands outspread.
and towers and palaces
Will crown your head.

He will set a gold circlet
On your brow.
And heaven, rejoicing
To you will bow.

(J. Manik Lederman, "Jerusalem")

# 8

# WHAT DOES THE LORD REQUIRE? THE CALL TO SOCIAL JUSTICE

And I tell you the good in man will win
Over all his wickedness, over all the wrongs he has done.
He will look at the pages of written history, and be amazed,
And then he will laugh and sing,
And the good that is in man, children in their cradles, will
    have won.

Here I stand, the Jew, marked by history, for who can count
    how long?
Wrapped in compassion as in a Tallith, staring every storm
    in the face
Write songs of pain, sing prayers of torment, refresh yourself
    with suffering.
Too much for one people, small and weak—it is enough to
Share out among the whole human race

But God has planted in me goodness, compassion, as a father
    loves his children,
So I writhe with pain, weep and sing, sing and weep,
For the blood knows the heart of the world is not made of stone,
The wonderful light of God's face is for all eternity stamped
    on it firm and deep.

And the heart feels that there is a day and an hour,
And a mountain called Zion
And then all the sufferings will gather there and will all
   become song.
Ringing out into every corner of the earth, from end to end,
And the nations will hear it, and like caravans in the desert
Will all to that mountain throng.

(A. Nissenson, "Not Stone")


When the poet A. Nissenson speaks about God, he does not elaborate on things we usually identify as "religious": prayer, ritual acts, beliefs, or expressions of piety. Rather, he is drawn to human behavior and acts of goodness. In this, Nissenson is part of a long tradition within Judaism.

## God Cares about How We Behave

Rabbi Israel Salanter was one of the great teachers of the Jewish community in eighteenth-century Eastern Europe. In addition to his teaching, he supervised the *kashrut*/compliance with Jewish dietary laws in his community. One year, as *Pesach*/Passover approached, he prepared to send his students to inspect the factory that produced matzah. Before they left, one student asked whether there was anything specific that they should look for. We might expect Rabbi Salanter to go into the fine points of separating leavened from unleavened products or scrupulously protecting the rainwater used in matzah from exposure to leavening products. There is much minutiae involved in matzah-making that he could have taught them. Instead, he replied, "Yes, the women who work there are poor, and their families depend on their income. Make sure they are well paid."

Two thousand years ago, the Rabbis engaged in the practice of searching for a *clal*—a single principle that expressed all the teachings of the Bible. What they chose reflects a lot about what these codifiers of Jewish tradition and practice considered important:

> Rabbi Simlai taught: Six hundred and thirteen command-ments were given to Moses. Then David reduced them to eleven in Psalm 15, beginning, "He who does what is right and speaks the truth in his heart." Micah reduced them to three when he wrote, "It has been told you, O man, what is good and what the Lord requires of you: act justly, love mercy, and walk humbly with your God" (Micah 6:8). Then came Isaiah and reduced them to two, "Keep justice and act with integrity" (Isaiah 56:1). Amos reduced them to one, "Seek me and live" (Amos 5:4). Habakuk also contained them in one, "The righteous shall live by his faith" (Habakuk 2:4). Akiba taught, "The great principle of the Torah is expressed in the commandment, 'Love your neigh-bor as you love yourself. I am the Lord'" (Leviticus 19:18). But Ben Azai taught a greater principle, "This is the book of the generations of man. When God made man, He made him in the likeness of God" (Genesis 5:1). (Babylonian Talmud Makkot 23b–24a)

What is striking about these various attempts to identify a single overarching principle is the consistency with which the Rabbis point to the verses in the Bible that deal with how human beings should treat one another. Much earlier, the prophet Isaiah put it even more succinctly:

> The Lord of Hosts is exalted by justice, and the Holy God is sanctified by righteousness. (Isaiah 5:16)

The Book of Psalms is of a piece with this approach to reli-gious life. In truth, Psalms differs greatly from what people might expect from a religious text. It does not talk in lofty, abstract terms. It includes virtually no narrative about the acts of God. Its focus is not in the heavens, but here on earth; its real subject, in many ways, is not God, but us. When it does talk about religious obligations, it speaks less about cult or rituals and more about right behavior. Psalm 50 makes a single point: What does God want from us?—only right behavior.

1 God, God the Lord, hath spoken, and called the earth
   From the rising of the sun unto the going down thereof.
2 Out of Zion, the perfection of beauty,
   God hath shined forth.
3 Our God cometh, and doth not keep silence;
   A fire devoureth before Him,
   And round about Him it stormeth mightily.
4 He calleth to the heavens above,
   And to the earth, that He may judge His people:
5 "Gather my saints together unto Me;
   Those that have made a covenant with Me by sacrifice."
6 And the heavens declare His righteousness;
   For God, He is judge. Selah.
7 "Hear, O My people, and I will speak;
   O Israel, and I will testify against thee:
   God, thy God, am I.
8 I will not reprove thee for thy sacrifices;
   And thy burnt-offerings are continually before Me.
9 I will take no bullock out of thy house,
   Nor he-goats out of thy folds.
10 For every beast of the forest is Mine,
   And the cattle upon a thousand hills.
11 I know all the fowls of the mountains;
   And the wild beasts of the field are Mine.
12 If I were hungry, I would not tell thee;

For the world is Mine, and the fulness thereof.
13 Do I eat the flesh of bulls,
Or drink the blood of goats?
14 Offer unto God the sacrifice of thanksgiving;
And pay thy vows unto the Most High;
15 And call upon Me in the day of trouble;
I will deliver thee, and thou shalt honour Me."
16 But unto the wicked God saith:
"What hast thou to do to declare My statutes,
And that thou hast taken My covenant in thy mouth?
17 Seeing thou hatest instruction,
And castest My words behind thee.
18 When thou sawest a thief, thou hadst company with him,
And with adulterers as thy portion.
19 Thou hast let loose thy mouth for evil,
And thy tongue frameth deceit.
20 Thou sittest and speaketh against thy brother;
Thou slanderest thine own mother's son.
21 These things hast thou done, and should I have kept silence?
Thou hadst thought that I was altogether such a one as thyself;
But I will reprove thee, and set the cause before thine eyes.
22 Now consider this, ye that forget God,
Lest I tear in pieces, and there be none to deliver.
23 Who so offereth the sacrifice of thanksgiving honoreth Me;
And to him that ordereth his way aright
Will I show the salvation of God."

(Psalm 50:1–23)

For all its lofty language and beautiful imagery, Psalm 50 makes a straightforward assertion. Our conduct is of supreme importance to God. In this, Psalm 50 sounds very much like the Prophets quoted in chapter 2, who teach that God does not care about our sacrifices, only our deeds. We see this in just two examples of many in the Bible:

I hate, I despise your feasts, and I will take no delight in your
solemn assemblies. Yea, though ye offer Me burnt-offerings
and your meal-offerings, I will not accept them; neither will
I regard the peace-offerings of your fat beasts. Take thou
away from Me the noise of thy songs; and let Me not hear
the melody of thy psalteries. But let justice well up as waters,
and righteousness as a mighty stream. (Amos 5:21–24)

For I desire mercy, and not sacrifice, and the knowledge of
God rather than burnt-offerings. (Hosea 6:6)

This is an attitude we hear echoed in Psalm 40:

7 Sacrifice and meal-offering Thou hast no delight in;
  Mine ears hast Thou opened;
  Burnt-offering and sin-offering hast Thou not required.
8 Then said I: "Lo, I am come
  With a scroll of a book which is prescribed for me;
9 I delight to do Thy will, O my God;
  Yea, Thy law is in my inmost parts."

(Psalm 40:7–9)

These verses from Psalm 40 go beyond what we read in Psalm
50. They reject the centrality of sacrifice and underscore the
importance of our acts. Psalm 40 teaches that we must take the
"scroll," the "teaching," into our very selves. The Hebrew word
*Torah*, here translated as "law," is better understood as "teaching."
Torah is described as God's will, which is "prescribed for me." And
what are the contents of this Torah? It contains the righteousness
that the psalmist preaches in the congregation. In these verses,
sacrifice has been replaced by righteous behavior; the primary
locus of religious life has been relocated from the altar to our
"inmost parts." The personal internalizing of our religious life in

Psalm 40 sounds very much like a powerful teaching in the Book of Deuteronomy:

> For this commandment which I command thee this day, it is not too hard for thee, neither is it far off. It is not in heaven, that thou shouldest say: "Who shall go up for us to heaven, and bring it unto us, and make us to hear it, that we may do it?" Neither is it beyond the sea, that thou shouldest say: "Who shall go over the sea for us, and bring it unto us, and make us to hear it, that we may do it?" But the word is very nigh unto thee, in thy mouth, and in thy heart, that thou mayest do it. (Deuteronomy 30:11–14)

Perhaps it is echoes of this idea that we hear in a rather perplexing incident in the career of the prophet Ezekiel:

> And He said unto me: "Son of man, eat that which thou findest; eat this scroll, and go speak to the house of Israel." So I opened my mouth, and He caused me to eat that scroll. And He said unto me: "Son of man, cause thy belly to eat, and fill thy bowels with this scroll that I give thee." Then did I eat it; and it was in my mouth as honey for sweetness. (Ezekiel 3:1–3)

It is not enough to go through the gestures of ritual. We must take the teaching into our very selves and live it out in our lives.

## Making God's Qualities Our Own

The master key to the riddle of how we are to live our lives is displayed in Psalm 11:

> For the Lord is righteous, He loveth righteousness;
> The upright shall behold His face.
>
> (Psalm 11:7)

The words sound very much like those in the Book of Leviticus:

> Speak unto all the congregation of the children of Israel,
> and say unto them: "Ye shall be holy; for I the Lord your
> God am holy." (Leviticus 19:2)

Although they are short, the profound implications of these verses cannot be stated strongly enough. God wants us to behave as God's own self behaves. God wants us to treat others in the way we want to be treated by God. The full implication of understanding God in these terms becomes clear. We are to embody in our-selves the very qualities we recognize in God, qualities that include *rachum*/compassion, *chanun*/caring, *chesed*/steadfastness, *tzedek*/righteousness, and *mishpat*/justice. To be a person of faith means to take these qualities into oneself and become like God. The conduct expected of us is consistent with the character attributes we associate with God. We hear the echo of this idea in some other vers-es in Psalms:

> 26 With the merciful Thou dost show Thyself merciful,
>    With the upright man Thou dost show Thyself upright;
> 27 With the pure Thou dost show Thyself pure;
>    And with the crooked Thou dost show Thyself subtle.
> 28 For Thou dost save the afflicted people;
>    But the haughty eyes Thou dost humble.
>    (Psalm 18:26–28)

> 4 Do good, O Lord, unto the good,
>   And to them that are upright in their hearts.
> 5 But as for such as turn aside unto their crooked ways,
>   The Lord will lead them away with the workers of iniquity....
>   (Psalm 125:4–5)

As God is, so are we expected to be. All the teachings in Psalms about how we are to behave grow out of this fundamental vision.

## Personal Ethical Behavior

The very first words in the Book of Psalms are about the reward that comes to us when we have conducted ourselves properly:

¹ Happy is the man that hath not walked in the counsel of
   the wicked,
   Nor stood in the way of sinners,
   Nor sat in the seat of the scornful.
² But his delight is in the Torah of the Lord;
   And in His Torah doth he meditate day and night.

(Psalm 1:1–2)

Interestingly, the phrase "*ashrei ha'ish*/happy is the man" echoes throughout the Book of Psalms:

Happy is the man unto whom the Lord counteth not iniquity,
And in whose spirit there is no guile.

(Psalm 32:2)

Happy are they that keep justice,
That do righteousness at all times.

(Psalm 106:3)

¹ Happy are they that are upright in the way,
   Who walk in the Torah of the Lord.
² Happy are they that keep His testimonies,
   That seek Him with the whole heart.
³ Yea, they do no unrighteousness;
   They walk in His ways.

(Psalm 119:1–3)

It is significant that the Book of Psalms begins on the note of individual behavior. It serves to underscore the very personal nature of the book, and it reminds the reader that the ultimate expression of our religious lives is in our conduct. Psalm 112 begins on a similar note and then directs our attention to what we can do to achieve it:

> ¹ Happy is the man that feareth the Lord,
> That delighteth greatly in His commandments....
> ⁴ Unto the upright He shineth as a light in the darkness,
> Gracious, and full of compassion, and righteous.
> ⁵ Well is it with the man that dealeth graciously and lendeth,
> That ordereth his affairs rightfully....
> ⁹ He hath scattered abroad, he hath given to the poor;
> His righteousness endureth forever;
> His horn shall be exalted in honor.
>
> (Psalm 112:1, 4–5, 9)

The special theme of Psalm 112 is a description of the qualities of a God-fearing person—really, God-revering is a better translation. It is important for us to know that the "he" of verse 4 can be understood in two very different ways. It might refer to God shining as a light. In that case, it speaks about how God deals kindly with the good person. But because the subject of all the other verses is the good person himself, it is more likely that this verse is part of the description of the God-revering person. In that case, what becomes significant is that the words describing this person are adjectives usually used to describe God: *chanun*/gracious, *rachum*/compassionate, and *tzedek*/righteous. So this verse, and the situation it describes, is a perfect example of the good person embodying in himself (and herself) the qualities that we understand as God's attributes. The good person is accorded the same accolade that is usually reserved for God: "His righteousness endureth forever." The good person of Psalm 112 has internalized the commandments in which they delight.

The psalm speaks about some specific actions in which this good person engages: lending to people in need and giving to the poor. Such a person's righteousness endures forever. The phrase "his horn shall be exalted" means that he can hold his head high with pride. That is how this phrase is used in Psalm 92:

> But my horn hast Thou exalted like the horn of the wild-ox;
> I am anointed with rich oil.
>
> (Psalm 92:11)

Certainly this person has every right to feel pride, knowing that his conduct has brought him close to God. Indeed, his actions embody the very best of God's qualities.

The message of all these verses is the centrality of our own personal conduct. This same understanding infuses Psalm 15:

> ¹ Lord, who shall sojourn in Thy tabernacle?
> Who shall dwell upon Thy holy mountain?
> ² He that walketh uprightly, and worketh righteousness,
> And speakcth truth in his heart;
> ³ That hath no slander upon his tongue,
> Nor doeth evil to his fellow,
> Nor taketh up a reproach against his neighbor;
> ⁴ In whose eyes a vile person is despised,
> But he honoreth them that fear the Lord;
> He that sweareth to his own hurt, and changeth not;
> ⁵ He that putteth not out his money on interest,
> Nor taketh a bribe against the innocent,
> He that doeth these things shall never be moved.
>
> (Psalm 15:1–5)

The question that begins this psalm seems to be about Jerusalem, the earthly city, which we discussed in the previous chapter. But in a deeper sense, the "holy mountain" is really a metaphor. The question is about who will be allowed to inhabit God's precincts. The answer has nothing to do with sacrifice or ritual. Rather, the person who is honored is one whose conduct is exemplary. Such a person "shall never be moved," in contrast to the wicked person in Psalm 10:

He saith in his heart: "I shall not be moved,
I who to all generations shall not be in adversity."
(Psalm 10:6)

The wicked imagine that they are invulnerable, but in the end they perish. It is the righteous who, in the end, shall thrive. When verse 5 of Psalm 15 asserts that the righteous shall prosper, we are reminded that we have seen this same idea in many other psalms, such as Psalm 37:

The righteous shall inherit the land,
And dwell therein forever.
(Psalm 37:29)

The Talmud (Makkot 23b–24a) says that Psalm 15 contains all the *mitzvoth*/commandments of the Torah. It also says that when Rabban Gamliel read Psalm 15, he wept, for it made him aware of his own inadequacies. Psalm 15 can cause all of us to look at our own behavior. It is a powerful yardstick. We hear much the same idea repeated in Psalm 24:

3 Who shall ascend into the mountain of the Lord?
And who shall stand in His holy place?
4 He that hath clean hands, and a pure heart;

> Who hath not taken My name in vain
> And hath not sworn deceitfully.
> 5 He shall receive a blessing from the Lord,
> And righteousness from the God of his salvation.
>
> (Psalm 24:3–5)

Here again, the psalm begins by asking who deserves to dwell in intimacy with God. And, as in Psalm 15, the answer lies in personal conduct. Our individual behavior is the measure by which we are judged and by which we can gauge our closeness with God.

The Book of Psalms can be very explicit about how we should live our lives:

> Depart from evil, and do good;
> Seek peace, and pursue it.
>
> (Psalm 34:15)

Psalm 37 also promises a reward for fulfilling these instructions:

> Depart from evil, and do good;
> And dwell forevermore.
>
> (Psalm 37:27)

Both of these verses sound very much like the injunctions stated by the prophet Isaiah:

> Wash you, and make you clean, put away the evil of your doings from before Mine eyes, cease to do evil; learn to do good; seek justice, relieve the oppressed, judge the fatherless, plead for the widow. (Isaiah 1:16–17)

## Guard Your Words

Psalms seems to have special sensitivity to one particular category of personal behavior: the abuse of words. The wicked are frequently characterized as having mouths that are like weapons:

> 3 Why boastest thou thyself of evil, O mighty man?
> The mercy of God endureth continually.
> 4 Thy tongue deviseth destruction;
> Like a sharp razor, working deceitfully.
> 5 Thou lovest evil more than good;
> Falsehood rather than speaking righteousness,
> 6 Thou lovest all devouring words,
> The deceitful tongue.
>
> (Psalm 52:3–6)

> My soul is among lions, I do lie down among them that are
> aflame;
> Even the sons of men, whose teeth are spears and arrows,
> And their tongues a sharp sword.
>
> (Psalm 57:5)

> 19 Thou hast let loose thy mouth for evil,
> And thy tongue frameth deceit.
> 20 Thou sittest and speakest slander against thy brother;
> Thou slanderest thine own mother's son.
>
> (Psalm 50:19–20)

> For the sin of their mouth, and the words of their lips,
> Let them even be taken in their pride,
> And for cursing and lying which they speak.
>
> (Psalm 59:13)

Ferocious as the creatures described may appear, their only weapons are words: lies, slander, and expressions of hatred and ill will. In contrast to the vicious person, the psalmist implores:

I said: "I will take heed to my ways,
That I sin not with my tongue;
I will keep a curb upon my mouth,
While the wicked is before me."

(Psalm 39:2)

Even more powerfully, Psalm 34 enjoins us to turn away from the evil of harmful speech:

Who is the man that desireth life,
And loveth days, that he may see good therein?
Keep thy tongue from evil,
And thy lips from speaking guile.

(Psalm 34:13–14)

Psalm 34 is a forceful outcry against what may be the most common kind of destructive behavior. Most of us do not murder or steal. Most don't willfully inflict physical injury on others. But if we look at our lives, we see that, despite our best intentions, we are guilty of lying or speaking angry words. Most of us, at some time, engage in gossip or slander.

The frequency of this form of wickedness shaped the career of one of the most intriguing figures of modern Jewish life. The Chafetz Chayim was probably the outstanding rabbi in Eastern Europe in the late nineteenth and early twentieth centuries. When he was in his thirties, he anonymously published a 300-page volume attacking the evils of gossip, slander, and other abuses of the tongue. He took the title for the book from the verses we have just cited in Psalm 34—*Chafetz Chayim*/who desires life (verse 13).

When his identity as the author was discovered, the community attached the name of the book to his person, and so he was known for the rest of his long life. The Chafetz Chayim devoted his entire career to preaching against the evils that were the subject of his book. Indeed, he came to be revered throughout the Jewish community of Europe for his piety and for exemplifying in his own life the values he wrote about. He once said, "Grant that I should say nothing that is unnecessary."

## Visions of the Just Society

The ethical concerns in the Book of Psalms are not limited to the realm of personal conduct. Many psalms deal with the values of society at large and how we should live our collective life. God, whose actions we are to emulate, is described in Psalm 99 as a king:

> ³ Let them praise ...
> ⁴ The king who loveth justice—
> Thou hast established equity,
> Thou hast executed justice and righteousness in Jacob.
> (Psalm 99:3–4)

Given this understanding of the divine King, there can be little doubt about how the expectations of a human king's behavior would be depicted in the Book of Psalms. We find the aspirations of a king represented in Psalm 101:

> ¹ I will sing of mercy and justice;
> Unto Thee, O Lord, will I sing praises.
> ² I will give heed unto the way of integrity;
> Oh when wilt Thou come unto me?
> I will walk within my house in the integrity of my heart.

³ I will set no base thing before mine eyes;
   I hate the doing of things crooked;
   It shall not cleave unto me.
⁴ A perverse heart shall depart from me;
   I will know no evil thing.
⁵ Who so slandereth his neighbor in secret, him will I
      destroy;
   Who so is haughty of eye and proud of heart, him will I not
      suffer.
⁶ Mine eyes are upon the faithful of the land, that they may
      dwell with me;
   He that walketh in a way of integrity, he shall minister unto
      me.
⁷ He that worketh deceit shall not dwell in my house;
   He that speaketh falsehood shall not be established before
      mine eyes.
⁸ Morning by morning will I destroy all the wicked of the
      land;
   To cut off all the workers of iniquity from the city of the
      Lord.

(Psalm 101:1–8)

The human king's first thoughts are of mercy and justice, qualities attributed to God. The king aspires to integrity and repudiates all that is base or "crooked." Slander, deceit, and lying are singled out for special repudiation.

A more extensive and detailed description of what is expected of a king is found in Psalm 72:

² That he may judge Thy people with righteousness,
   And Thy poor with justice.
³ Let the mountains bear peace to the people,
   And the hills, through righteousness.

4 May he judge the poor of the people,
And save the children of the needy,
And crush the oppressor....
7 In his days let the righteous flourish,
And abundance of peace, till the moon be no more....
12 For he will deliver the needy when he crieth;
The poor also, and him that hath no helper.
13 He will have pity on the poor and needy
And the souls of the needy he will save.
14 He will redeem their soul from oppression and violence,
And precious will their blood be in his sight;
15 That they may live, and that he may give them of the gold
of Sheba,
That they may pray for him continually,
Yea, bless him all the day.

(Psalm 72:2–4, 7, 12–15)

Other verses in this psalm speak of hopes for the king's might and respect among the nations and ask that he be blessed with riches. These are conventional enough wishes on behalf of any ruler (or government). The verses that I have singled out, however, reflect a remarkable social vision. Clearly, Psalm 72 understands that a ruler must be especially vigilant about the needs of the most marginal members of society.

Just as Psalms reflects expectations about the behavior of a king, so too does it express an understanding of how judges should conduct themselves:

He that putteth not out his money on interest,
Nor taketh a bribe against the innocent.
He that doeth these things shall never be moved.

(Psalm 15:5)

Do ye indeed speak as a righteous company?
Do ye judge with equity the sons of men?

(Psalm 58:2)

Psalm 82 offers a more extensive reflection on how judges are supposed to discharge their responsibilities:

1 God standeth in the congregation of God;
   In the midst of the judges He judgeth:
2 "How long will ye judge unjustly,
   And respect the persons of the wicked?" Selah.
3 Judge the poor and fatherless;
   Do justice to the afflicted and destitute.
4 Rescue the poor and needy;
   Deliver them out of the hand of the wicked.
5 They know not, neither do they understand;
   They go about in darkness;
   All the foundations of the earth are moved.
6 I said: "Ye are godlike beings,
   And all of you sons of the Most High.
7 Nevertheless ye shall die like men,
   And fall like one of the princes."
8 Arise, O God, judge the earth;
   For Thou shalt possess all the nations.

(Psalm 82:1–8)

Psalm 82 begins and ends with the image of God as the supreme judge, conveying the sense that God sits in judgment on human judges. They are condemned for judging unfairly and favoring the powerful. They are expected to be attentive to the needs of the poor and fatherless, the afflicted and destitute, the poor and needy. As we saw in Psalm 72, the most marginal members of society should be the special concern of those in power.

The understanding of the role of a judge in Psalm 82 corresponds to values expressed earlier in the Bible:

> Thou shalt not utter a false report; put not thy hand with the wicked to be an unrighteous witness. Thou shalt not follow a multitude to do evil; neither shalt thou bear witness in a cause to turn aside after a multitude to pervert justice. Neither shalt thou favor a poor man in his cause.... Thou shalt not wrest the judgment of thy poor in his cause. Keep thee far from a false matter; and the innocent and righteous slay thou not; for I will not justify the wicked. And thou shalt take no gift; for a gift blindeth them that have sight, and perverteth the words of the righteous. (Exodus 23:1–3, 6–8)

> Ye shall do no unrighteousness in judgment; thou shalt not respect the person of the poor, nor favor the person of the mighty; but in righteousness shalt thou judge thy neighbor. (Leviticus 19:15)

Psalm 82 concludes with God as the ultimate judge. This image is found in the Book of Genesis when Abraham challenges God's intention to destroy the cities of Sodom and Gomorrah, including any righteous people living there, along with the wicked. Abraham demands, "Shall not the Judge of all the earth do justly?" (Genesis 18:25). The image of God as judge is found at the conclusion of Psalm 58 as well:

> And men shall say: "Verily there is a reward for the righteous; Verily there is a God that judgeth in the earth."
>
> (Psalm 58:12)

# The Cause of the Poor and the Needy

Clearly, there were people at special risk in the society reflected in the Bible. Psalm 109 describes a wicked person as someone who lacks compassion for the needy:

> Because that he remembered not to do kindness,
> But persecuted the poor and needy man,
> And the broken in heart he was ready to slay.
>
> (Psalm 109:16)

There is a deeply cynical Yiddish proverb that says, "God loves the poor—and helps the rich." This is diametrically opposite the biblical understanding and is at odds with what we find in the Book of Psalms. The fact is that throughout the Bible, and throughout the Book of Psalms, we encounter what can only be characterized as a preferential bias in favor of the poor:

> For the needy shall not always be forgotten,
> Nor the expectation of the poor perish forever.
>
> (Psalm 9:19)

> Ye would put to shame the counsel of the poor,
> But the Lord is his refuge.
>
> (Psalm 14:6)

These sentiments are consistent with a sentiment we find in the Book of Proverbs:

> One may oppress the poor, yet will their gain increase; one may give to the rich, yet will want come. (Proverbs 22:16)

Repeatedly, Psalms asserts that God hears the cries of the poor and needy:

For the Lord hearkeneth unto the needy,
And despiseth not His prisoners.

(Psalm 69:34)

For He hath not despised nor abhorred the lowliness of the
   poor;
Neither hath He hid His face from him;
But when he cried out unto Him, He heard.

(Psalm 22:25)

The assertion that God hears the cries of the needy is reminiscent of a section in the Book of Exodus:

And a stranger shalt thou not wrong, neither shalt thou oppress him; for ye were strangers in the land of Egypt. Ye shall not afflict any widow, or fatherless child. If thou afflict them in any wise—for if they cry at all unto Me, I will surely hear their cry—My wrath shall wax hot, and I will kill you with the sword; and your wives shall be widows, and your children fatherless. (Exodus 22:20–23)

And of one in Proverbs:

Rob not the weak, because he is weak, neither crush the poor in the gate; for the Lord will plead their cause, and despoil of life those that despoil them. (Proverbs 22:22–23)

God not only hears the cries of the poor and needy, God responds to them, even vigorously.

This poor man cried, and the Lord heard,
And saved him out of all his troubles.

(Psalm 34:7)

I know the Lord will maintain the cause of the poor,
And the right of the needy.

(Psalm 140:13)

30 I will give great thanks unto the Lord with my mouth;
Yea, I will praise Him among the multitude;
31 Because He standeth at the right hand of the needy,
To save him from them that judge his soul.

(Psalm 109:30–31)

All my bones shall say: "Lord, who is like unto Thee,
Who deliverest the poor from him that is too strong for him,
Yea, the poor and the needy from him that spoileth him?"

(Psalm 35:10)

"For the oppression of the poor, for the sighing of the needy,
Now I will arise," saith the Lord;
"I will set him in safety at whom they puff."

(Psalm 12:6)

In Psalm 113, we encounter God taking care of the poor and needy in a way that completely overcomes their marginality and reverses their position in the social order:

7 Who raiseth up the poor out of the dust,
And lifteth up the needy out of the dunghill;
8 That He may set him with princes,
Even with the princes of His people.

(Psalm 113:7–8)

Perhaps most striking about the way Psalms presents the cause of the poor is the way it depicts their special relationship with God.

In Psalm 14, when God is represented as speaking about *ami*/my people, the word is used to refer to the poor:

¹ The fool hath said in his heart: "There is no God";
They have dealt corruptly, they have done abominably;
There is none that doeth good.
² The Lord looked forth from heaven upon the children of men,
To see if there was any man of understanding, that did seek
after God.
³ They are all corrupt, they are together become impure;
There is none that doeth good, no, not one.
⁴ "Shall not all the workers of iniquity know it,
Who eat up my people as they eat bread,
And call not upon the Lord?"
⁵ There are they in great fear;
For God is with the righteous generation.
⁶ Ye would put to shame the counsel of the poor,
But the Lord is his refuge.

(Psalm 14:1–6)

Not only are the poor depicted as "My people," but also those who oppress them are seen as virtually rejecting God. These same verses are repeated in Psalm 53:1–6. This identification of God's people as the poor is consistent with a social vision that is encountered elsewhere in the Bible:

If thou lend money to any of My people, even to the poor among thee, thou shalt not treat him as a creditor; neither shall ye lay upon him interest. (Exodus 22:24)

"What mean ye that ye crush My people, and grind the face of the poor?" saith the Lord, the God of hosts. (Isaiah 3:15)

# The Needs of the Helpless

Everything we have examined to this point should not be taken to suggest that God's concern is limited to the poor. All those who are marginal and helpless are depicted as the object of God's concern, care, and active assistance. Thus, we read of the oppressed:

> The Lord executeth righteousness,
> And acts of justice for all that are oppressed.
>
> (Psalm 103:6)

and those who are characterized as "humble" or humbled by the circumstances of their lives:

> 9 Thou didst cause sentence to be heard from heaven;
> And the earth feared, and was still,
> 10 When God arose in judgment,
> To save all the humble of the earth.
>
> (Psalm 76:9–10)

A more inclusive list of the objects of God's concern is presented in Psalm 10:

> 12 Arise, O Lord; O God, lift up Thy hand;
> Forget not the humble.
> 13 Wherefore doth the wicked contemn God,
> And say in his heart: "Thou wilt not require"?
> 14 Thou hast seen; for Thou beholdest trouble and vexation to
> requite them with Thy hand;
> Unto Thee the helpless committeth himself;
> Thou hast been the helper of the fatherless....
> 17 Lord, Thou hast heard the desire of the humble:
> Thou wilt direct their heart, Thou wilt cause Thine ear to attend;

18 To right the fatherless and oppressed,
That man who is of the earth may be terrible no more.

(Psalm 10:12–14, 17–18)

We find a similarly inclusive list in Psalm 146:

7 Who executeth justice for the oppressed;
Who giveth bread to the hungry.
The Lord looseth the prisoners;
8 The Lord openeth the eyes of the blind;
The Lord raiseth up them that are bowed down;
The Lord loveth the righteous;
9 The Lord preserveth the strangers;
He upholdeth the fatherless and the widow;
But the way of the wicked He maketh crooked.

(Psalm 146:7–9)

God is represented as especially concerned with the humble, the stranger, the widow, and the fatherless. They were the most defenseless members of biblical society, virtually helpless. They had no given place in the communal structure and no one to defend them, if not God. Perhaps that is why they are mentioned repeatedly as special recipients of God's concern in so many psalms:

A father to the fatherless, and a judge of the widows,
Is God in His holy habitation.

(Psalm 68:6)

3 Lord, how long shall the wicked,
How long shall the wicked exult?
4 They gush out, they speak arrogancy;
All the workers of iniquity bear themselves loftily.
5 They crush Thy people, O Lord,

And afflict Thy heritage.
6 They slay the widow and the stranger,
And murder the fatherless.
7 And they say: "The Lord will not see,
Neither will the God of Jacob give heed."

(Psalm 94:3–7)

Psalm 94 resembles Psalm 14 in that it sees those most in need as having a special relationship with God. In the parallelism of verses 5 and 6, we are to see the widow, the fatherless, and the stranger as God's people. Also, like Psalm 14, the wicked ones are depicted as scoffing at God, virtually rejecting God (verse 7). We have already encountered this kind of "functional atheism of the wicked" in a number of psalms. God's concern for the most marginal members of society involves a kind of paradox, put into words by the prophet Isaiah:

For thus saith the High and Lofty One that inhabiteth eternity, whose name is Holy; I dwell in the high and holy place with him also that is of a contrite and humble spirit, to revive the spirit of the humble, and to revive the heart of the contrite ones. (Isaiah 57:15)

The notion that God has special concern for the helpless—and that as a result, we, who want to be like God, need to reach out to them—is a vision that the Book of Psalms shares with other parts of the Bible. We see it in many places:

When thou reapest thy harvest in thy field, and hast forgot a sheaf in the field, thou shalt not go back to fetch it; it shall be for the stranger, for the fatherless, and for the widow. (Deuteronomy 24:19)

> For the Lord your God, He is a God of gods, and Lord of lords, the great God, the mighty and the awful, who regardeth not persons, nor taketh reward. He doth execute justice for the fatherless and widow, and loveth the stranger, giving him food and raiment. Love ye therefore the stranger; for ye were strangers in the land of Egypt. (Deuteronomy 10:17–19)

> Execute ye justice and righteousness, and deliver the spoiled out of the hand of the oppressor; and do no wrong, do no violence to the stranger, the fatherless, nor the widow; neither shed innocent blood in this place. (Jeremiah 22:3)

The sum of all these statements is a clear vision of what makes for a just society.

The Book of Psalms was part of a particular vision of what society should be. The God whom the people worshipped was a God who had special concern for the most marginal and vulnerable members of society. The king who ruled and the judges who administered justice were expected to show special concern for the needy and the dispossessed. The kind of shared collective life that would be built on such a vision is clear. The implication of such teachings for our own behavior is equally clear. We, too, are expected to build a society that extends itself to those who cannot take care of themselves. The values of this worldview are expressed in terms of how God is understood in the Bible:

> Thus saith the Lord: "Let not the wise man glory in his wisdom, neither let the mighty man glory in his might, let not the rich man glory in his riches; but let him that glorieth glory in this, that he understandeth, and knoweth Me, that I am the Lord who exercises mercy, justice, and righteousness, in the earth; for in these things I delight," saith the Lord. (Jeremiah 9:22–23)

These values are reflected in the most exalted hopes for society:

> Sow to yourselves according to righteousness, reap accord-
> ing to mercy, break up your fallow ground; for it is time to
> seek the Lord, till He come and cause righteousness to rain
> upon you. (Hosea 10:12)

These values are translated into concrete demands placed upon us
as members of society:

> If there be among you a needy man, one of thy brethren,
> within any of thy gates, in thy land which the Lord thy God
> giveth thee, thou shalt not harden thy heart, nor shut thy
> hand from thy needy brother.... For the poor shall never
> cease out of the land; therefore I command thee, saying:
> "Thou shalt surely open thy hand unto thy poor and needy
> brother in thy land." (Deuteronomy 15:7, 11)

In the biblical understanding, justice is the foundation upon
which society is built. Without it, none of the other structures
would stand.

> Beggars in the stories of old
> Wandered ragged up and down
> From town to village, back to town,
> From one house to another.
>
> And the stories always ended
> With the children being told
> How the beggars were rewarded
> With crowns of purest gold.
>
> (Itzik Manger, "Fairy Tales")

# A Personal Afterword

With the completion of this book, I conclude a project that has captivated me from the time it began percolating in my mind until the last word was finally set on paper. The entire undertaking began when I realized that, though I had a full and extensive seminary and graduate school education, I really did not understand the reasons why generations of people have loved and cherished the Book of Psalms. Perhaps I needed more years in the school of life.

When I reached the point where I was ready to enter the Book of Psalms, I studied them closely so that I could understand them. By the time I was done, I discovered that my heart and soul had been moved. It occurred to me that I found things in Psalms that could benefit other people as well. I came to understand that the Book of Psalms was beloved because it gave people strength and hope in the face of challenges that inevitably confront us all. I decided to write a book that would open the door to the treasure-house of human spirit that is the Book of Psalms. In my first book, *Bringing the Psalms to Life: How to Understand and Use the Book of Psalms*, I looked at how Psalms can help us face the various crises that characterize our lives. But after I completed that book, I realized that there was much more in Psalms that I had left unexplored.

I realized that even as Psalms was helping people face the challenges of their lives, it was shaping the way they understood fundamental religious issues. The Book of Psalms provided an important source for how readers understood God and their place in the world. I was drawn to the idea of Psalms as a resource that could help people explore their spiritual lives and create personal theologies. Psalms does offer us ways of meeting God and thinking about God. Psalms also throws us into the deepest issues that challenge and test our faith, and it helps us find ways to move toward a deeper understanding of our beliefs. As I read books that explored the Book of Psalms, I did not find any that presented it in those terms. I felt that before I could consider myself to have done justice to my engagement with Psalms, I would have to put those issues before people as well.

Some people may feel that this book is less personal than the first. Although the first book talks about what we call personal crises, this book is no less intimate and immediate. I believe that human beings are innately spiritual creatures. Religious issues are very much a part of who we are. If we are to be fully realized people, we need to come to terms with questions of faith, belief, and our relationship with God. We have as urgent a need to wrestle with the perplexing issues of faith as we do to cope with illness and adversity. Therefore, the issues in this book are every bit as compelling and fundamental to our lives as those in the first book. For me, the experience of writing this book was just as challenging and personal. Many people have told me that my first book spoke directly to them. I hope this book does as well.

Now that I have had the opportunity to explore the Book of Psalms from two different perspectives, I feel that my project is complete. I have a few more things that I might still want to say about Psalms, but most of what I wanted to share is on these pages. Like every author, I suspect, I write in order to learn. But I write, as well, in the hope that what I have learned from my own studies is helpful to others as they confront challenges in their lives. I hope I have given you some keys to unlock the mysteries of Psalms and enable it to become a resource for making your life more whole and lovely. I am thankful to God for the privilege of undertaking, and completing, this project. Now this undertaking is out of my hands and in yours. I hope and pray that you find it valuable.

I conclude with some final words of prayer from the Book of Psalms:

May the words of my mouth
And the meditations of my heart
Be acceptable in Thy sight, O Lord,
My rock and my redeemer.

(Psalm 19:15)

# Index of Hebrew Scripture References

| | |
|---|---|
| 32 | *60* |
| 32:15–18 | *60* |
| 34:5 | *202* |

## Judges

| | |
|---|---|
| 1 | *61* |
| 2:10 | *170* |

## 2 Samuel

| | |
|---|---|
| 5:9 | *77* |
| 6:12f. | *77* |
| 7:12–16 | *79* |

## 1 Kings

| | |
|---|---|
| 2:10 | *170* |
| 5:11 | *242* |
| 8:1 | *77* |
| 8:12–13, 27 | *242* |
| 14:31 | *170* |

## 2 Kings

| | |
|---|---|
| 16:9 | *232* |

## Isaiah

| | |
|---|---|
| 1:11–17 | *42* |
| 1:16–17 | *263* |
| 1:18 | *213* |
| 2:2–3 | *242* |

| | |
|---|---|
| 3:15 | *274* |
| 5:16 | *253* |
| 10:9ff. | *232* |
| 17:1 | *231* |
| 38:18–19 | *215* |
| 43:10–12 | *50* |
| 48:10 | *147* |
| 54:7–8 | *61* |
| 55:12 | *9* |
| 56:1 | *253* |
| 57:15 | *277* |
| 60:21 | *143* |

## Jeremiah

| | |
|---|---|
| 9:22–23 | *278* |
| 12:1 | *111* |
| 14:9 | *207* |
| 17:5–8 | *135* |
| 17:8 | *37* |
| 22:3 | *278* |
| 32:35 | *61* |

## Ezekiel

| | |
|---|---|
| 3:1–4 | *257* |

## Hosea

| | |
|---|---|
| 6:6 | *42, 256* |
| 10:12 | *279* |

## Amos

| | |
|---|---|
| 1:4ff | *232* |
| 5:4 | *253* |
| 5:8 | *20* |
| 5:21–24 | *42, 256* |

## Micah

| | |
|---|---|
| 4:1–2 | *242* |
| 6:8 | *253* |

## Psalms

| | |
|---|---|
| 1:1 | *133* |
| 1:1–2 | *259* |
| 1:2 | *34* |
| 1:3 | *37, 67, 133* |
| 1:4 | *134* |
| 1:6 | *36* |
| 2:6 | *243* |
| 3:4 | *191* |
| 3:8 | *206* |
| 6:4 | *115* |
| 6:4–6 | *214* |
| 7:7 | *206* |
| 7:11 | *191* |
| 7:16–17 | *126* |
| 8:4–5 | *11* |
| 8:5 | *xi* |

# *Bar/Bat Mitzvah*

**The Bar/Bat Mitzvah Memory Book**
An Album for Treasuring the Spiritual Celebration
*By Rabbi Jeffrey K. Salkin and Nina Salkin*
A unique album for preserving the spiritual memories of the day, and for recording plans for the Jewish future ahead. Contents include space for creating or recording family history; teachings received from rabbi, cantor, and others; mitzvot and *tzedakot* chosen and carried out, etc.
8 x 10, 48 pp, Deluxe Hardcover, 2-color text, ribbon marker, ISBN 1-58023-111-X **$19.95**

**Bar/Bat Mitzvah Basics:** A Practical Family Guide to Coming of Age Together
*Edited by Helen Leneman. Foreword by Rabbi Jeffrey K. Salkin.*
6 x 9, 240 pp, Quality PB, ISBN 1-58023-151-9 **$18.95**

**For Kids—Putting God on Your Guest List:** How to Claim the Spiritual Meaning
of Your Bar or Bat Mitzvah *By Rabbi Jeffrey K. Salkin*
6 x 9, 144 pp, Quality PB, ISBN 1-58023-015-6 **$14.95** *For ages 11–12*

**Putting God on the Guest List:** How to Reclaim the Spiritual Meaning of Your
Child's Bar or Bat Mitzvah *By Rabbi Jeffrey K. Salkin*
6 x 9, 224 pp, Quality PB, ISBN 1-879045-59-1 **$16.95**

**Tough Questions Jews Ask:** A Young Adult's Guide to Building a Jewish Life
*By Rabbi Edward Feinstein* 6 x 9, 160 pp, Quality PB, ISBN 1-58023-139-X **$14.95** *For ages 13 & up*
Also Available: **Tough Questions Jews Ask Teacher's Guide**
8½ x 11, 72 pp, PB, ISBN 1-58023-187-X **$8.95**

# *Bible Study/Midrash*

**Hineini in Our Lives:** Learning How to Respond to Others through 14 Biblical Texts,
and Personal Stories *By Norman J. Cohen*
6 x 9, 240 pp, Hardcover, ISBN 1-58023-131-4 **$23.95**

**Ancient Secrets:** Using the Stories of the Bible to Improve Our Everyday Lives
*By Rabbi Levi Meier, Ph.D.* 5½ x 8½, 288 pp, Quality PB, ISBN 1-58023-064-4 **$16.95**

**Moses—The Prince, the Prophet** His Life, Legend & Message for Our Lives
*By Rabbi Levi Meier, Ph.D.*
6 x 9, 224 pp, Quality PB, ISBN 1-58023-069-5 **$16.95**; Hardcover, ISBN 1-58023-013-X **$23.95**

**Self, Struggle & Change:** Family Conflict Stories in Genesis and Their Healing Insights
for Our Lives *By Norman J. Cohen* 6 x 9, 224 pp, Quality PB, ISBN 1-879045-66-4 **$16.95**

**Voices from Genesis:** Guiding Us through the Stages of Life *By Norman J. Cohen*
6 x 9, 192 pp, Quality PB, ISBN 1-58023-118-7 **$16.95**

# *Congregation Resources*

**Becoming a Congregation of Learners:** Learning as a Key to Revitalizing
Congregational Life *By Isa Aron, Ph.D. Foreword by Rabbi Lawrence A. Hoffman.*
6 x 9, 304 pp, Quality PB, ISBN 1-58023-089-X **$19.95**

**Finding a Spiritual Home:** How a New Generation of Jews Can Transform the
American Synagogue *By Rabbi Sidney Schwarz*
6 x 9, 352 pp, Quality PB, ISBN 1-58023-185-3 **$19.95**

**Jewish Pastoral Care:** A Practical Handbook from Traditional & Contemporary Sources
*Edited by Rabbi Dayle A. Friedman* 6 x 9, 464 pp, Hardcover, ISBN 1-58023-078-4 **$35.00**

**The Self-Renewing Congregation:** Organizational Strategies for Revitalizing
Congregational Life *By Isa Aron, Ph.D. Foreword by Dr. Ron Wolfson.*
6 x 9, 304 pp, Quality PB, ISBN 1-58023-166-7 **$19.95**

# Children's Books

## Because Nothing Looks Like God
*By Lawrence and Karen Kushner*
What is God like? The first collaborative work by husband-and-wife team Lawrence and Karen Kushner introduces children to the possibilities of spiritual life. Real-life examples of happiness and sadness invite us to explore, together with our children, the questions we all have about God, no matter what our age.
11 x 8½, 32 pp, Full-color illus., Hardcover, ISBN 1-58023-092-X **$16.95** *For ages 4 & up*

Also Available: **Because Nothing Looks Like God Teacher's Guide**
8½ x 11, 22 pp, PB, ISBN 1-58023-140-3 **$6.95** *For ages 5–8*
    **Board Book Companions to Because Nothing Looks Like God**
    5 x 5, 24 pp, Full-color illus., SkyLight Paths Board Books, **$7.95** each *For ages 0–4*
**What Does God Look Like?** ISBN 1-893361-23-3
**How Does God Make Things Happen?** ISBN 1-893361-24-1
**Where Is God?** ISBN 1-893361-17-9

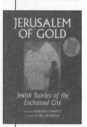

## The 11th Commandment: Wisdom from Our Children
*by The Children of America*
"If there were an Eleventh Commandment, what would it be?" Children of many religious denominations across America answer this question—in their own drawings and words.
8 x 10, 48 pp, Full-color illus., Hardcover, ISBN 1-879045-46-X **$16.95** *For all ages*

## Jerusalem of Gold: Jewish Stories of the Enchanted City
*Retold by Howard Schwartz. Full-color illus. by Neil Waldman.*
A beautiful and engaging collection of historical and legendary stories for children. Each celebrates the magical city that has served as a beacon for the Jewish imagination for three thousand years. Draws on Talmud, midrash, Jewish folklore, and mystical and Hasidic sources.
8 x 10, 64 pp, Full-color illus., Hardcover, ISBN 1-58023-149-7 **$18.95** *For ages 7 & up*

### The Book of Miracles: A Young Person's Guide to Jewish Spiritual Awareness
*By Lawrence Kushner. All-new illustrations by the author.*
6 x 9, 96 pp, 2-color illus., Hardcover, ISBN 1-879045-78-8 **$16.95** *For ages 9–13*

### In Our Image: God's First Creatures
*By Nancy Sohn Swartz*
9 x 12, 32 pp, Full-color illus., Hardcover, ISBN 1-879045-99-0 **$16.95** *For ages 4 & up*

# *From* SKYLIGHT PATHS PUBLISHING

## Becoming Me: A Story of Creation
*By Martin Boroson. Full-color illus. by Christopher Gilvan-Cartwright.*
Told in the personal "voice" of the Creator, a story about creation and relationship that is about each one of us. In simple words and with radiant illustrations, the Creator tells an intimate story about love, about friendship and playing, about our world—and about ourselves.
8 x 10, 32 pp, Full-color illus., Hardcover, ISBN 1-893361-11-X **$16.95** *For ages 4 & up*

### Ten Amazing People: And How They Changed the World
*By Maura D. Shaw. Foreword by Dr. Robert Coles. Full-color illus. by Stephen Marchesi.*
Black Elk • Dorothy Day • Malcolm X • Mahatma Gandhi • Martin Luther King, Jr. • Mother Teresa • Janusz Korczak • Desmond Tutu • Thich Nhat Hanh • Albert Schweitzer • This vivid, inspirational, and authoritative book will open new possibilities for children by telling the stories of how ten of the past century's greatest leaders changed the world in important ways.
8½ x 11, 48 pp, Full-color illus., Hardcover, ISBN 1-893361-47-0 **$17.95** *For ages 7 & up*

### Where Does God Live? *By August Gold and Matthew J. Perlman*
Using simple, everyday examples that children can relate to, this colorful book helps young readers develop a personal understanding of God.
10 x 8½, 32 pp, Full-color photo illus., Quality PB, ISBN 1-893361-39-X **$8.95** *For ages 3–6*

# Children's Books
# by Sandy Eisenberg Sasso

## Adam & Eve's First Sunset: God's New Day
Engaging new story explores fear and hope, faith and gratitude in ways that will delight kids and adults—inspiring us to bless each of God's days and nights.
9 x 12, 32 pp, Full-color illus., Hardcover, ISBN 1-58023-177-2 **$17.95** *For ages 4 & up*

## But God Remembered: Stories of Women from Creation to the Promised Land
Four different stories of women—Lillith, Serach, Bityah, and the Daughters of Z—teach us important values through their faith and actions.
9 x 12, 32 pp, Full-color illus., Hardcover, ISBN 1-879045-43-5 **$16.95** *For ages 8 & up*

## Cain & Abel: Finding the Fruits of Peace
*Full-color illus. by Joani Keller Rothenberg*
Shows children that we have the power to deal with anger in positive ways. Provides questions for kids and adults to explore together.
9 x 12, 32 pp, Full-color illus., Hardcover, ISBN 1-58023-123-3 **$16.95** *For ages 5 & up*

## God in Between
*Full-color illus. by Sally Sweetland*
If you wanted to find God, where would you look? This magical, mythical tale teaches that God can be found where we are: within all of us and the relationships between us.
9 x 12, 32 pp, Full-color illus., Hardcover, ISBN 1-879045-86-9 **$16.95** *For ages 4 & up*

## God's Paintbrush
Wonderfully interactive, invites children of all faiths and backgrounds to encounter God through moments in their own lives. Provides questions adult and child can explore together.
11 x 8½, 32 pp, Full-color illus., Hardcover, ISBN 1-879045-22-2 **$16.95** *For ages 4 & up*

### Also Available: God's Paintbrush Teacher's Guide
8½ x 11, 32 pp, PB, ISBN 1-879045-57-5 **$8.95**

### God's Paintbrush Celebration Kit
A Spiritual Activity Kit for Teachers and Students of All Faiths, All Backgrounds
Additional activity sheets available:
8-Student Activity Sheet Pack (40 sheets/5 sessions), ISBN 1-58023-058-X **$19.95**
Single-Student Activity Sheet Pack (5 sessions), ISBN 1-58023-059-8 **$3.95**

## In God's Name
*Full-color illus. by Phoebe Stone*
Like an ancient myth in its poetic text and vibrant illustrations, this award-winning modern fable about the search for God's name celebrates the diversity and, at the same time, the unity of all people.
9 x 12, 32 pp, Full-color illus., Hardcover, ISBN 1-879045-26-5 **$16.95** *For ages 4 & up*

### Also Available as a Board Book: What Is God's Name?
5 x 5, 24 pp, Board, Full-color illus., ISBN 1-893361-10-1 **$7.95** *For ages 0–4 (A SkyLight Paths book)*

### Also Available: In God's Name video and study guide
Computer animation, original music, and children's voices. 18 min. **$29.99**

### Also Available in Spanish: El nombre de Dios
9 x 12, 32 pp, Full-color illus., Hardcover, ISBN 1-893361-63-2 **$16.95** *(A SkyLight Paths book)*

## Noah's Wife: The Story of Naamah
When God tells Noah to bring the animals of the world onto the ark, God also calls on Naamah, Noah's wife, to save each plant on Earth. Based on an ancient text.
9 x 12, 32 pp, Full-color illus., Hardcover, ISBN 1-58023-134-9 **$16.95** *For ages 4 & up*

### Also Available as a Board Book: Naamah, Noah's Wife
5 x 5, 24 pp, Full-color illus., Board, ISBN 1-893361-56-X **$7.95** *For ages 0–4 (A SkyLight Paths book)*

### For Heaven's Sake: Finding God in Unexpected Places
9 x 12, 32 pp, Full-color illus., Hardcover, ISBN 1-58023-054-7 **$16.95** *For ages 4 & up*

### God Said Amen: Finding the Answers to Our Prayers
9 x 12, 32 pp, Full-color illus., Hardcover, ISBN 1-58023-080-6 **$16.95** *For ages 4 & up*

# Current Events/History

**The Story of the Jews:** A 4,000-Year Adventure—A Graphic History Book
*Written & illustrated by Stan Mack*
Through witty, illustrated narrative, we visit all the major happenings from biblical times to the twenty-first century. Celebrates the major characters and events that have shaped the Jewish people and culture.
6 x 9, 288 pp, illus., Quality PB, ISBN 1-58023-155-1 **$16.95**

**The Jewish Prophet:** Visionary Words from Moses and Miriam to Henrietta Szold and A. J. Heschel   *By Rabbi Michael J. Shire*   6½ x 8½, 128 pp, 123 full-color illus., Hardcover, ISBN 1-58023-168-3 **$25.00**

**Shared Dreams:** Martin Luther King, Jr. & the Jewish Community
*By Rabbi Marc Schneier. Preface by Martin Luther King III.*
6 x 9, 240 pp, Hardcover, ISBN 1-58023-062-8 **$24.95**

**"Who Is a Jew?":** Conversations, Not Conclusions   *By Meryl Hyman*
6 x 9, 272 pp, Quality PB, ISBN 1-58023-052-0 **$16.95**

# Ecology

**Ecology & the Jewish Spirit:** Where Nature & the Sacred Meet
*Edited by Ellen Bernstein*   6 x 9, 288 pp, Quality PB, ISBN 1-58023-082-2 **$16.95**

**Torah of the Earth:** Exploring 4,000 Years of Ecology in Jewish Thought
Vol. 1:  Biblical Israel: One Land, One People; Rabbinic Judaism: One People, Many Lands
Vol. 2:  Zionism: One Land, Two Peoples; Eco-Judaism: One Earth, Many Peoples
*Edited by Rabbi Arthur Waskow*
Vol. 1:  6 x 9, 272 pp, Quality PB, ISBN 1-58023-086-5 **$19.95**
Vol. 2:  6 x 9, 336 pp, Quality PB, ISBN 1-58023-087-3 **$19.95**

# Grief/Healing

**Against the Dying of the Light:** A Parent's Story of Love, Loss and Hope
*By Leonard Fein*
In this unusual exploration of heartbreak and healing, Leonard Fein chronicles the sudden death of his 30-year-old daughter and shares the hard-earned wisdom that emerges in the face of loss and grief.
5½ x 8½, 176 pp, Hardcover, ISBN 1-58023-110-1 **$19.95**

**Grief in Our Seasons:** A Mourner's Kaddish Companion   *By Rabbi Kerry M. Olitzky*
4½ x 6½, 448 pp, Quality PB, ISBN 1-879045-55-9 **$15.95**

**Healing of Soul, Healing of Body:** Spiritual Leaders Unfold the Strength & Solace in Psalms   *Edited by Rabbi Simkha Y. Weintraub, C.S.W.*
6 x 9, 128 pp, 2-color illus. text, Quality PB, ISBN 1-879045-31-1 **$14.95**

**Jewish Paths toward Healing and Wholeness:** A Personal Guide to Dealing with Suffering   *By Rabbi Kerry M. Olitzky. Foreword by Debbie Friedman.*
6 x 9, 192 pp, Quality PB, ISBN 1-58023-068-7 **$15.95**

**Mourning & Mitzvah, 2nd Edition:** A Guided Journal for Walking the Mourner's Path through Grief to Healing   *By Anne Brener, L.C.S.W.*
7½ x 9, 304 pp, Quality PB, ISBN 1-58023-113-6 **$19.95**

**The Perfect Stranger's Guide to Funerals and Grieving Practices**
A Guide to Etiquette in Other People's Religious Ceremonies   *Edited by Stuart M. Matlins*
6 x 9, 240 pp, Quality PB, ISBN 1-893361-20-9 **$16.95**   *(A SkyLight Paths book)*

**Tears of Sorrow, Seeds of Hope:** A Jewish Spiritual Companion for Infertility and Pregnancy Loss   *By Rabbi Nina Beth Cardin*
6 x 9, 192 pp, Hardcover, ISBN 1-58023-017-2 **$19.95**

**A Time to Mourn, A Time to Comfort:** A Guide to Jewish Bereavement and Comfort   *By Dr. Ron Wolfson*   7 x 9, 336 pp, Quality PB, ISBN 1-879045-96-6 **$18.95**

**When a Grandparent Dies:** A Kid's Own Remembering Workbook for Dealing with Shiva and the Year Beyond   *By Nechama Liss-Levinson, Ph.D.*
8 x 10, 48 pp, 2-color text, Hardcover, ISBN 1-879045-44-3 **$15.95**   *For ages 7–13*

# Abraham Joshua Heschel

**The Earth Is the Lord's:** The Inner World of the Jew in Eastern Europe
5½ x 8, 128 pp, Quality PB, ISBN 1-879045-42-7 **$14.95**

**Israel:** An Echo of Eternity *New Introduction by Susannah Heschel*
5½ x 8, 272 pp, Quality PB, ISBN 1-879045-70-2 **$19.95**

**A Passion for Truth:** Despair and Hope in Hasidism
5½ x 8, 352 pp, Quality PB, ISBN 1-879045-41-9 **$18.95**

# *Holidays/Holy Days*

**7th Heaven:** Celebrating Shabbat with Rebbe Nachman of Breslov
*By Moshe Mykoff with the Breslov Research Institute*
Based on the teachings of Rebbe Nachman of Breslov. Explores the art of consciously observing Shabbat and understanding in-depth many of the day's traditional spiritual practices.
5⅛ x 8¼, 224 pp, Deluxe PB w/flaps, ISBN 1-58023-175-6 **$18.95**

**The Women's Passover Companion**
Women's Reflections on the Festival of Freedom
*Edited by Rabbi Sharon Cohen Anisfeld, Tara Mohr, and Catherine Spector*
A groundbreaking collection that captures the voices of Jewish women who engage in a provocative conversation about women's relationships to Passover as well as the roots and meanings of women's seders.
6 x 9, 352 pp, Hardcover, ISBN 1-58023-128-4 **$24.95**

**The Women's Seder Sourcebook**
Rituals & Readings for Use at the Passover Seder
*Edited by Rabbi Sharon Cohen Anisfeld, Tara Mohr, and Catherine Spector*
This practical guide gathers the voices of more than one hundred women in readings, personal and creative reflections, commentaries, blessings, and ritual suggestions that can be incorporated into your Passover celebration as supplements to or substitutes for traditional passages of the haggadah.
6 x 9, 384 pp, Hardcover, ISBN 1-58023-136-5 **$24.95**

**Hanukkah, 2nd Edition:** The Family Guide to Spiritual Celebration
*By Dr. Ron Wolfson. Edited by Joel Lurie Grishaver.*
7 x 9, 240 pp, illus., Quality PB, ISBN 1-58023-122-5 **$18.95**

**The Jewish Gardening Cookbook:** Growing Plants & Cooking for
Holidays & Festivals *By Michael Brown*
6 x 9, 224 pp, 30+ illus., Quality PB, ISBN 1-58023-116-0 **$16.95**;
Hardcover, ISBN 1-58023-004-0 **$21.95**

**Passover, 2nd Edition:** The Family Guide to Spiritual Celebration
*By Dr. Ron Wolfson with Joel Lurie Grishaver*
7 x 9, 352 pp, Quality PB, ISBN 1-58023-174-8 **$19.95**

**Shabbat, 2nd Edition:** The Family Guide to Preparing for and Celebrating the Sabbath
*By Dr. Ron Wolfson* 7 x 9, 320 pp, illus., Quality PB, ISBN 1-58023-164-0 **$19.95**

**Sharing Blessings:** Children's Stories for Exploring the Spirit of the Jewish Holidays
*By Rahel Musleah and Michael Klayman*
8½ x 11, 64 pp, Full-color illus., Hardcover, ISBN 1-879045-71-0 **$18.95** *For ages 6 & up*

**The Jewish Family Fun Book:** Holiday Projects, Everyday Activities,
and Travel Ideas with Jewish Themes
*By Danielle Dardashti and Roni Sarig. Illus. by Avi Katz.*
With almost 100 easy-to-do activities to re-invigorate age-old Jewish customs and make them fun for the whole family, this complete sourcebook details activities for fun at home and away from home, including meaningful everyday and holiday crafts, recipes, travel guides, enriching entertainment and much, much more. Illustrated.
6 x 9, 288 pp, 70+ b/w illus. & diagrams, Quality PB, ISBN 1-58023-171-3 **$18.95**

# Inspiration

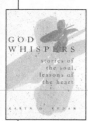

## God in All Moments
### Mystical & Practical Spiritual Wisdom from Hasidic Masters
*Edited and translated by Or N. Rose with Ebn D. Leader*

Hasidic teachings on how to be mindful in religious practice and how to cultivate everyday ethical behavior—*hanhagot*.

5½ x 8½, 240 pp, Quality PB, ISBN 1-58023-186-1 **$16.95**

**The Dance of the Dolphin:** Finding Prayer, Perspective and Meaning in the Stories of Our Lives *By Karyn D. Kedar* 6 x 9, 176 pp, Hardcover, ISBN 1-58023-154-3 **$19.95**

**The Empty Chair:** Finding Hope and Joy—Timeless Wisdom from a Hasidic Master, Rebbe Nachman of Breslov *Adapted by Moshe Mykoff and the Breslov Research Institute* 4 x 6, 128 pp, 2-color text, Deluxe PB w/flaps, ISBN 1-879045-67-2 **$9.95**

**The Gentle Weapon:** Prayers for Everyday and Not-So-Everyday Moments— Timeless Wisdom from the Teachings of the Hasidic Master, Rebbe Nachman of Breslov *Adapted by Moshe Mykoff and S. C. Mizrahi, together with the Breslov Research Institute* 4 x 6, 144 pp, 2-color text, Deluxe PB w/flaps, ISBN 1-58023-022-9 **$9.95**

**God Whispers:** Stories of the Soul, Lessons of the Heart *By Karyn D. Kedar* 6 x 9, 176 pp, Quality PB, ISBN 1-58023-088-1 **$15.95**

**An Orphan in History:** One Man's Triumphant Search for His Jewish Roots *By Paul Cowan. Afterword by Rachel Cowan.* 6 x 9, 288 pp, Quality PB, ISBN 1-58023-135-7 **$16.95**

**Restful Reflections:** Nighttime Inspiration to Calm the Soul, Based on Jewish Wisdom *By Rabbi Kerry M. Olitzky & Rabbi Lori Forman* 4½ x 6½, 448 pp, Quality PB, ISBN 1-58023-091-1 **$15.95**

**Sacred Intentions:** Daily Inspiration to Strengthen the Spirit, Based on Jewish Wisdom *By Rabbi Kerry M. Olitzky and Rabbi Lori Forman* 4½ x 6½, 448 pp, Quality PB, ISBN 1-58023-061-X **$15.95**

# Kabbalah/Mysticism/Enneagram

## Seek My Face: A Jewish Mystical Theology
*By Dr. Arthur Green*

This classic work of contemporary Jewish theology, revised and updated, is a profound, deeply personal statement of the lasting truths of Jewish mysticism and the basic faith claims of Judaism. A tool for anyone seeking the elusive presence of God in the world. 6 x 9, 304 pp, Quality PB, ISBN 1-58023-130-6 **$19.95**

## Zohar: Annotated & Explained
*Translation and annotation by Dr. Daniel C. Matt. Foreword by Andrew Harvey, SkyLight Illuminations series editor.*

Offers insightful yet unobtrusive commentary to the masterpiece of Jewish mysticism that explains references and mystical symbols, shares wisdom of spiritual masters, and clarifies the *Zohar*'s bold claim: We have always been taught that we need God, but in order to manifest in the world, God needs us. 5½ x 8½, 160 pp, Quality PB, ISBN 1-893361-51-9 **$15.95** *(A SkyLight Paths book)*

**Cast in God's Image:** Discover Your Personality Type Using the Enneagram and Kabbalah *By Rabbi Howard A. Addison* 7 x 9, 176 pp, Quality PB, Layflat binding, 20+ journaling exercises, ISBN 1-58023-124-1 **$16.95**

**Ehyeh: A Kabbalah for Tomorrow** *By Dr. Arthur Green* 6 x 9, 224 pp, Hardcover, ISBN 1-58023-125-X **$21.95**

**The Enneagram and Kabbalah:** Reading Your Soul *By Rabbi Howard A. Addison* 6 x 9, 176 pp, Quality PB, ISBN 1-58023-001-6 **$15.95**

**Finding Joy:** A Practical Spiritual Guide to Happiness *By Dannel I. Schwartz with Mark Hass* 6 x 9, 192 pp, Quality PB, ISBN 1-58023-009-1 **$14.95**; Hardcover, ISBN 1-879045-53-2 **$19.95**

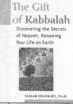

**The Gift of Kabbalah:** Discovering the Secrets of Heaven, Renewing Your Life on Earth *By Tamar Frankiel, Ph.D.* 6 x 9, 256 pp, Quality PB, ISBN 1-58023-141-1 **$16.95**; Hardcover, ISBN 1-58023-108-X **$21.95**

**The Way Into Jewish Mystical Tradition** *By Lawrence Kushner* 6 x 9, 224 pp, Hardcover, ISBN 1-58023-029-6 **$21.95**

# Life Cycle

## Parenting

**The New Jewish Baby Album:** Creating and Celebrating the Beginning of a Spiritual Life—A Jewish Lights Companion
*By the Editors at Jewish Lights. Foreword by Anita Diamant. Preface by Sandy Eisenberg Sasso.*
A spiritual keepsake that will be treasured for generations. More than just a memory book, *shows you how—and why it's important*—to create a Jewish home and a Jewish life. Includes sections to describe naming ceremony, space to write encouragements, and pages for writing original blessings, prayers, and meaningful quotes throughout.
8 x 10, 64 pp, Deluxe Padded Hardcover, Full-color illus., ISBN 1-58023-138-1 **$19.95**

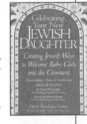

**The Jewish Pregnancy Book:** A Resource for the Soul, Body & Mind during Pregnancy, Birth & the First Three Months
*By Dr. Sandy Falk, M.D., and Rabbi Daniel Judson, with Steven A. Rapp*
Includes medical information on fetal development, pre-natal testing and more, from a liberal Jewish perspective; prenatal *aleph-bet* yoga; and ancient and modern prayers and rituals for each stage of pregnancy.
7 x 10, 144 pp, Quality PB, Layflat binding, b/w illus., ISBN 1-58023-178-0 **$16.95**

**Celebrating Your New Jewish Daughter:** Creating Jewish Ways to Welcome Baby Girls into the Covenant—New and Traditional Ceremonies
*By Debra Nussbaum Cohen* 6 x 9, 272 pp, Quality PB, ISBN 1-58023-090-3 **$18.95**

**The New Jewish Baby Book:** Names, Ceremonies & Customs—A Guide for Today's Families  *By Anita Diamant*  6 x 9, 336 pp, Quality PB, ISBN 1-879045-28-1 **$18.95**

**Parenting As a Spiritual Journey:** Deepening Ordinary and Extraordinary Events into Sacred Occasions  *By Rabbi Nancy Fuchs-Kreimer*
6 x 9, 224 pp, Quality PB, ISBN 1-58023-016-4 **$16.95**

**Embracing the Covenant:** Converts to Judaism Talk About Why & How
*Edited and with introductions by Rabbi Allan Berkowitz and Patti Moskovitz*
6 x 9, 192 pp, Quality PB, ISBN 1-879045-50-8 **$16.95**

**The Guide to Jewish Interfaith Family Life:** An InterfaithFamily.com Handbook
*Edited by Ronnie Friedland and Edmund Case* 6 x 9, 384 pp, Quality PB, ISBN 1-58023-153-5 **$18.95**

**Making a Successful Jewish Interfaith Marriage:** The Jewish Outreach Institute Guide to Opportunities, Challenges and Resources
*By Rabbi Kerry Olitzky with Joan Peterson Littman* 6 x 9, 176 pp, Quality PB, ISBN 1-58023-170-5 **$16.95**

**The Perfect Stranger's Guide to Wedding Ceremonies**
A Guide to Etiquette in Other People's Religious Ceremonies  *Edited by Stuart M. Matlins*
6 x 9, 208 pp, Quality PB, ISBN 1-893361-19-5 **$16.95**  *(A SkyLight Paths book)*

## How to Be a Perfect Stranger, 3rd Edition
The Essential Religious Etiquette Handbook
*Edited by Stuart M. Matlins and Arthur J. Magida*
The indispensable guidebook to help the well-meaning guest when visiting other people's religious ceremonies.
   A straightforward guide to the rituals and celebrations of the major religions and denominations in the United States and Canada from the perspective of an interested guest of any other faith, based on information obtained from authorities of each religion. Belongs in every living room, library, and office.
6 x 9, 432 pp, Quality PB, ISBN 1-893361-67-5 **$19.95**  *(A SkyLight Paths book)*

**Divorce Is a Mitzvah:** A Practical Guide to Finding Wholeness and Holiness When Your Marriage Dies  *By Rabbi Perry Netter. Afterword by Rabbi Laura Geller.*
6 x 9, 224 pp, Quality PB, ISBN 1-58023-172-1 **$16.95**

**A Heart of Wisdom:** Making the Jewish Journey from Midlife through the Elder Years
*Edited by Susan Berrin. Foreword by Harold Kushner.*  6 x 9, 384 pp, Quality PB, ISBN 1-58023-051-2 **$18.95**

**So That Your Values Live On:** Ethical Wills and How to Prepare Them
*Edited by Jack Riemer and Nathaniel Stampfer* 6 x 9, 272 pp, Quality PB, ISBN 1-879045-34-6 **$18.95**

# Meditation

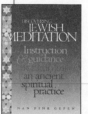

**The Handbook of Jewish Meditation Practices**
A Guide for Enriching the Sabbath and Other Days of Your Life
*By Rabbi David A. Cooper*
Easy-to-learn meditation techniques for use on the Sabbath and every day, to help us return to the roots of traditional Jewish spirituality where Shabbat is a state of mind and soul. 6 x 9, 208 pp, Quality PB, ISBN 1-58023-102-0 **$16.95**

**Discovering Jewish Meditation:** Instruction & Guidance for Learning an Ancient Spiritual Practice *By Nan Fink Gefen, Ph.D.* 6 x 9, 208 pp, Quality PB, ISBN 1-58023-067-9 **$16.95**

**A Heart of Stillness:** A Complete Guide to Learning the Art of Meditation
*By Rabbi David A. Cooper*
5½ x 8½, 272 pp, Quality PB, ISBN 1-893361-03-9 **$16.95** *(A SkyLight Paths book)*

**Meditation from the Heart of Judaism:** Today's Teachers Share Their Practices, Techniques, and Faith *Edited by Avram Davis*
6 x 9, 256 pp, Quality PB, ISBN 1-58023-049-0 **$16.95**

**Silence, Simplicity & Solitude:** A Complete Guide to Spiritual Retreat at Home
*By Rabbi David A. Cooper*
5½ x 8½, 336 pp, Quality PB, ISBN 1-893361-04-7 **$16.95** *(A SkyLight Paths book)*

**Three Gates to Meditation Practice:** A Personal Journey into Sufism, Buddhism, and Judaism *By Rabbi David A. Cooper*
5½ x 8½, 240 pp, Quality PB, ISBN 1-893361-22-5 **$16.95** *(A SkyLight Paths book)*

**The Way of Flame:** A Guide to the Forgotten Mystical Tradition of Jewish Meditation
*By Avram Davis* 4½ x 8, 176 pp, Quality PB, ISBN 1-58023-060-1 **$15.95**

# Ritual/Sacred Practice

**The Jewish Dream Book**
The Key to Opening the Inner Meaning of Your Dreams
*By Vanessa L. Ochs with Elizabeth Ochs; Full-color Illus. by Kristina Swarner*
Vibrant illustrations, instructions for how modern people can perform ancient Jewish dream practices, and dream interpretations drawn from the Jewish wisdom tradition help make this guide the ideal bedside companion for anyone who wants to further their understanding of their dreams—and themselves.
8 x 8, 120 pp, Full-color illus., Deluxe PB w/flaps, ISBN 1-58023-132-2 **$16.95**

**The Rituals & Practices of a Jewish Life:** A Handbook for Personal Spiritual Renewal *Edited by Rabbi Kerry M. Olitzky and Rabbi Daniel Judson*
6 x 9, 272 pp, illus., Quality PB, ISBN 1-58023-169-1 **$18.95**

**The Book of Jewish Sacred Practices:** CLAL's Guide to Everyday & Holiday Rituals & Blessings *Edited by Rabbi Irwin Kula and Vanessa L. Ochs, Ph.D.*
6 x 9, 368 pp, Quality PB, ISBN 1-58023-152-7 **$18.95**

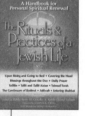

# Science Fiction/ Mystery & Detective Fiction

**Mystery Midrash:** An Anthology of Jewish Mystery & Detective Fiction
*Edited by Lawrence W. Raphael. Preface by Joel Siegel.*
6 x 9, 304 pp, Quality PB, ISBN 1-58023-055-5 **$16.95**

**Criminal Kabbalah:** An Intriguing Anthology of Jewish Mystery & Detective Fiction
*Edited by Lawrence W. Raphael. Foreword by Laurie R. King.*
6 x 9, 256 pp, Quality PB, ISBN 1-58023-109-8 **$16.95**

**More Wandering Stars:** An Anthology of Outstanding Stories of Jewish Fantasy and Science Fiction *Edited by Jack Dann. Introduction by Isaac Asimov.*
6 x 9, 192 pp, Quality PB, ISBN 1-58023-063-6 **$16.95**

**Wandering Stars:** An Anthology of Jewish Fantasy & Science Fiction
*Edited by Jack Dann. Introduction by Isaac Asimov.*
6 x 9, 272 pp, Quality PB, ISBN 1-58023-005-9 **$16.95**

# Spirituality

**The Alphabet of Paradise:** An A–Z of Spirituality for Everyday Life
*By Rabbi Howard Cooper*
In twenty-six engaging chapters, Cooper spiritually illuminates the subjects of our daily lives—A to Z—examining these sources by using an ancient Jewish mystical method of interpretation that reveals both the literal and more allusive meanings of each.   5 x 7¼, 224 pp, Quality PB, ISBN 1-893361-80-2 **$16.95** *(A SkyLight Paths book)*

**Does the Soul Survive?:** A Jewish Journey to Belief in Afterlife, Past Lives & Living with Purpose   *By Rabbi Elie Kaplan Spitz. Foreword by Brian L Weiss, M.D.*
Spitz relates his own experiences and those shared with him by people he has worked with as a rabbi, and shows us that belief in afterlife and past lives, so often approached with reluctance, is in fact true to Jewish tradition.
6 x 9, 288 pp, Quality PB, ISBN 1-58023-165-9 **$16.95**; Hardcover, ISBN 1-58023-094-6 **$21.95**

**First Steps to a New Jewish Spirit:** Reb Zalman's Guide to Recapturing the Intimacy & Ecstasy in Your Relationship with God
*By Rabbi Zalman M. Schachter-Shalomi with Donald Gropman*
An extraordinary spiritual handbook that restores psychic and physical vigor by introducing us to new models and alternative ways of practicing Judaism. Offers meditation and contemplation exercises for enriching the most important aspects of everyday life.   6 x 9, 144 pp, Quality PB, ISBN 1-58023-182-9 **$16.95**

**God in Our Relationships:** Spirituality between People from the Teachings of Martin Buber   *By Rabbi Dennis S. Ross*
On the eightieth anniversary of Buber's classic work, we can discover new answers to critical issues in our lives. Inspiring examples from Ross's own life—as congregational rabbi, father, hospital chaplain, social worker, and husband—illustrate Buber's difficult-to-understand ideas about how we encounter God and each other. 5½ x 8½, 160 pp, Quality PB, ISBN 1-58023-147-0 **$16.95**

**The Jewish Lights Spirituality Handbook:** A Guide to Understanding, Exploring & Living a Spiritual Life   *Edited by Stuart M. Matlins*
What exactly is "Jewish" about spirituality? How do I make it a part of my life? Fifty of today's foremost spiritual leaders share their ideas and experience with us.
6 x 9, 456 pp, Quality PB, ISBN 1-58023-093-8 **$18.95**; Hardcover, ISBN 1-58023-100-4 **$24.95**

**Bringing the Psalms to Life:** How to Understand and Use the Book of Psalms
*By Dr. Daniel F. Polish*
6 x 9, 208 pp, Quality PB, ISBN 1-58023-157-8 **$16.95**; Hardcover, ISBN 1-58023-077-6 **$21.95**

**God & the Big Bang:** Discovering Harmony between Science & Spirituality
*By Dr. Daniel C. Matt*  6 x 9, 216 pp, Quality PB, ISBN 1-879045-89-3 **$16.95**

**Godwrestling—Round 2:** Ancient Wisdom, Future Paths
*By Rabbi Arthur Waskow*  6 x 9, 352 pp, Quality PB, ISBN 1-879045-72-9 **$18.95**

**One God Clapping:** The Spiritual Path of a Zen Rabbi   *By Rabbi Alan Lew with Sherril Jaffe*
5½ x 8½, 336 pp, Quality PB, ISBN 1-58023-115-2 **$16.95**

**The Path of Blessing:** Experiencing the Energy and Abundance of the Divine
*By Rabbi Marcia Prager*  5½ x 8½, 240 pp., Quality PB, ISBN 1-58023-148-9 **$16.95**

**Six Jewish Spiritual Paths:** A Rationalist Looks at Spirituality   *By Rabbi Rifat Sonsino*
6 x 9, 208 pp, Quality PB, ISBN 1-58023-167-5 **$16.95**; Hardcover, ISBN 1-58023-095-4 **$21.95**

**Soul Judaism:** Dancing with God into a New Era
*By Rabbi Wayne Dosick*  5½ x 8½, 304 pp, Quality PB, ISBN 1-58023-053-9 **$16.95**

**Stepping Stones to Jewish Spiritual Living:** Walking the Path Morning, Noon, and Night   *By Rabbi James L Mirel and Karen Bonnell Werth*
6 x 9, 240 pp, Quality PB, ISBN 1-58023-074-1 **$16.95**; Hardcover, ISBN 1-58023-003-2 **$21.95**

**There Is No Messiah... and You're It:** The Stunning Transformation of Judaism's Most Provocative Idea   *By Rabbi Robert N. Levine, D.D.*
6 x 9, 192 pp, Hardcover, ISBN 1-58023-173-X **$21.95**

**These Are the Words:** A Vocabulary of Jewish Spiritual Life   *By Dr. Arthur Green*
6 x 9, 304 pp, Quality PB, ISBN 1-58023-107-1 **$18.95**

# Spirituality/Lawrence Kushner

**The Book of Letters:** A Mystical Hebrew Alphabet
Popular Hardcover Edition, 6 x 9, 80 pp, 2-color text, ISBN 1-879045-00-1 **$24.95**
Deluxe Gift Edition with slipcase, 9 x 12, 80 pp, 4-color text, Hardcover, ISBN 1-879045-01-X **$79.95**
Collector's Limited Edition, 9 x 12, 80 pp, gold foil embossed pages, w/limited edition silkscreened print, ISBN 1-879045-04-4 **$349.00**

**The Book of Miracles:** A Young Person's Guide to Jewish Spiritual Awareness
*All-new illustrations by the author*
6 x 9, 96 pp, 2-color illus., Hardcover, ISBN 1-879045-78-8 **$16.95** *For ages 9–13*

**The Book of Words:** Talking Spiritual Life, Living Spiritual Talk
6 x 9, 160 pp, Quality PB, ISBN 1-58023-020-2 **$16.95**

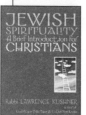

**Eyes Remade for Wonder:** A Lawrence Kushner Reader
*Introduction by Thomas Moore*
6 x 9, 240 pp, Quality PB, ISBN 1-58023-042-3 **$18.95;** Hardcover, ISBN 1-58023-014-8 **$23.95**

**God Was in This Place & I, i Did Not Know**
Finding Self, Spirituality and Ultimate Meaning
6 x 9, 192 pp, Quality PB, ISBN 1-879045-33-8 **$16.95**

**Honey from the Rock:** An Introduction to Jewish Mysticism
6 x 9, 176 pp, Quality PB, ISBN 1-58023-073-3 **$16.95**

**Invisible Lines of Connection:** Sacred Stories of the Ordinary
5½ x 8½, 160 pp, Quality PB, ISBN 1-879045-98-2 **$15.95**

**Jewish Spirituality—A Brief Introduction for Christians**
5½ x 8½, 112 pp, Quality PB Original, ISBN 1-58023-150-0 **$12.95**

**The River of Light:** Jewish Mystical Awareness
6 x 9, 192 pp, Quality PB, ISBN 1-58023-096-2 **$16.95**

**The Way Into Jewish Mystical Tradition**
6 x 9, 224 pp, Hardcover, ISBN 1-58023-029-6 **$21.95**

# Spirituality/Prayer

**Pray Tell:** A Hadassah Guide to Jewish Prayer
*By Rabbi Jules Harlow, with contributions from Tamara Cohen, Rochelle Furstenberg, Rabbi Daniel Gordis, Leora Tanenbaum, and many others*
A guide to traditional Jewish prayer enriched with insight and wisdom from a broad variety of viewpoints—from Orthodox, Conservative, Reform, and Reconstructionist Judaism to New Age and feminist. Offers fresh and modern slants on what it means to pray as a Jew, and how women and men might actually pray. 8½ x 11, 400 pp, Quality PB, ISBN 1-58023-163-2 **$29.95**

**My People's Prayer Book Series**
Traditional Prayers, Modern Commentaries
*Edited by Rabbi Lawrence A. Hoffman*
Provides diverse and exciting commentary to the traditional liturgy, helping modern men and women find new wisdom in Jewish prayer, and bring liturgy into their lives.

Each book includes Hebrew text, modern translation, and commentaries from all perspectives of the Jewish world.
Vol. 1—The *Sh'ma* and Its Blessings
7 x 10, 168 pp, Hardcover, ISBN 1-879045-79-6 **$23.95**
Vol. 2—The *Amidah*
7 x 10, 240 pp, Hardcover, ISBN 1-879045-80-X **$24.95**
Vol. 3—*P'sukei D'zimrah* (Morning Psalms)
7 x 10, 240 pp, Hardcover, ISBN 1-879045-81-8 **$24.95**
Vol. 4—*Seder K'riat Hatorah* (The Torah Service)
7 x 10, 264 pp, Hardcover, ISBN 1-879045-82-6 **$23.95**
Vol. 5—*Birkhot Hashachar* (Morning Blessings)
7 x 10, 240 pp, Hardcover, ISBN 1-879045-83-4 **$24.95**
Vol. 6—*Tachanun* and Concluding Prayers
7 x 10, 240 pp, Hardcover, ISBN 1-879045-84-2 **$24.95**
Vol. 7—Shabbat at Home
7 x 10, 240 pp (est), Hardcover, ISBN 1-879045-85-0 **$24.95**

# Spirituality/The Way Into... Series

The Way Into... Series offers an accessible and highly usable "guided tour" of the Jewish faith, people, history and beliefs—in total, an introduction to Judaism that will enable you to understand and interact with the sacred texts of the Jewish tradition. Each volume is written by a leading contemporary scholar and teacher, and explores one key aspect of Judaism. The Way Into... enables all readers to achieve a real sense of Jewish cultural literacy through guided study.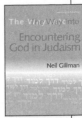

**The Way Into Encountering God in Judaism**   By Neil Gillman
6 x 9, 240 pp, Hardcover, ISBN 1-58023-025-3 **$21.95**

Also Available: **The Jewish Approach to God: A Brief Introduction for Christians**
By Neil Gillman 5½ x 8½, 192 pp, Quality PB, ISBN 1-58023-190-X **$16.95**

**The Way Into Jewish Mystical Tradition**   By Lawrence Kushner
6 x 9, 224 pp, Hardcover, ISBN 1-58023-029-6 **$21.95**

**The Way Into Jewish Prayer**   By Lawrence A. Hoffman
6 x 9, 224 pp, Hardcover, ISBN 1-58023-027-X **$21.95**

**The Way Into Torah**   By Norman J. Cohen
6 x 9, 176 pp, Hardcover, ISBN 1-58023-028-8 **$21.95**

# Spirituality in the Workplace

**Being God's Partner**
How to Find the Hidden Link Between Spirituality and Your Work
By Rabbi Jeffrey K. Salkin. Introduction by Norman Lear.
6 x 9, 192 pp, Quality PB, ISBN 1-879045-65-6 **$17.95**

**The Business Bible:** 10 New Commandments for Bringing Spirituality & Ethical Values into the Workplace   By Rabbi Wayne Dosick
5½ x 8½, 208 pp, Quality PB, ISBN 1-58023-101-2 **$14.95**

# Spirituality and Wellness

**Aleph-Bet Yoga**
Embodying the Hebrew Letters for Physical and Spiritual Well-Being
By Steven A. Rapp. Foreword by Tamar Frankiel, Ph.D., and Judy Greenfeld. Preface by Hart Lazer
7 x 10, 128 pp, b/w photos, Quality PB, Layflat binding, ISBN 1-58023-162-4 **$16.95**

**Entering the Temple of Dreams**
Jewish Prayers, Movements, and Meditations for the End of the Day
By Tamar Frankiel, Ph.D., and Judy Greenfeld
7 x 10, 192 pp, illus., Quality PB, ISBN 1-58023-079-2 **$16.95**

**Minding the Temple of the Soul**
Balancing Body, Mind, and Spirit through Traditional Jewish Prayer, Movement, and Meditation   By Tamar Frankiel, Ph.D., and Judy Greenfeld
7 x 10, 184 pp, illus., Quality PB, ISBN 1-879045-64-8 **$16.95**
Audiotape of the Blessings and Meditations: 60 min. **$9.95**
Videotape of the Movements and Meditations: 46 min. **$20.00**

# Spirituality/Women's Interest

**Lifecycles, Vol. 1:** Jewish Women on Life Passages & Personal Milestones
*Edited and with introductions by Rabbi Debra Orenstein*
6 x 9, 480 pp, Quality PB, ISBN 1-58023-018-0 **$19.95**

**Lifecycles, Vol. 2:** Jewish Women on Biblical Themes in Contemporary Life
*Edited and with introductions by Rabbi Debra Orenstein and Rabbi Jane Rachel Litman*
6 x 9, 464 pp, Quality PB, ISBN 1-58023-019-9 **$19.95**

**Moonbeams:** A Hadassah Rosh Hodesh Guide  *Edited by Carol Diament, Ph.D.*
8½ x 11, 240 pp, Quality PB, ISBN 1-58023-099-7 **$20.00**

**ReVisions:** Seeing Torah through a Feminist Lens  *By Rabbi Elyse Goldstein*
5½ x 8½, 224 pp, Quality PB, ISBN 1-58023-117-9 **$16.95**

**White Fire:** A Portrait of Women Spiritual Leaders in America
*By Rabbi Malka Drucker. Photographs by Gay Block.*
7 x 10, 320 pp, 30+ b/w photos, Hardcover, ISBN 1-893361-64-0 **$24.95** *(A SkyLight Paths book)*

**Women of the Wall:** Claiming Sacred Ground at Judaism's Holy Site
*Edited by Phyllis Chesler and Rivka Haut*
6 x 9, 496 pp, b/w photos, Hardcover, ISBN 1-58023-161-6 **$34.95**

**The Women's Torah Commentary:** New Insights from Women Rabbis on the 54
Weekly Torah Portions  *Edited by Rabbi Elyse Goldstein*
6 x 9, 496 pp, Hardcover, ISBN 1-58023-076-8 **$34.95**

**The Year Mom Got Religion:** One Woman's Midlife Journey into Judaism
*By Lee Meyerhoff Hendler*
6 x 9, 208 pp, Quality PB, ISBN 1-58023-070-9 **$15.95**; Hardcover, ISBN 1-58023-000-8 **$19.95**

See Holidays for *The Women's Passover Companion: Women's Reflections on the Festival of Freedom* and *The Women's Seder Sourcebook: Rituals & Readings for Use at the Passover Seder.*

# Theology/Philosophy

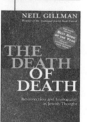

**Aspects of Rabbinic Theology**
*By Solomon Schechter. New Introduction by Dr. Neil Gillman.*
6 x 9, 448 pp, Quality PB, ISBN 1-879045-24-9 **$19.95**

**Broken Tablets:** Restoring the Ten Commandments and Ourselves
*Edited by Rachel S. Mikva. Introduction by Lawrence Kushner. Afterword by Arnold Jacob Wolf.*
6 x 9, 192 pp, Quality PB, ISBN 1-58023-158-6 **$16.95**; Hardcover, ISBN 1-58023-066-0 **$21.95**

**Creating an Ethical Jewish Life**
A Practical Introduction to Classic Teachings on How to Be a Jew
*By Dr. Byron L. Sherwin and Seymour J. Cohen*
6 x 9, 336 pp, Quality PB, ISBN 1-58023-114-4 **$19.95**

**The Death of Death:** Resurrection and Immortality in Jewish Thought
*By Dr. Neil Gillman*  6 x 9, 336 pp, Quality PB, ISBN 1-58023-081-4 **$18.95**

**Evolving Halakhah:** A Progressive Approach to Traditional Jewish Law
*By Rabbi Dr. Moshe Zemer*
6 x 9, 480 pp, Quality PB, ISBN 1-58023-127-6 **$29.95**; Hardcover, ISBN 1-58023-002-4 **$40.00**

**Hasidic Tales: Annotated & Explained**
*By Rabbi Rami Shapiro. Foreword by Andrew Harvey, SkyLight Illuminations series editor.*
5½ x 8½, 192 pp, Quality PB, ISBN 1-893361-86-1 **$16.95** *(A SkyLight Paths Book)*

**A Heart of Many Rooms:** Celebrating the Many Voices within Judaism
*By Dr. David Hartman*
6 x 9, 352 pp, Quality PB, ISBN 1-58023-156-X **$19.95**; Hardcover, ISBN 1-58023-048-2 **$24.95**

**Judaism and Modern Man:** An Interpretation of Jewish Religion
*By Will Herberg. New Introduction by Dr. Neil Gillman.*
5½ x 8½, 336 pp, Quality PB, ISBN 1-879045-87-7 **$18.95**

**Keeping Faith with the Psalms:** Deepen Your Relationship with God Using the
Book of Psalms  *By Daniel F. Polish*
6 x 9, 272 pp, Hardcover, ISBN 1-58023-179-9 **$24.95**

*(continued next page)*

# Theology/Philosophy *(continued)*

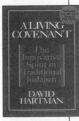

**The Last Trial**
On the Legends and Lore of the Command to Abraham to Offer Isaac as a Sacrifice
*By Shalom Spiegel. New Introduction by Judah Goldin.*
6 x 9, 208 pp, Quality PB, ISBN 1-879045-29-X **$18.95**

**A Living Covenant:** The Innovative Spirit in Traditional Judaism
*By Dr. David Hartman* 6 x 9, 368 pp, Quality PB, ISBN 1-58023-011-3 **$18.95**

**Love and Terror in the God Encounter**
The Theological Legacy of Rabbi Joseph B. Soloveitchik
*By Dr. David Hartman*
6 x 9, 240 pp, Quality PB, ISBN 1-58023-176-4 **$19.95**; Hardcover, ISBN 1-58023-112-8 **$25.00**

**Seeking the Path to Life**
Theological Meditations on God and the Nature of People, Love, Life and Death
*By Rabbi Ira F. Stone* 6 x 9, 160 pp, Quality PB, ISBN 1-879045-47-8 **$14.95**

**The Spirit of Renewal:** Finding Faith after the Holocaust
*By Rabbi Edward Feld* 6 x 9, 224 pp, Quality PB, ISBN 1-879045-40-0 **$16.95**

**Tormented Master:** *The Life and Spiritual Quest of Rabbi Nahman of Bratslav*
*By Dr. Arthur Green* 6 x 9, 416 pp, Quality PB, ISBN 1-879045-11-7 **$19.95**

**Your Word Is Fire:** The Hasidic Masters on Contemplative Prayer
*Edited and translated by Dr. Arthur Green and Barry W. Holtz*
6 x 9, 160 pp, Quality PB, ISBN 1-879045-25-7 **$15.95**

# Travel

**Israel—A Spiritual Travel Guide:** A Companion for the Modern Jewish Pilgrim
*By Rabbi Lawrence A. Hoffman*
4¾ x 10, 256 pp, Quality PB, illus., ISBN 1-879045-56-7 **$18.95**

Also Available: **The Israel Mission Leader's Guide**
*Prepared with the assistance of Rabbi Elliott Kleinman*
5½ x 8½, 16 pp, PB, ISBN 1-58023-085-7 **$4.95**

# 12 Steps

**100 Blessings Every Day**
Daily Twelve Step Recovery Affirmations, Exercises for Personal Growth &
Renewal Reflecting Seasons of the Jewish Year
*By Rabbi Kerry M. Olitzky. Foreword by Rabbi Neil Gillman.*
Using a one-day-at-a-time monthly format, this guide reflects on the rhythm of
the Jewish calendar to help bring insight to recovery from addictions and com-
pulsive behaviors of all kinds. Its exercises help us move from *thinking* to *doing*.
4¼ x 6¼, 432 pp, Quality PB, ISBN 1-879045-30-3 **$14.95**

**Recovery from Codependence:** A Jewish Twelve Steps Guide to Healing Your Soul
*By Rabbi Kerry M. Olitzky* 6 x 9, 160 pp, Quality PB, ISBN 1-879045-32-X **$13.95**

**Renewed Each Day:** Daily Twelve Step Recovery Meditations Based on the Bible
*By Rabbi Kerry M. Olitzky and Aaron Z.*
Vol. 1—Genesis & Exodus:
6 x 9, 224 pp, Quality PB, ISBN 1-879045-12-5 **$14.95**
Vol. 2—Leviticus, Numbers & Deuteronomy:
6 x 9, 280 pp, Quality PB, ISBN 1-879045-13-3 **$14.95**

**Twelve Jewish Steps to Recovery**
A Personal Guide to Turning from Alcoholism & Other Addictions—Drugs, Food,
Gambling, Sex...
*By Rabbi Kerry M. Olitzky and Stuart A. Copans, M.D. Preface by Abraham J. Twerski, M.D.*
6 x 9, 144 pp, Quality PB, ISBN 1-879045-09-5 **$14.95**

## About Jewish Lights

People of all faiths and backgrounds yearn for books that attract, engage, educate, and spiritually inspire.

Our principal goal is to stimulate thought and help all people learn about who the Jewish People are, where they come from, and what the future can be made to hold. While people of our diverse Jewish heritage are the primary audience, our books speak to people in the Christian world as well and will broaden their understanding of Judaism and the roots of their own faith.

We bring to you authors who are at the forefront of spiritual thought and experience. While each has something different to say, they all say it in a voice that you can hear.

Our books are designed to welcome you and then to engage, stimulate, and inspire. We judge our success not only by whether or not our books are beautiful and commercially successful, but by whether or not they make a difference in your life.

For your information and convenience, at the back of this book we have provided a list of other Jewish Lights books you might find interesting and useful. They cover all the categories of your life:

| | |
|---|---|
| Bar/Bat Mitzvah | Life Cycle |
| Bible Study / Midrash | Meditation |
| Children's Books | Parenting |
| Congregation Resources | Prayer |
| Current Events / History | Ritual / Sacred Practice |
| Ecology | Spirituality |
| Fiction: Mystery, Science Fiction | Theology / Philosophy |
| Grief / Healing | Travel |
| Holidays / Holy Days | Twelve Steps |
| Inspiration | Women's Interest |
| Kabbalah / Mysticism / Enneagram | |

Stuart M. Matlins, Publisher

*Or phone, fax, mail or e-mail to:* **JEWISH LIGHTS Publishing**
Sunset Farm Offices, Route 4 • P.O. Box 237 • Woodstock, Vermont 05091
Tel: (802) 457-4000 • Fax: (802) 457-4004 • www.jewishlights.com
*Credit card orders:* (800) 962-4544 (8:30AM–5:30PM ET Monday–Friday)
Generous discounts on quantity orders. SATISFACTION GUARANTEED. Prices subject to change.

**For more information about each book, visit our website at www.jewishlights.com**